JLA

The Hypothetical Woman

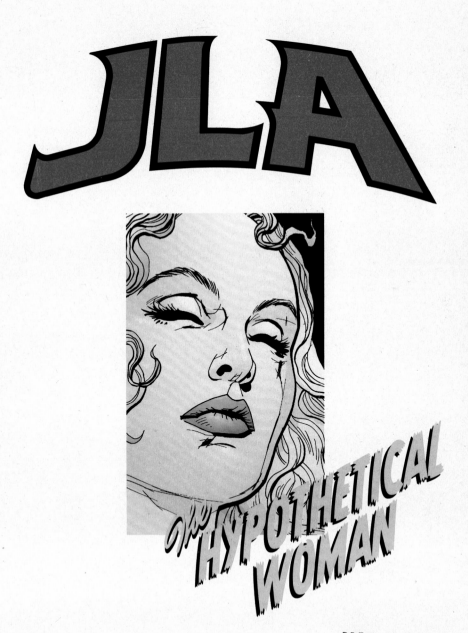

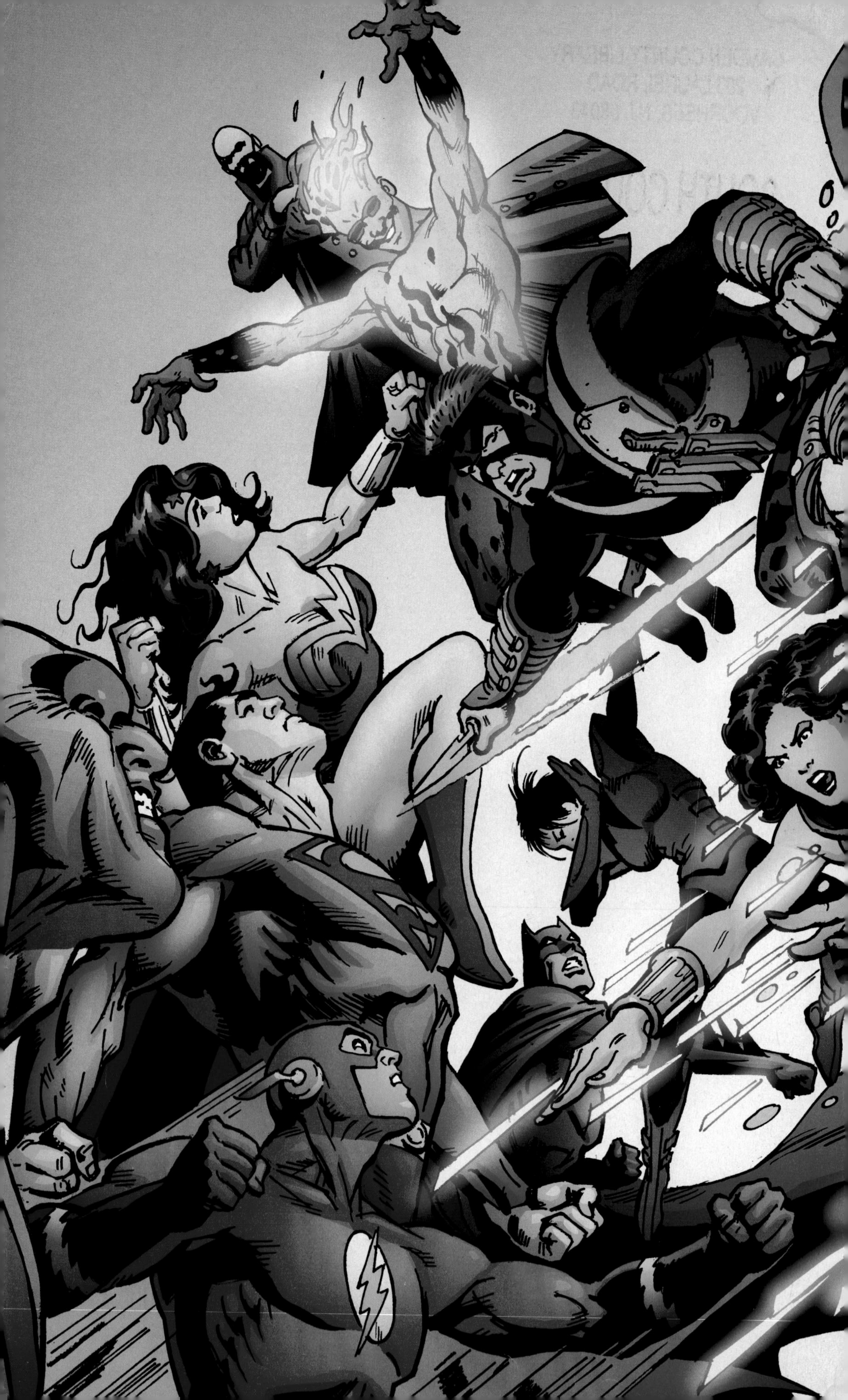

JLA

The HYPOTHETICAL WOMAN

Writer
GAIL SIMONE

Penciller
JOSÉ LUIS GARCÍA-LÓPEZ

Inkers
Klaus Janson (parts 1-3)
Sean Phillips (parts 4-6)

Colorist
David Baron

Letterers
Pat Brosseau
Rob Leigh

Original Covers
José Luis García-López with David Baron

Cover by José Luis García-López with David Baron

JLA: THE HYPOTHETICAL WOMAN

Published by DC Comics. Cover and compilation copyright © 2008
DC Comics. All Rights Reserved.

Originally published in single magazine form as JLA CLASSIFIED
#16-21. Copyright © 2006 DC Comics. All Rights Reserved.
All characters, their distinctive likenesses and related elements
featured in this publication are trademarks of DC Comics.
The stories, characters and incidents featured in this publication
are entirely fictional. DC Comics does not read or accept
unsolicited submissions of ideas, stories or artwork.

DC Comics, 1700 Broadway, New York, NY 10019
A Warner Bros. Entertainment Company
Printed in Canada. First Printing.

ISBN: 978-1-4012-1629-0

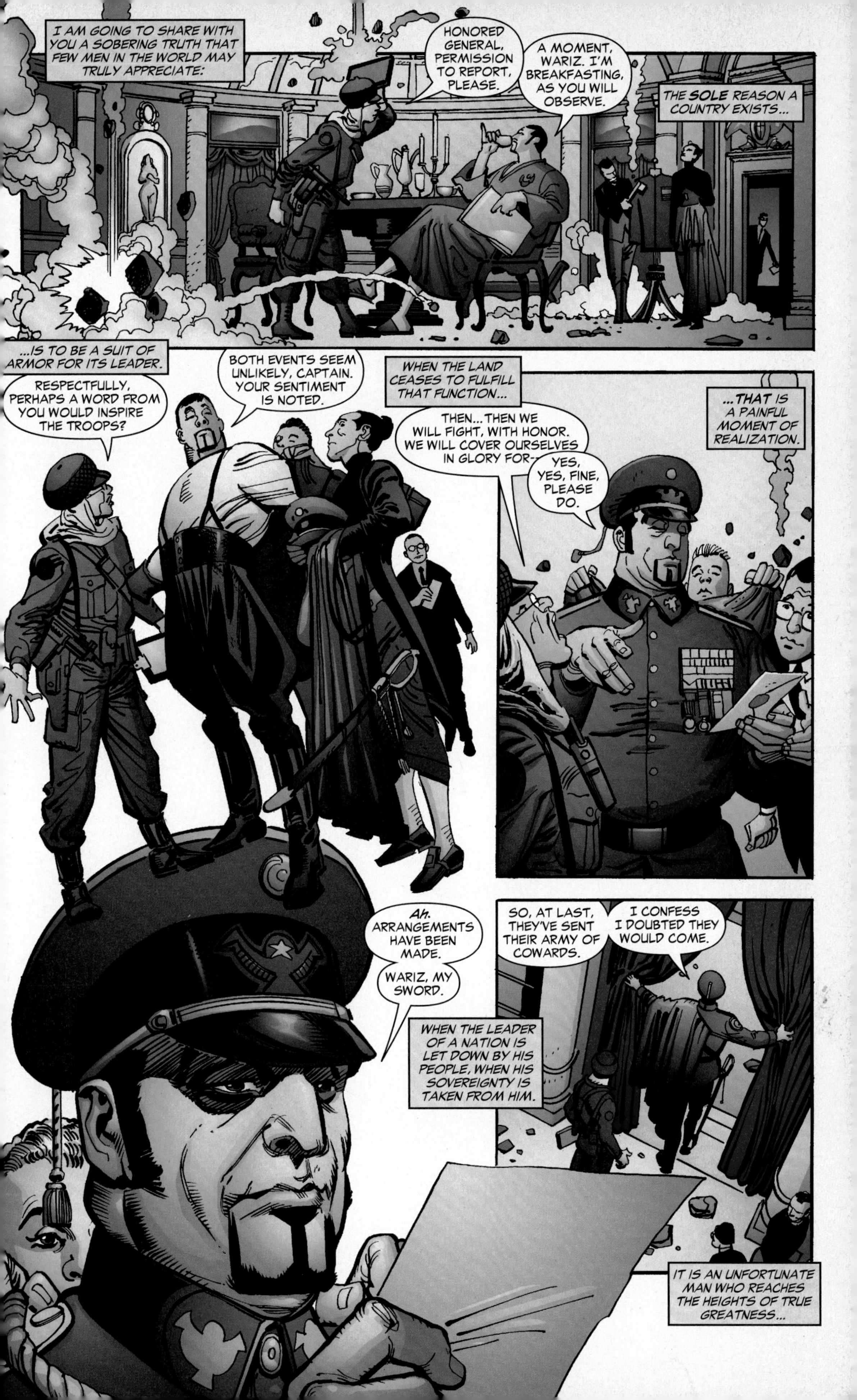
I AM GOING TO SHARE WITH YOU A SOBERING TRUTH THAT FEW MEN IN THE WORLD MAY TRULY APPRECIATE:
HONORED GENERAL, PERMISSION TO REPORT, PLEASE.
A MOMENT, WARIZ. I'M BREAKFASTING, AS YOU WILL OBSERVE.
THE SOLE REASON A COUNTRY EXISTS...
...IS TO BE A SUIT OF ARMOR FOR ITS LEADER.
RESPECTFULLY, PERHAPS A WORD FROM YOU WOULD INSPIRE THE TROOPS?
BOTH EVENTS SEEM UNLIKELY, CAPTAIN. YOUR SENTIMENT IS NOTED.
WHEN THE LAND CEASES TO FULFILL THAT FUNCTION...
THEN... THEN WE WILL FIGHT, WITH HONOR. WE WILL COVER OURSELVES IN GLORY FOR--
YES, YES, FINE, PLEASE DO.
...THAT IS A PAINFUL MOMENT OF REALIZATION.
Ah. ARRANGEMENTS HAVE BEEN MADE.
WARIZ, MY SWORD.
WHEN THE LEADER OF A NATION IS LET DOWN BY HIS PEOPLE, WHEN HIS SOVEREIGNTY IS TAKEN FROM HIM.
SO, AT LAST, THEY'VE SENT THEIR ARMY OF COWARDS.
I CONFESS I DOUBTED THEY WOULD COME.
IT IS AN UNFORTUNATE MAN WHO REACHES THE HEIGHTS OF TRUE GREATNESS...

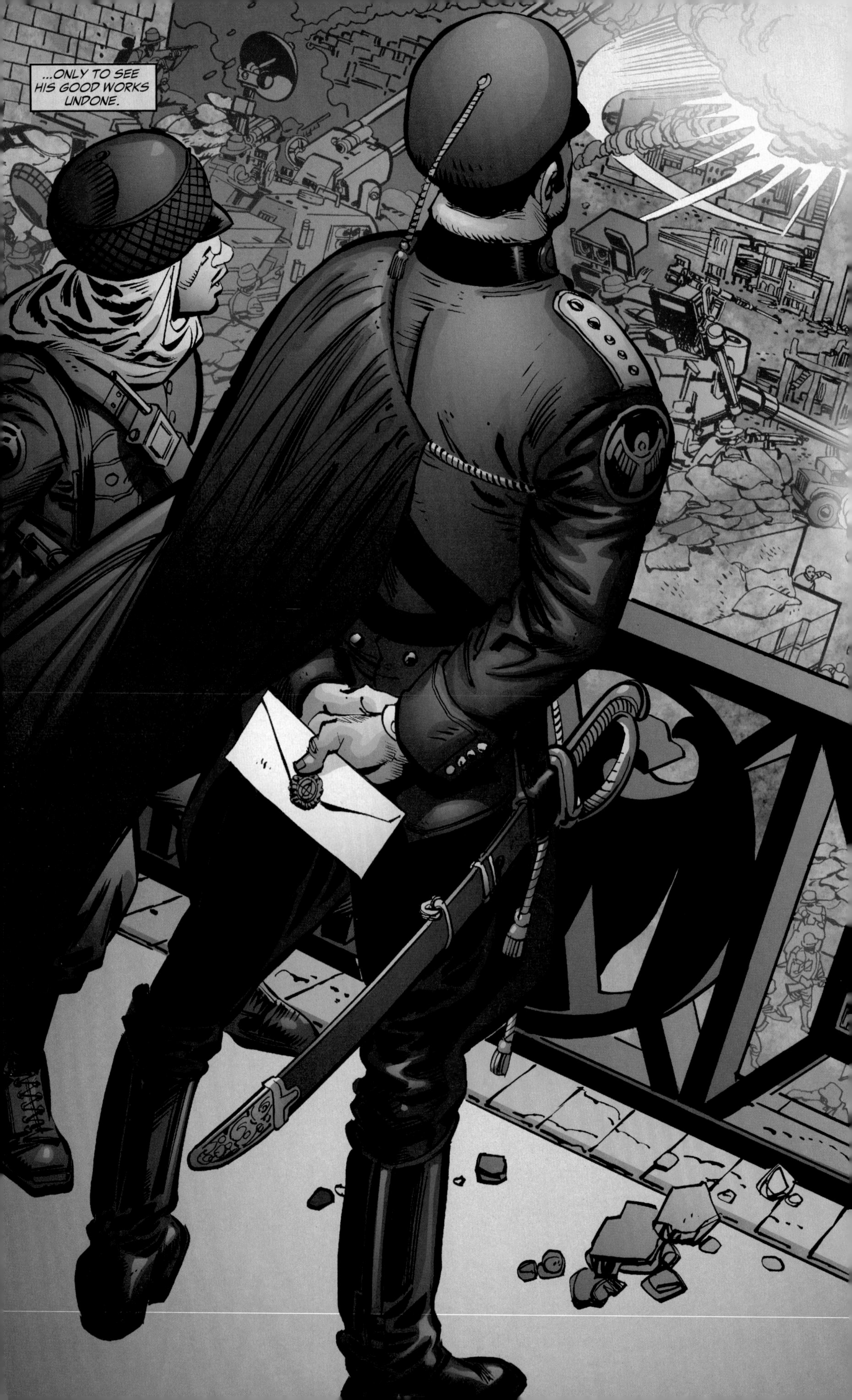
...ONLY TO SEE HIS GOOD WORKS UNDONE.

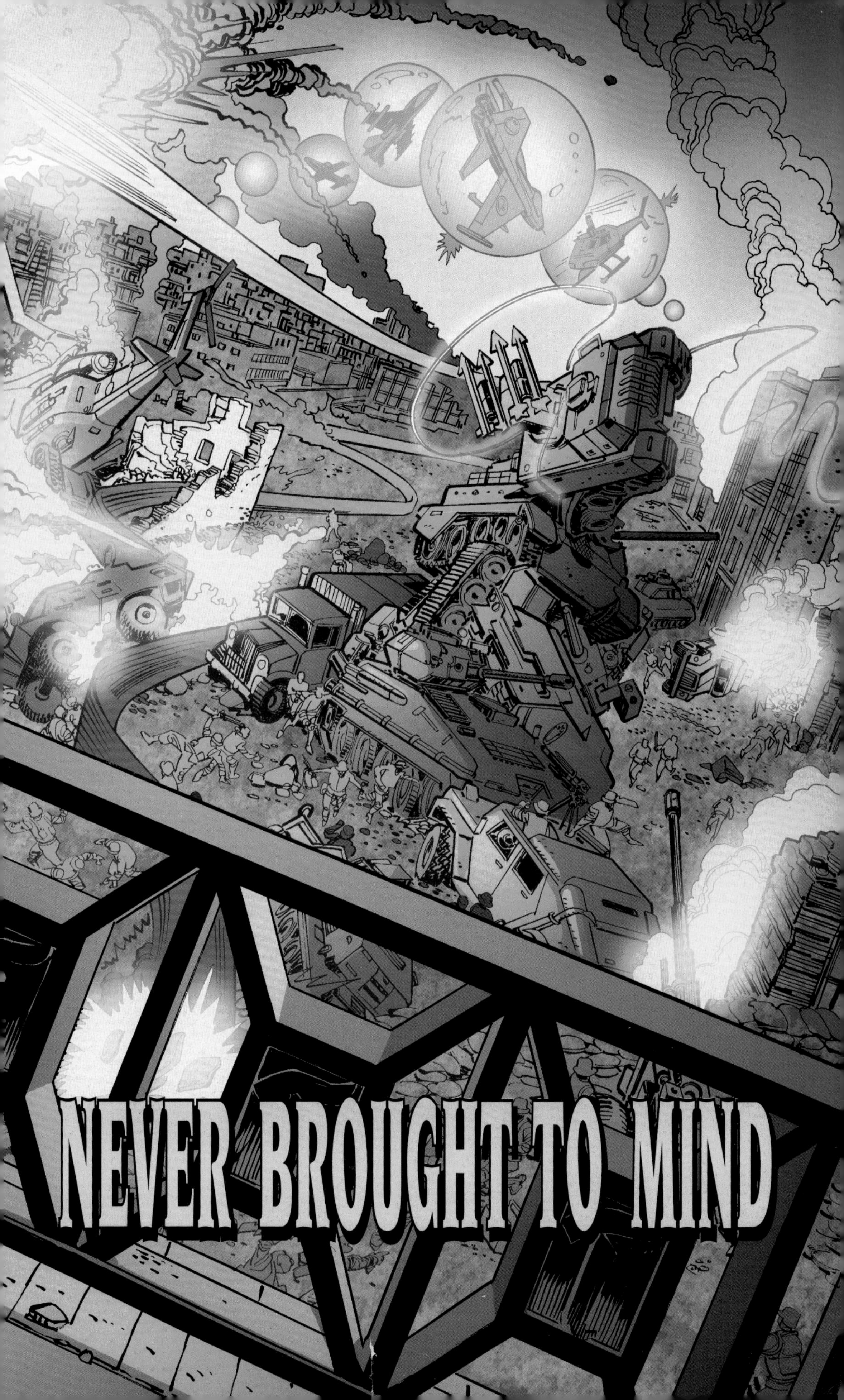
NEVER BROUGHT TO MIND

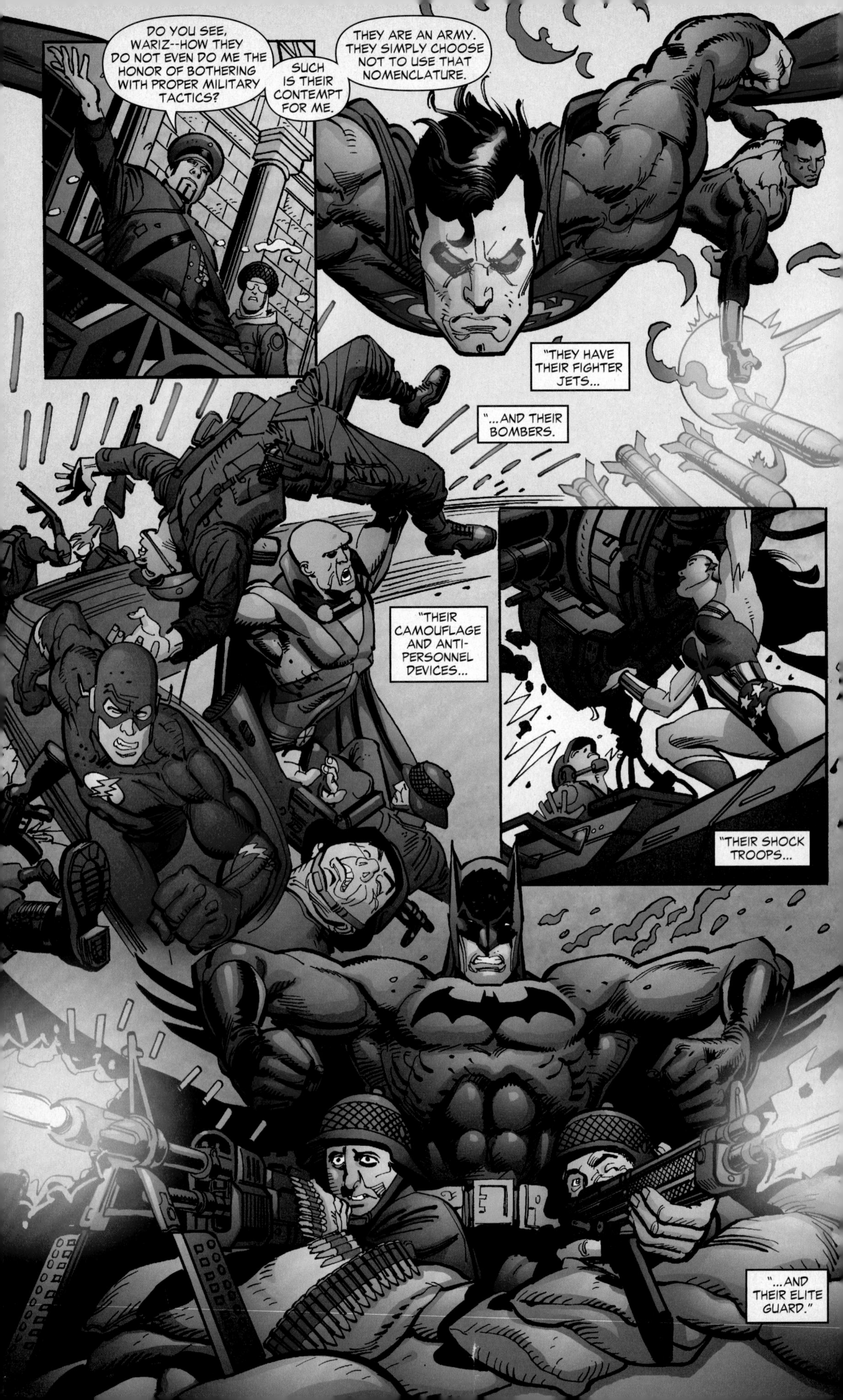
DO YOU SEE, WARIZ--HOW THEY DO NOT EVEN DO ME THE HONOR OF BOTHERING WITH PROPER MILITARY TACTICS?
SUCH IS THEIR CONTEMPT FOR ME.
THEY ARE AN ARMY. THEY SIMPLY CHOOSE NOT TO USE THAT NOMENCLATURE.
"THEY HAVE THEIR FIGHTER JETS...
"...AND THEIR BOMBERS.
"THEIR CAMOUFLAGE AND ANTI-PERSONNEL DEVICES...
"THEIR SHOCK TROOPS...
"...AND THEIR ELITE GUARD."

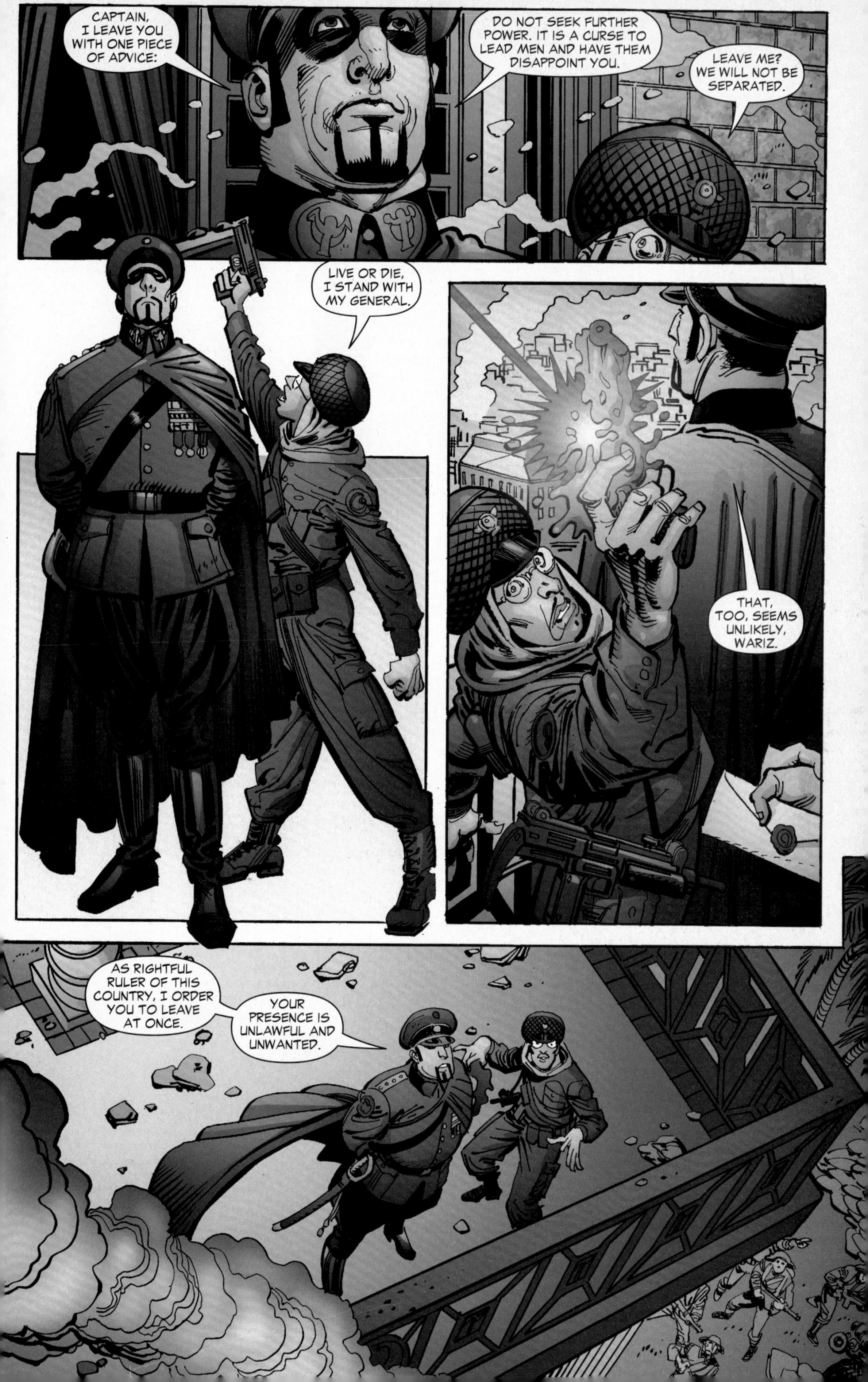
CAPTAIN, I LEAVE YOU WITH ONE PIECE OF ADVICE:
DO NOT SEEK FURTHER POWER. IT IS A CURSE TO LEAD MEN AND HAVE THEM DISAPPOINT YOU.
LEAVE ME? WE WILL NOT BE SEPARATED.
LIVE OR DIE, I STAND WITH MY GENERAL.
THAT, TOO, SEEMS UNLIKELY, WARIZ.
AS RIGHTFUL RULER OF THIS COUNTRY, I ORDER YOU TO LEAVE AT ONCE.
YOUR PRESENCE IS UNLAWFUL AND UNWANTED.

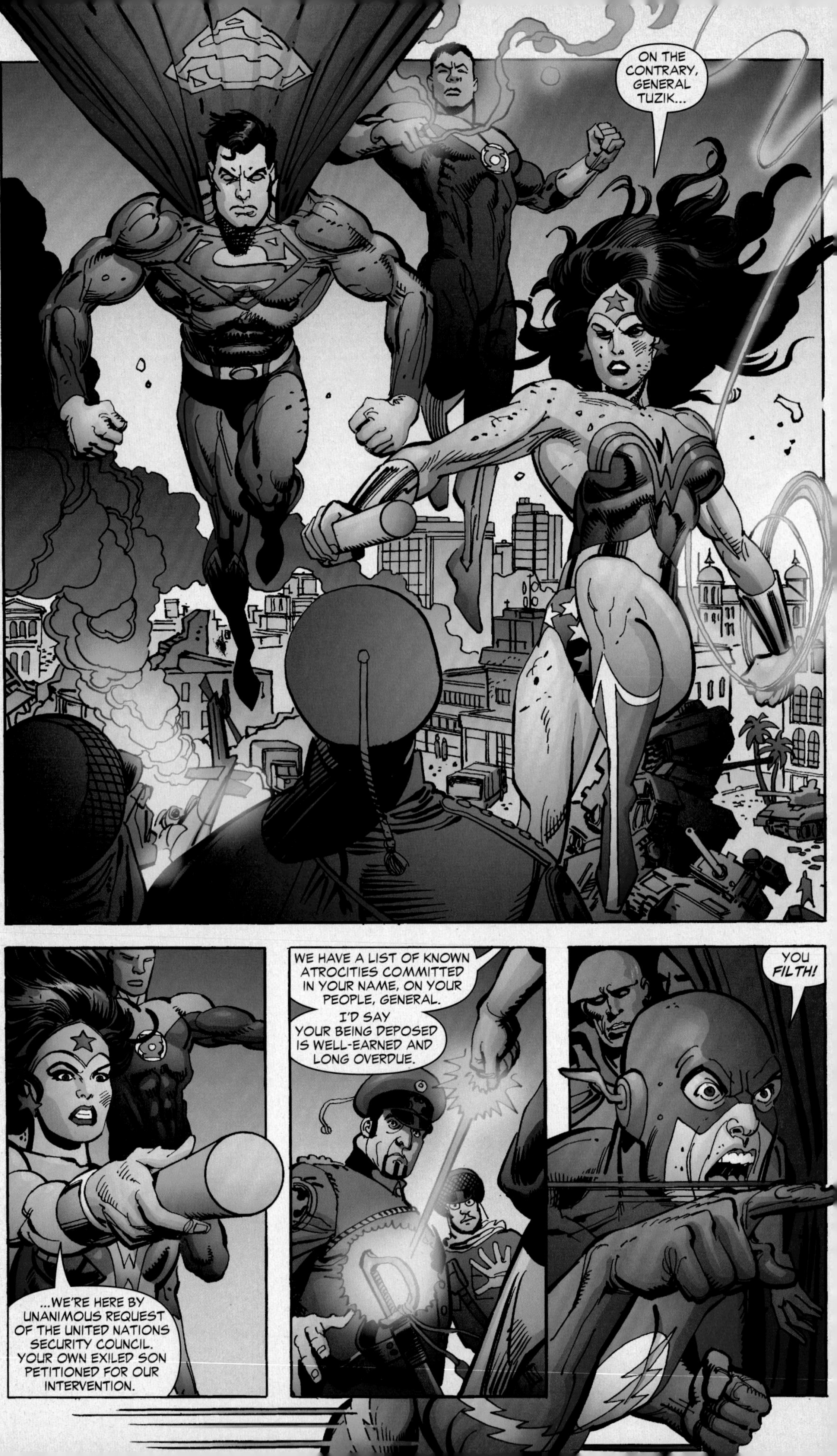
ON THE CONTRARY, GENERAL TUZIK...
...WE'RE HERE BY UNANIMOUS REQUEST OF THE UNITED NATIONS SECURITY COUNCIL. YOUR OWN EXILED SON PETITIONED FOR OUR INTERVENTION.
WE HAVE A LIST OF KNOWN ATROCITIES COMMITTED IN YOUR NAME, ON YOUR PEOPLE, GENERAL.
I'D SAY YOUR BEING DEPOSED IS WELL-EARNED AND LONG OVERDUE.
YOU *FILTH!*

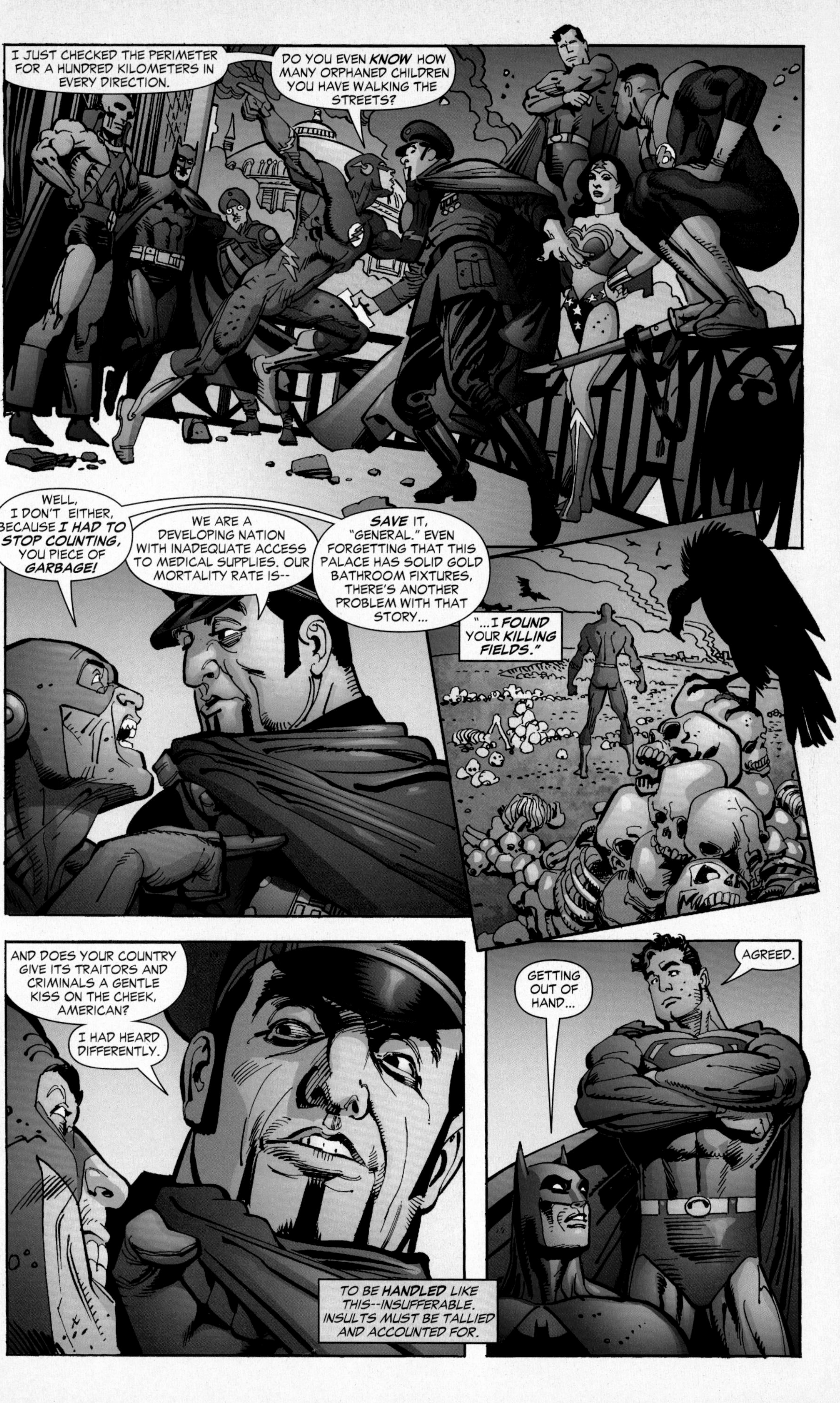
I JUST CHECKED THE PERIMETER FOR A HUNDRED KILOMETERS IN EVERY DIRECTION.
DO YOU EVEN KNOW HOW MANY ORPHANED CHILDREN YOU HAVE WALKING THE STREETS?
WELL, I DON'T EITHER, BECAUSE I HAD TO STOP COUNTING, YOU PIECE OF GARBAGE!
WE ARE A DEVELOPING NATION WITH INADEQUATE ACCESS TO MEDICAL SUPPLIES. OUR MORTALITY RATE IS--
SAVE IT, "GENERAL." EVEN FORGETTING THAT THIS PALACE HAS SOLID GOLD BATHROOM FIXTURES, THERE'S ANOTHER PROBLEM WITH THAT STORY...
"...I FOUND YOUR KILLING FIELDS."
AND DOES YOUR COUNTRY GIVE ITS TRAITORS AND CRIMINALS A GENTLE KISS ON THE CHEEK, AMERICAN?
I HAD HEARD DIFFERENTLY.
TO BE HANDLED LIKE THIS--INSUFFERABLE. INSULTS MUST BE TALLIED AND ACCOUNTED FOR.
GETTING OUT OF HAND...
AGREED.

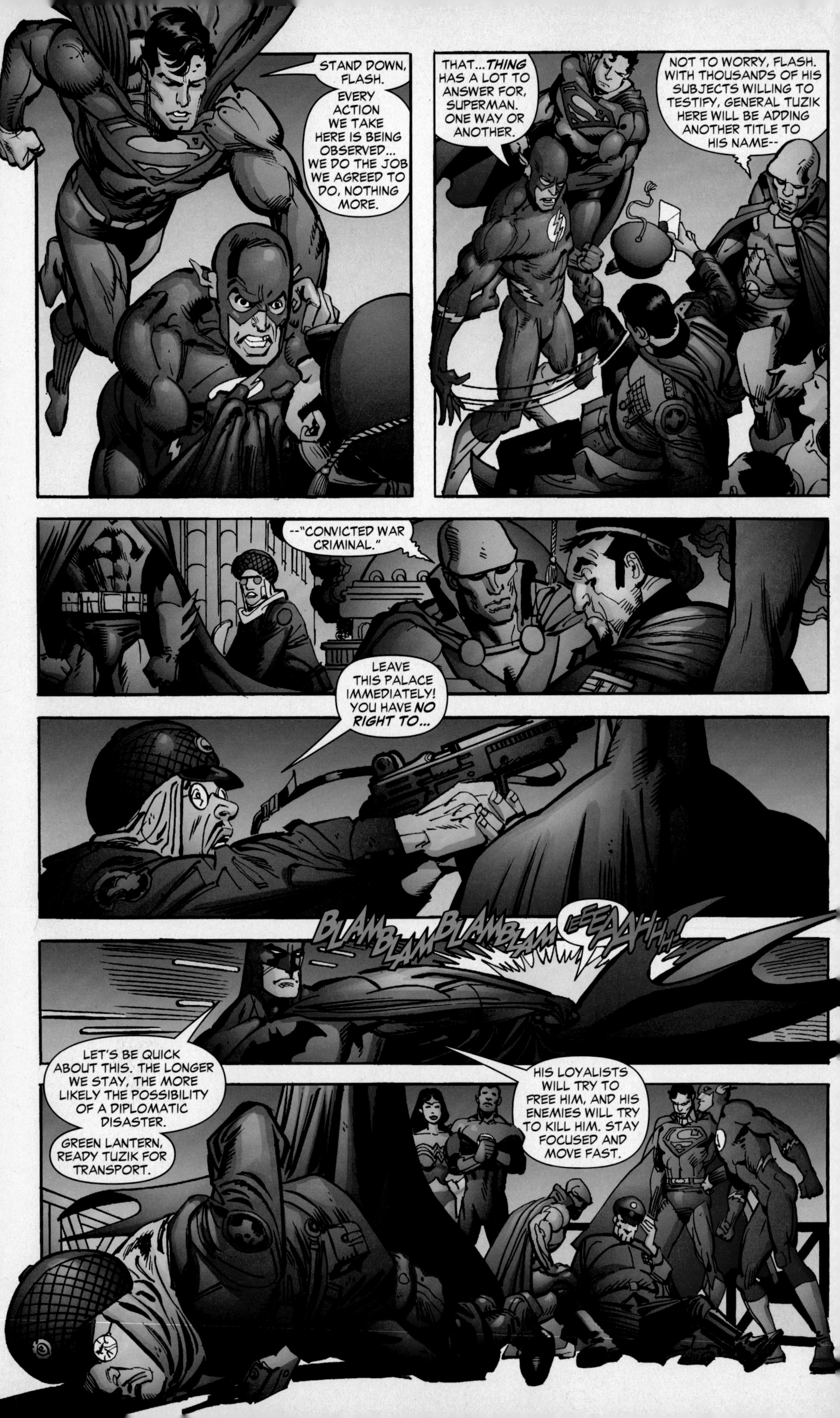
STAND DOWN, FLASH.
EVERY ACTION WE TAKE HERE IS BEING OBSERVED... WE DO THE JOB WE AGREED TO DO, NOTHING MORE.
THAT...THING HAS A LOT TO ANSWER FOR, SUPERMAN. ONE WAY OR ANOTHER.
NOT TO WORRY, FLASH. WITH THOUSANDS OF HIS SUBJECTS WILLING TO TESTIFY, GENERAL TUZIK HERE WILL BE ADDING ANOTHER TITLE TO HIS NAME--
--"CONVICTED WAR CRIMINAL."
LEAVE THIS PALACE IMMEDIATELY! YOU HAVE NO RIGHT TO...
BLAMBLAMBLAMBLAM
EEEAAHHH!
LET'S BE QUICK ABOUT THIS. THE LONGER WE STAY, THE MORE LIKELY THE POSSIBILITY OF A DIPLOMATIC DISASTER.
GREEN LANTERN, READY TUZIK FOR TRANSPORT.
HIS LOYALISTS WILL TRY TO FREE HIM, AND HIS ENEMIES WILL TRY TO KILL HIM. STAY FOCUSED AND MOVE FAST.

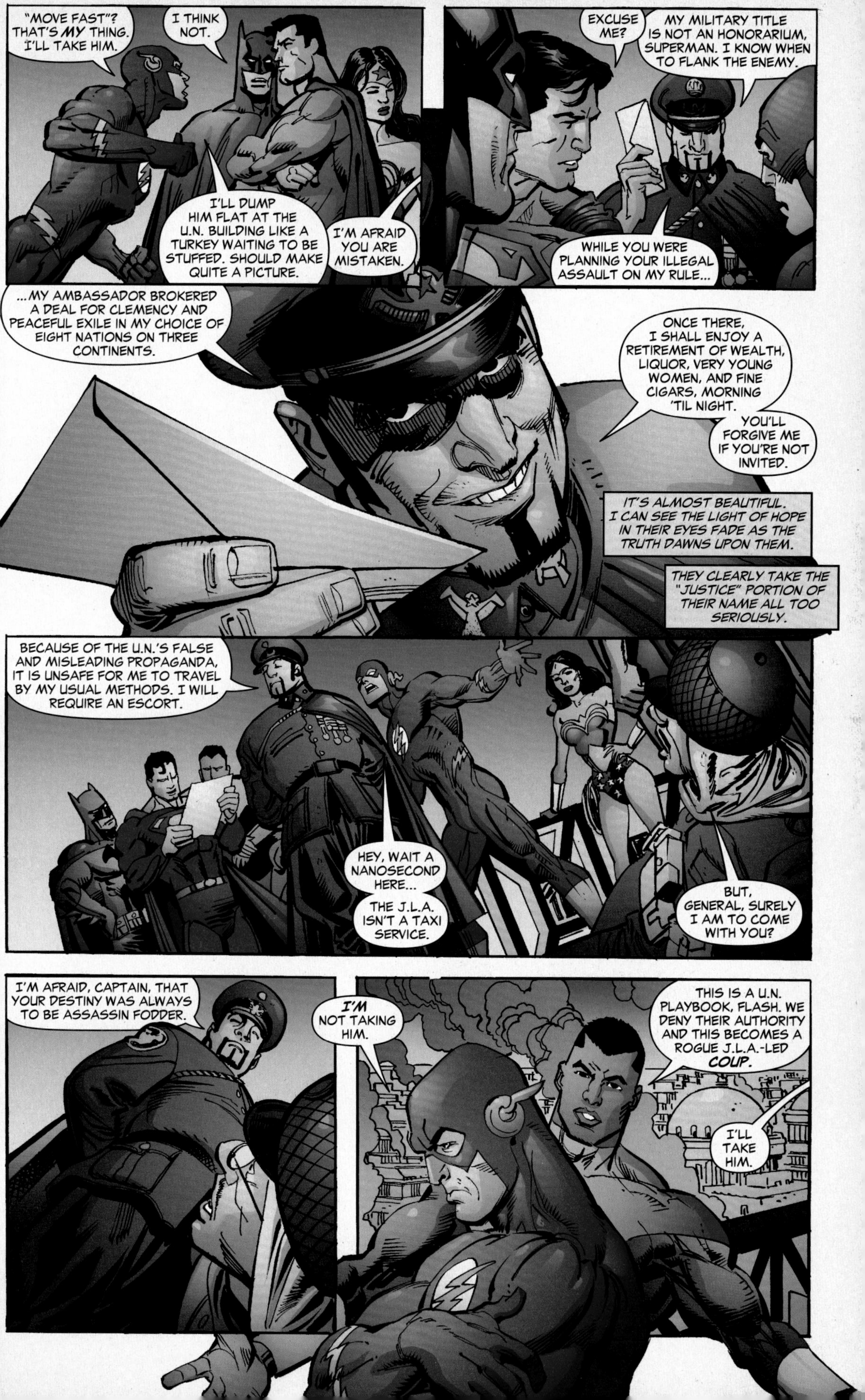
"MOVE FAST"? THAT'S *MY* THING. I'LL TAKE HIM.
I THINK NOT.
I'LL DUMP HIM FLAT AT THE U.N. BUILDING LIKE A TURKEY WAITING TO BE STUFFED. SHOULD MAKE QUITE A PICTURE.
I'M AFRAID YOU ARE MISTAKEN.
EXCUSE ME?
MY MILITARY TITLE IS NOT AN HONORARIUM, SUPERMAN. I KNOW WHEN TO FLANK THE ENEMY.
WHILE YOU WERE PLANNING YOUR ILLEGAL ASSAULT ON MY RULE...
...MY AMBASSADOR BROKERED A DEAL FOR CLEMENCY AND PEACEFUL EXILE IN MY CHOICE OF EIGHT NATIONS ON THREE CONTINENTS.
ONCE THERE, I SHALL ENJOY A RETIREMENT OF WEALTH, LIQUOR, VERY YOUNG WOMEN, AND FINE CIGARS, MORNING 'TIL NIGHT.
YOU'LL FORGIVE ME IF YOU'RE NOT INVITED.
IT'S ALMOST BEAUTIFUL. I CAN SEE THE LIGHT OF HOPE IN THEIR EYES FADE AS THE TRUTH DAWNS UPON THEM.
THEY CLEARLY TAKE THE "JUSTICE" PORTION OF THEIR NAME ALL TOO SERIOUSLY.
BECAUSE OF THE U.N.'S FALSE AND MISLEADING PROPAGANDA, IT IS UNSAFE FOR ME TO TRAVEL BY MY USUAL METHODS. I WILL REQUIRE AN ESCORT.
HEY, WAIT A NANOSECOND HERE...
THE J.L.A. ISN'T A TAXI SERVICE.
BUT, GENERAL, SURELY I AM TO COME WITH YOU?
I'M AFRAID, CAPTAIN, THAT YOUR DESTINY WAS ALWAYS TO BE ASSASSIN FODDER.
I'M NOT TAKING HIM.
THIS IS A U.N. PLAYBOOK, FLASH. WE DENY THEIR AUTHORITY AND THIS BECOMES A ROGUE J.L.A.-LED *COUP*.
I'LL TAKE HIM.

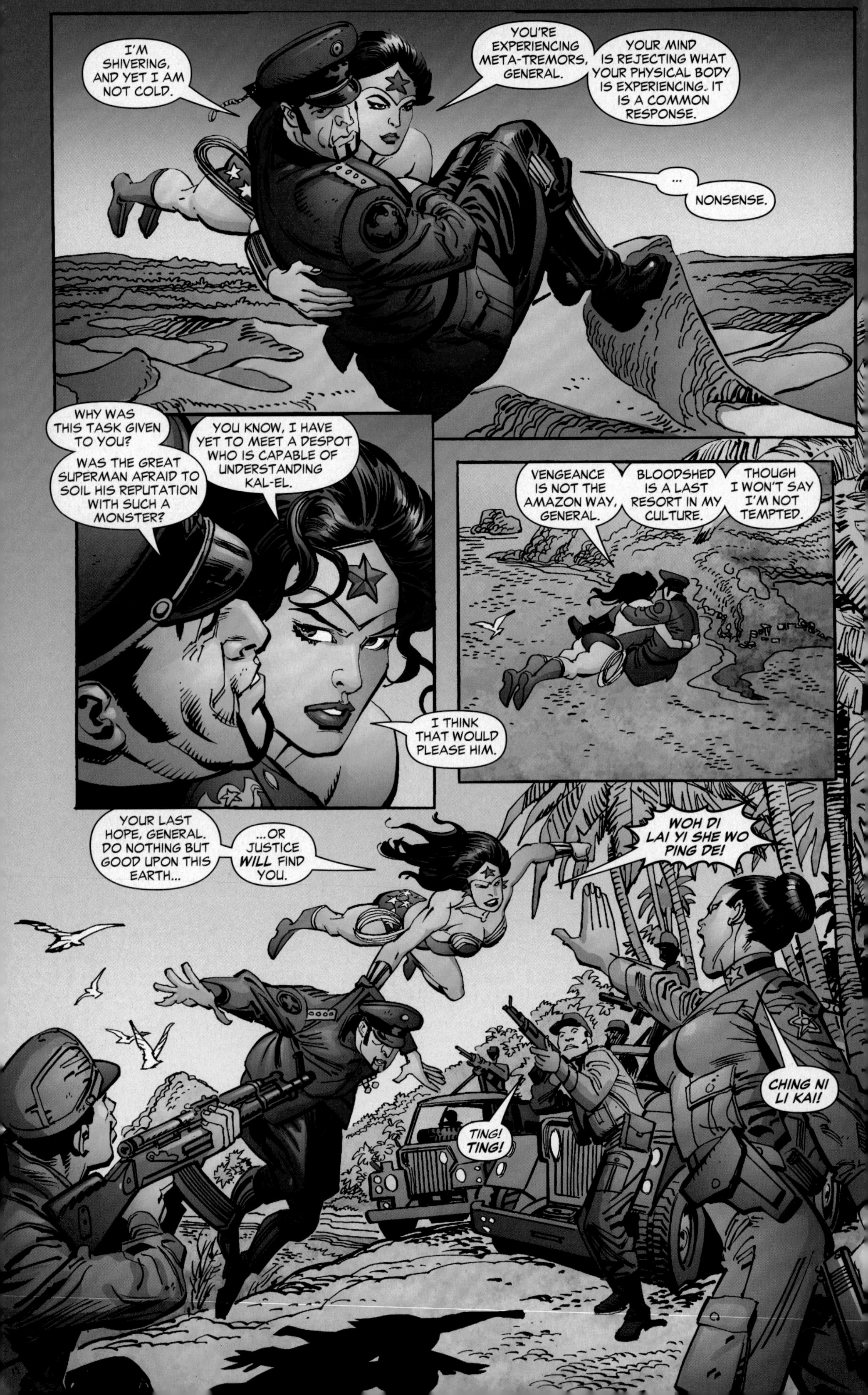
I'M SHIVERING, AND YET I AM NOT COLD.
YOU'RE EXPERIENCING META-TREMORS, GENERAL.
YOUR MIND IS REJECTING WHAT YOUR PHYSICAL BODY IS EXPERIENCING. IT IS A COMMON RESPONSE.
... NONSENSE.
WHY WAS THIS TASK GIVEN TO YOU?
WAS THE GREAT SUPERMAN AFRAID TO SOIL HIS REPUTATION WITH SUCH A MONSTER?
YOU KNOW, I HAVE YET TO MEET A DESPOT WHO IS CAPABLE OF UNDERSTANDING KAL-EL.
I THINK THAT WOULD PLEASE HIM.
VENGEANCE IS NOT THE AMAZON WAY, GENERAL.
BLOODSHED IS A LAST RESORT IN MY CULTURE.
THOUGH I WON'T SAY I'M NOT TEMPTED.
YOUR LAST HOPE, GENERAL. DO NOTHING BUT GOOD UPON THIS EARTH...
...OR JUSTICE **WILL** FIND YOU.
WOH DI LAI YI SHE WO PING DE!
CHING NI LI KAI!
TING! TING!

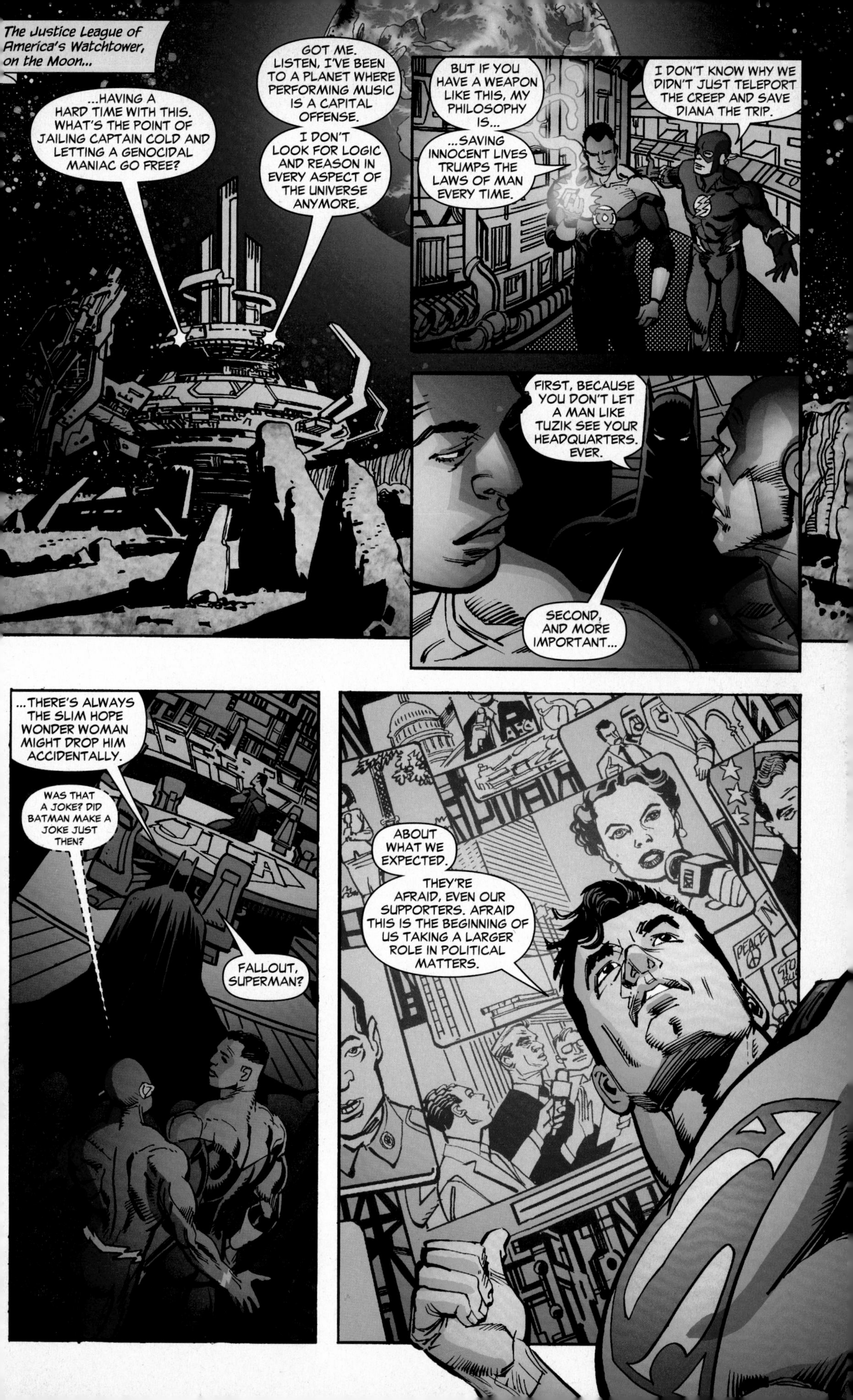
The Justice League of America's Watchtower, on the Moon...
...HAVING A HARD TIME WITH THIS. WHAT'S THE POINT OF JAILING CAPTAIN COLD AND LETTING A GENOCIDAL MANIAC GO FREE?
GOT ME. LISTEN, I'VE BEEN TO A PLANET WHERE PERFORMING MUSIC IS A CAPITAL OFFENSE.
I DON'T LOOK FOR LOGIC AND REASON IN EVERY ASPECT OF THE UNIVERSE ANYMORE.
BUT IF YOU HAVE A WEAPON LIKE THIS, MY PHILOSOPHY IS...
...SAVING INNOCENT LIVES TRUMPS THE LAWS OF MAN EVERY TIME.
I DON'T KNOW WHY WE DIDN'T JUST TELEPORT THE CREEP AND SAVE DIANA THE TRIP.
FIRST, BECAUSE YOU DON'T LET A MAN LIKE TUZIK SEE YOUR HEADQUARTERS. EVER.
SECOND, AND MORE IMPORTANT...
...THERE'S ALWAYS THE SLIM HOPE WONDER WOMAN MIGHT DROP HIM ACCIDENTALLY.
WAS THAT A JOKE? DID BATMAN MAKE A JOKE JUST THEN?
FALLOUT, SUPERMAN?
ABOUT WHAT WE EXPECTED.
THEY'RE AFRAID, EVEN OUR SUPPORTERS. AFRAID THIS IS THE BEGINNING OF US TAKING A LARGER ROLE IN POLITICAL MATTERS.

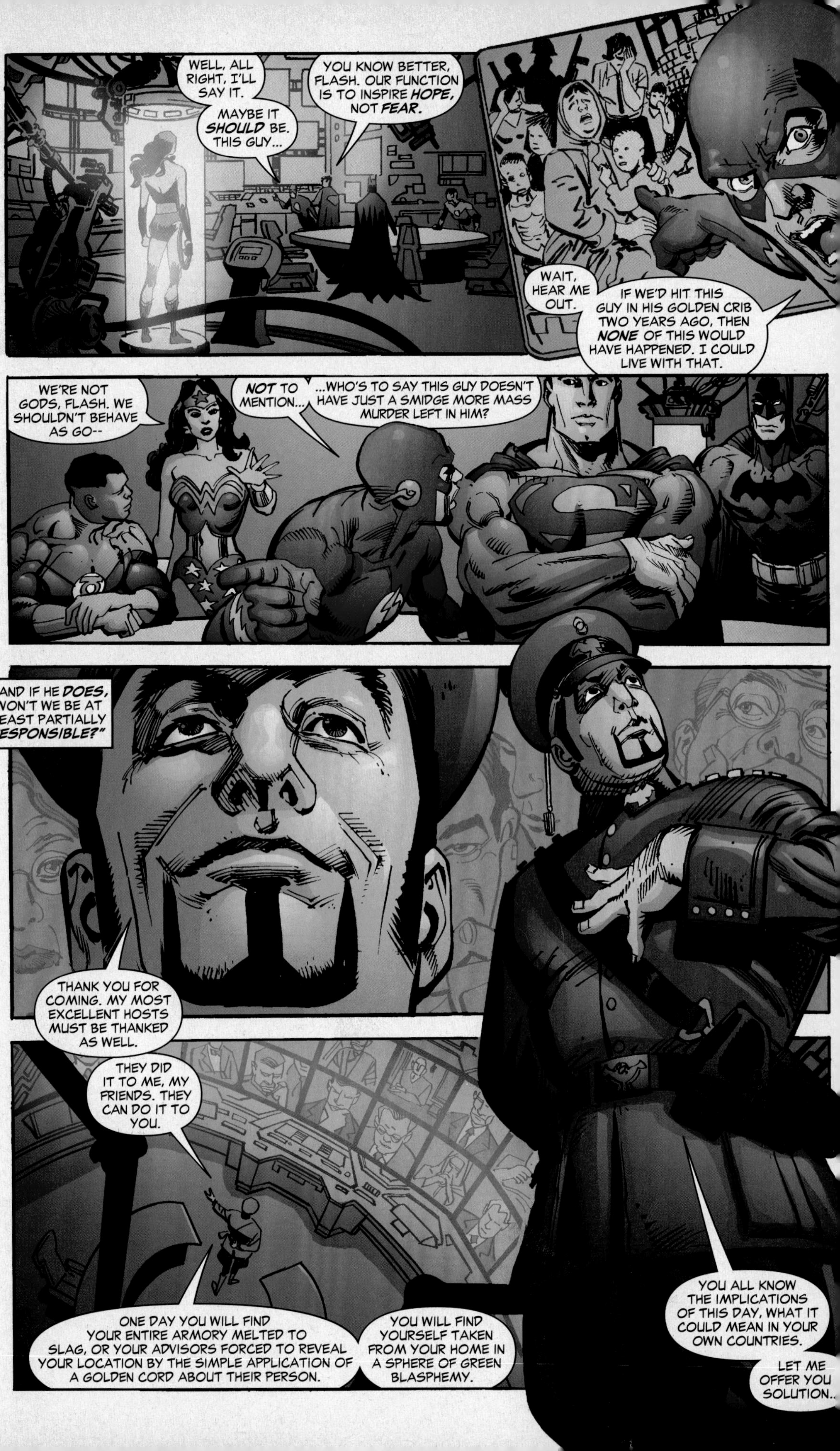

WELL, ALL RIGHT, I'LL SAY IT.
MAYBE IT SHOULD BE. THIS GUY...
YOU KNOW BETTER, FLASH. OUR FUNCTION IS TO INSPIRE HOPE, NOT FEAR.
WAIT, HEAR ME OUT.
IF WE'D HIT THIS GUY IN HIS GOLDEN CRIB TWO YEARS AGO, THEN NONE OF THIS WOULD HAVE HAPPENED. I COULD LIVE WITH THAT.
WE'RE NOT GODS, FLASH. WE SHOULDN'T BEHAVE AS GO--
NOT TO MENTION...
...WHO'S TO SAY THIS GUY DOESN'T HAVE JUST A SMIDGE MORE MASS MURDER LEFT IN HIM?
"AND IF HE DOES, WON'T WE BE AT LEAST PARTIALLY RESPONSIBLE?"
THANK YOU FOR COMING. MY MOST EXCELLENT HOSTS MUST BE THANKED AS WELL.
THEY DID IT TO ME, MY FRIENDS. THEY CAN DO IT TO YOU.
ONE DAY YOU WILL FIND YOUR ENTIRE ARMORY MELTED TO SLAG, OR YOUR ADVISORS FORCED TO REVEAL YOUR LOCATION BY THE SIMPLE APPLICATION OF A GOLDEN CORD ABOUT THEIR PERSON.
YOU WILL FIND YOURSELF TAKEN FROM YOUR HOME IN A SPHERE OF GREEN BLASPHEMY.
YOU ALL KNOW THE IMPLICATIONS OF THIS DAY, WHAT IT COULD MEAN IN YOUR OWN COUNTRIES.
LET ME OFFER YOU SOLUTION...

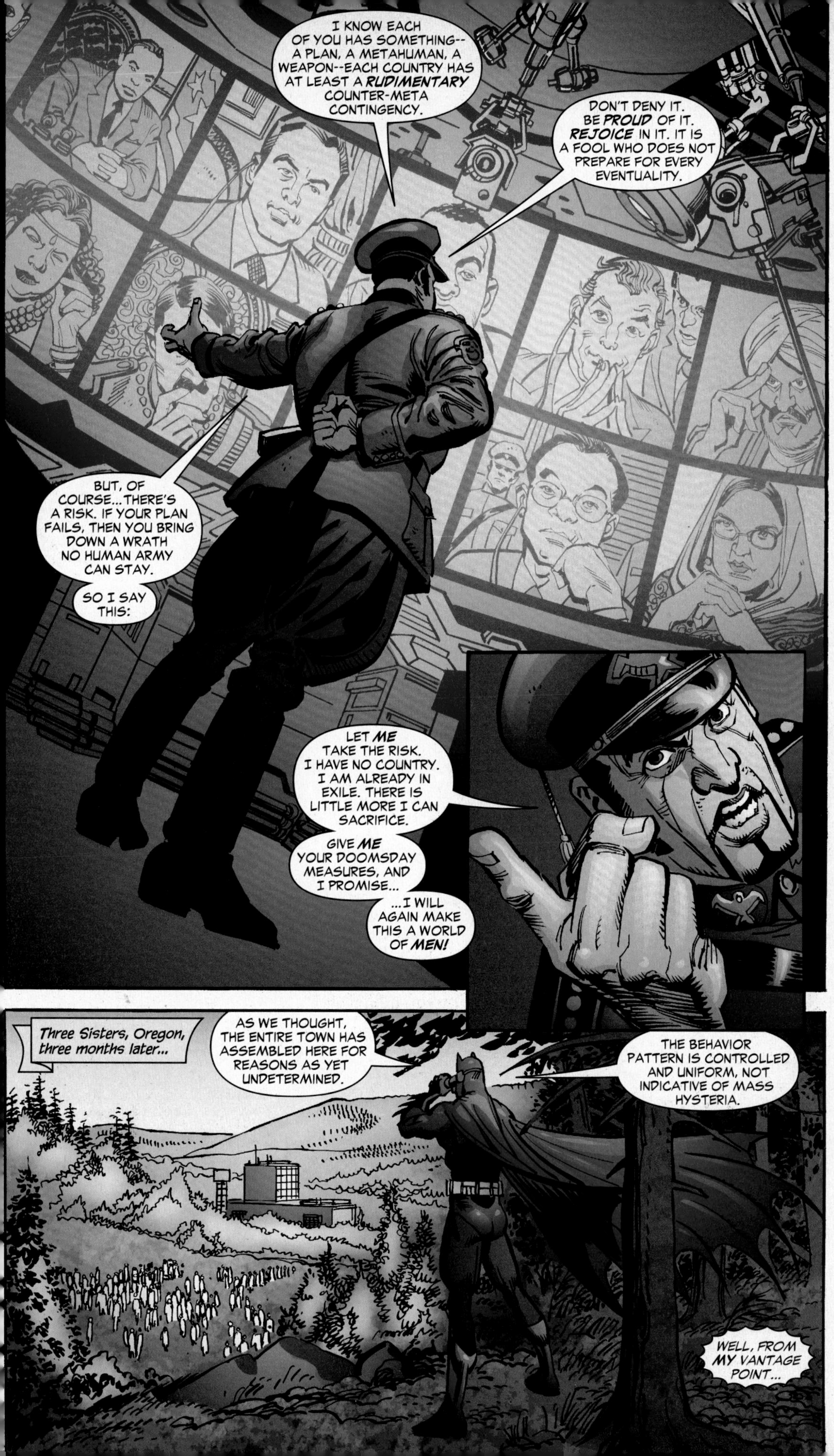

I KNOW EACH OF YOU HAS SOMETHING-- A PLAN, A METAHUMAN, A WEAPON--EACH COUNTRY HAS AT LEAST A ***RUDIMENTARY*** COUNTER-META CONTINGENCY.
DON'T DENY IT. BE ***PROUD*** OF IT. ***REJOICE*** IN IT. IT IS A FOOL WHO DOES NOT PREPARE FOR EVERY EVENTUALITY.
BUT, OF COURSE...THERE'S A RISK. IF YOUR PLAN FAILS, THEN YOU BRING DOWN A WRATH NO HUMAN ARMY CAN STAY.
SO I SAY THIS:
LET ***ME*** TAKE THE RISK. I HAVE NO COUNTRY. I AM ALREADY IN EXILE. THERE IS LITTLE MORE I CAN SACRIFICE.
GIVE ***ME*** YOUR DOOMSDAY MEASURES, AND I PROMISE...
...I WILL AGAIN MAKE THIS A WORLD OF ***MEN!***
Three Sisters, Oregon, three months later...
AS WE THOUGHT, THE ENTIRE TOWN HAS ASSEMBLED HERE FOR REASONS AS YET UNDETERMINED.
THE BEHAVIOR PATTERN IS CONTROLLED AND UNIFORM, NOT INDICATIVE OF MASS HYSTERIA.
WELL, FROM ***MY*** VANTAGE POINT...

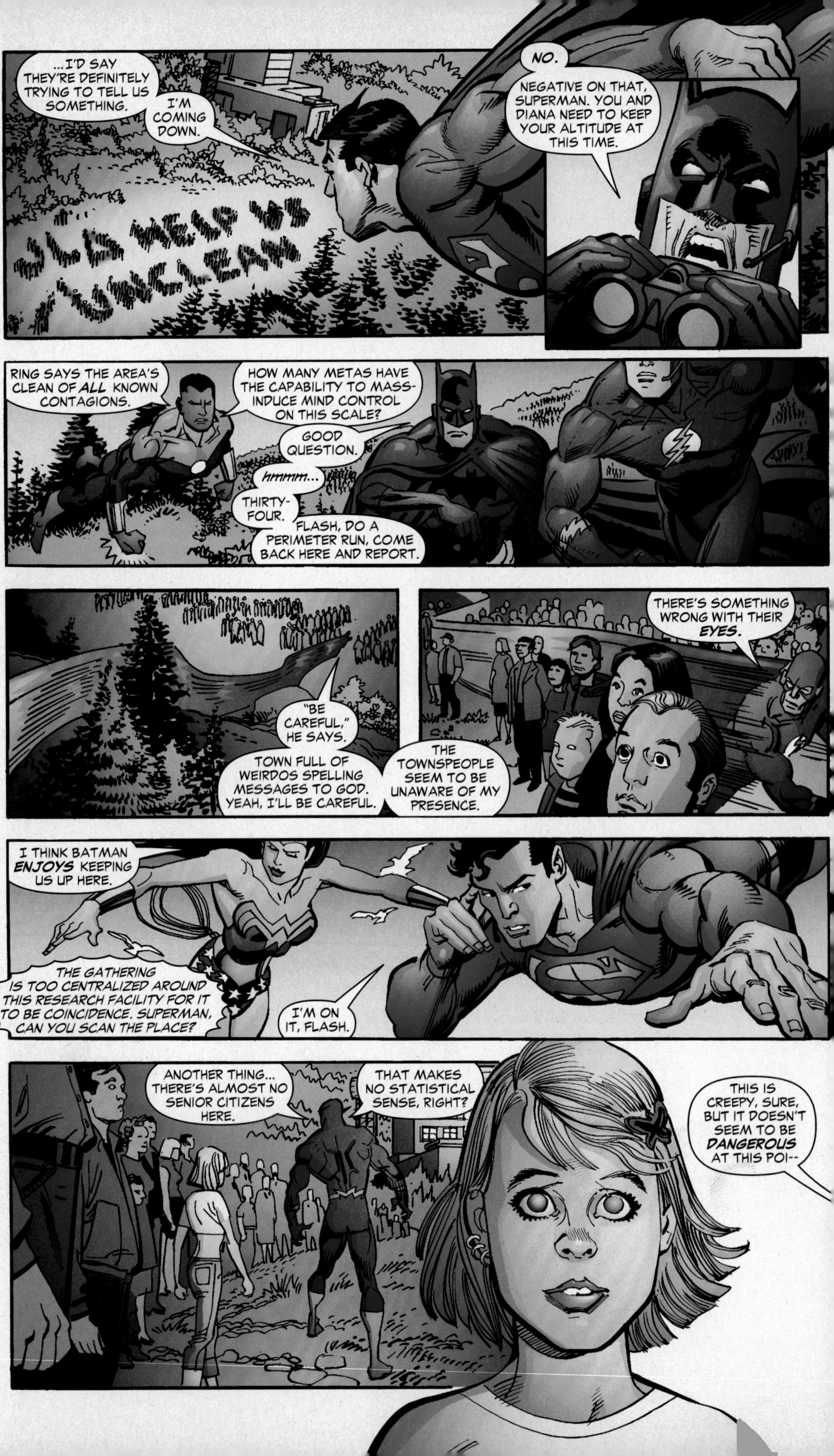
...I'D SAY THEY'RE DEFINITELY TRYING TO TELL US SOMETHING.
I'M COMING DOWN.
NO.
NEGATIVE ON THAT, SUPERMAN. YOU AND DIANA NEED TO KEEP YOUR ALTITUDE AT THIS TIME.
RING SAYS THE AREA'S CLEAN OF ALL KNOWN CONTAGIONS.
HOW MANY METAS HAVE THE CAPABILITY TO MASS-INDUCE MIND CONTROL ON THIS SCALE?
GOOD QUESTION.
hmmm...
THIRTY-FOUR.
FLASH, DO A PERIMETER RUN, COME BACK HERE AND REPORT.
"BE CAREFUL," HE SAYS.
TOWN FULL OF WEIRDOS SPELLING MESSAGES TO GOD. YEAH, I'LL BE CAREFUL.
THERE'S SOMETHING WRONG WITH THEIR EYES.
THE TOWNSPEOPLE SEEM TO BE UNAWARE OF MY PRESENCE.
I THINK BATMAN ENJOYS KEEPING US UP HERE.
THE GATHERING IS TOO CENTRALIZED AROUND THIS RESEARCH FACILITY FOR IT TO BE COINCIDENCE. SUPERMAN, CAN YOU SCAN THE PLACE?
I'M ON IT, FLASH.
ANOTHER THING... THERE'S ALMOST NO SENIOR CITIZENS HERE.
THAT MAKES NO STATISTICAL SENSE, RIGHT?
THIS IS CREEPY, SURE, BUT IT DOESN'T SEEM TO BE DANGEROUS AT THIS POI--

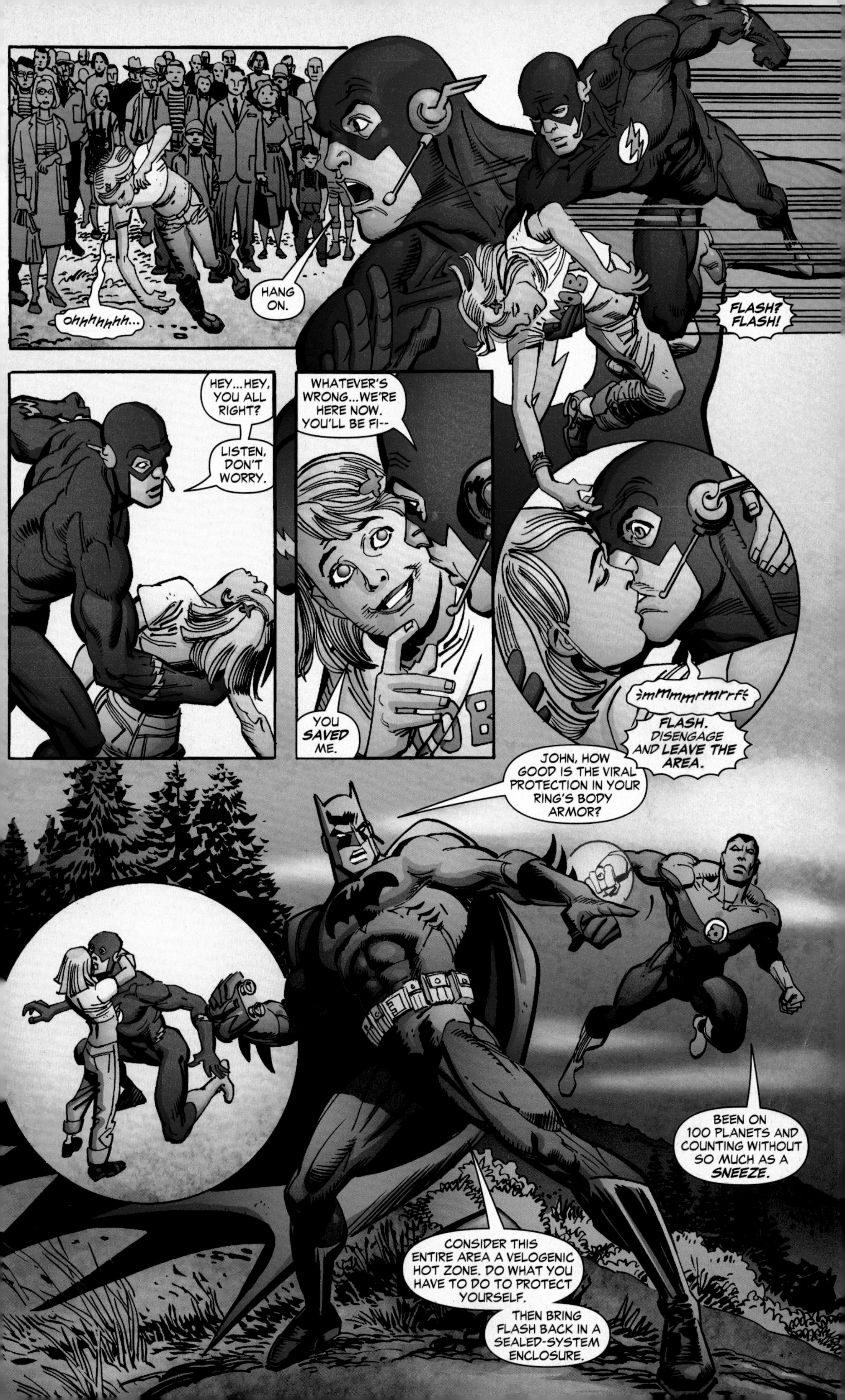
HANG ON.
ohhhhhhh...
FLASH? FLASH!
HEY...HEY, YOU ALL RIGHT?
LISTEN, DON'T WORRY.
WHATEVER'S WRONG...WE'RE HERE NOW. YOU'LL BE FI--
YOU SAVED ME.
mMMmmrmrrf
FLASH. DISENGAGE AND LEAVE THE AREA.
JOHN, HOW GOOD IS THE VIRAL PROTECTION IN YOUR RING'S BODY ARMOR?
BEEN ON 100 PLANETS AND COUNTING WITHOUT SO MUCH AS A SNEEZE.
CONSIDER THIS ENTIRE AREA A VELOGENIC HOT ZONE. DO WHAT YOU HAVE TO DO TO PROTECT YOURSELF.
THEN BRING FLASH BACK IN A SEALED-SYSTEM ENCLOSURE.

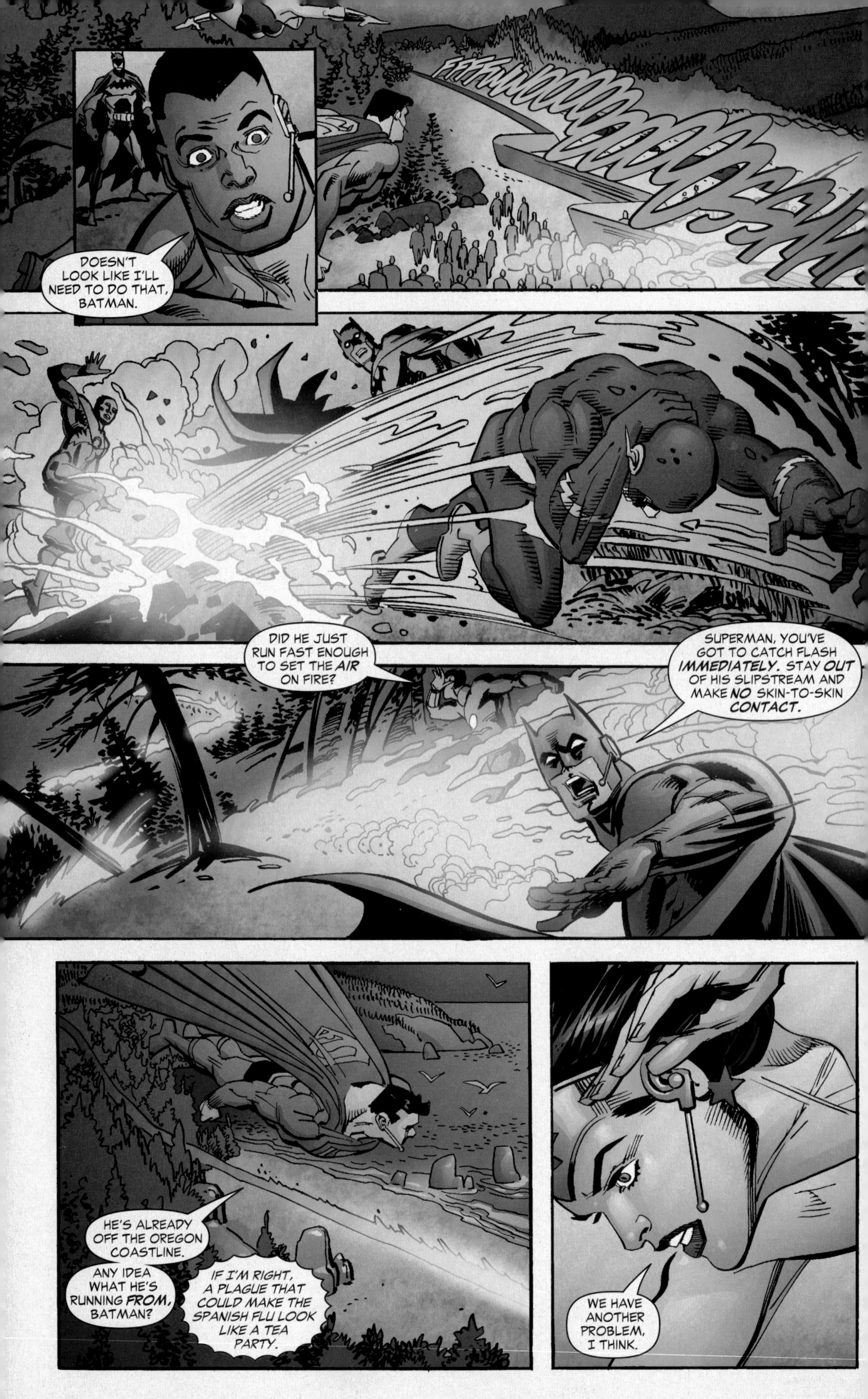
DOESN'T LOOK LIKE I'LL NEED TO DO THAT, BATMAN.
FFFFWOOOOOOOOOOOOOSSHHH
DID HE JUST RUN FAST ENOUGH TO SET THE *AIR* ON FIRE?
SUPERMAN, YOU'VE GOT TO CATCH FLASH *IMMEDIATELY*. STAY *OUT* OF HIS SLIPSTREAM AND MAKE *NO* SKIN-TO-SKIN *CONTACT*.
HE'S ALREADY OFF THE OREGON COASTLINE.
ANY IDEA WHAT HE'S RUNNING *FROM*, BATMAN?
IF I'M RIGHT, A PLAGUE THAT COULD MAKE THE SPANISH FLU LOOK LIKE A TEA PARTY.
WE HAVE ANOTHER PROBLEM, I THINK.

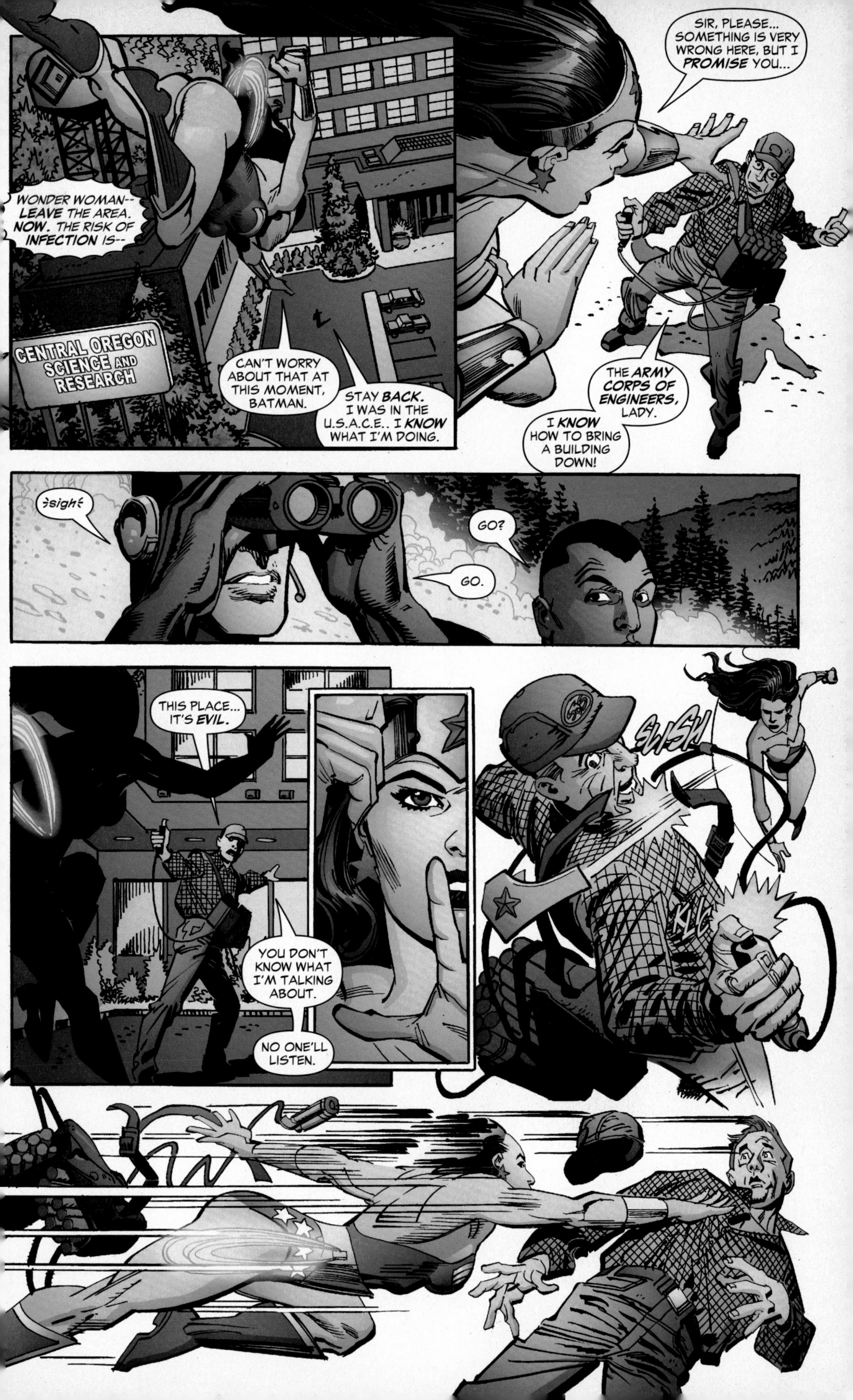
WONDER WOMAN-- LEAVE THE AREA. NOW. THE RISK OF INFECTION IS--
CENTRAL OREGON SCIENCE AND RESEARCH
CAN'T WORRY ABOUT THAT AT THIS MOMENT, BATMAN.
STAY BACK. I WAS IN THE U.S.A.C.E.. I KNOW WHAT I'M DOING.
SIR, PLEASE... SOMETHING IS VERY WRONG HERE, BUT I PROMISE YOU...
THE ARMY CORPS OF ENGINEERS, LADY.
I KNOW HOW TO BRING A BUILDING DOWN!
sigh
GO?
GO.
THIS PLACE... IT'S EVIL.
YOU DON'T KNOW WHAT I'M TALKING ABOUT.
NO ONE'LL LISTEN.
SWISH

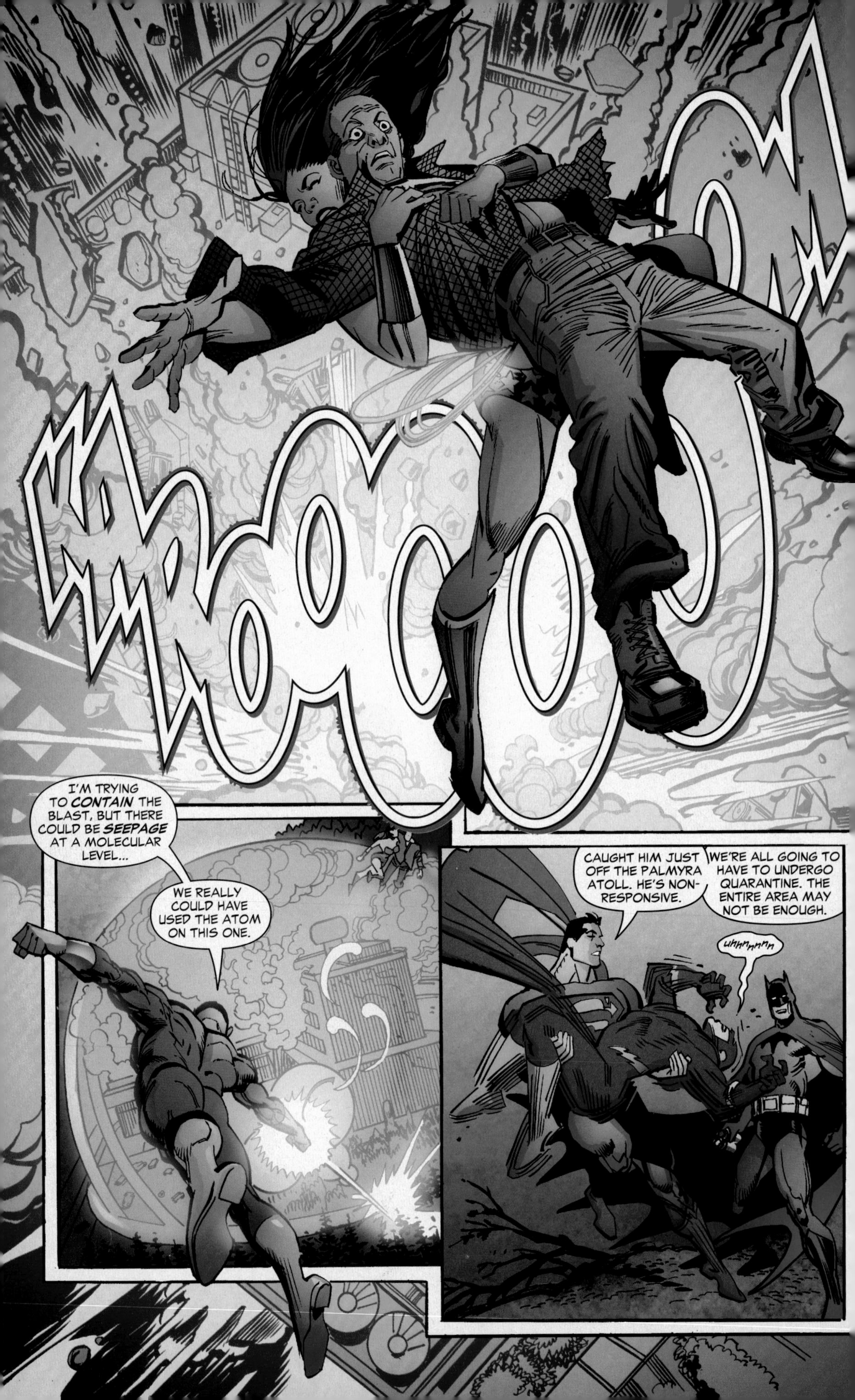
KA-ROOOOOOM
I'M TRYING TO CONTAIN THE BLAST, BUT THERE COULD BE SEEPAGE AT A MOLECULAR LEVEL...
WE REALLY COULD HAVE USED THE ATOM ON THIS ONE.
CAUGHT HIM JUST OFF THE PALMYRA ATOLL. HE'S NON-RESPONSIVE.
WE'RE ALL GOING TO HAVE TO UNDERGO QUARANTINE. THE ENTIRE AREA MAY NOT BE ENOUGH.
uhhnnnnn

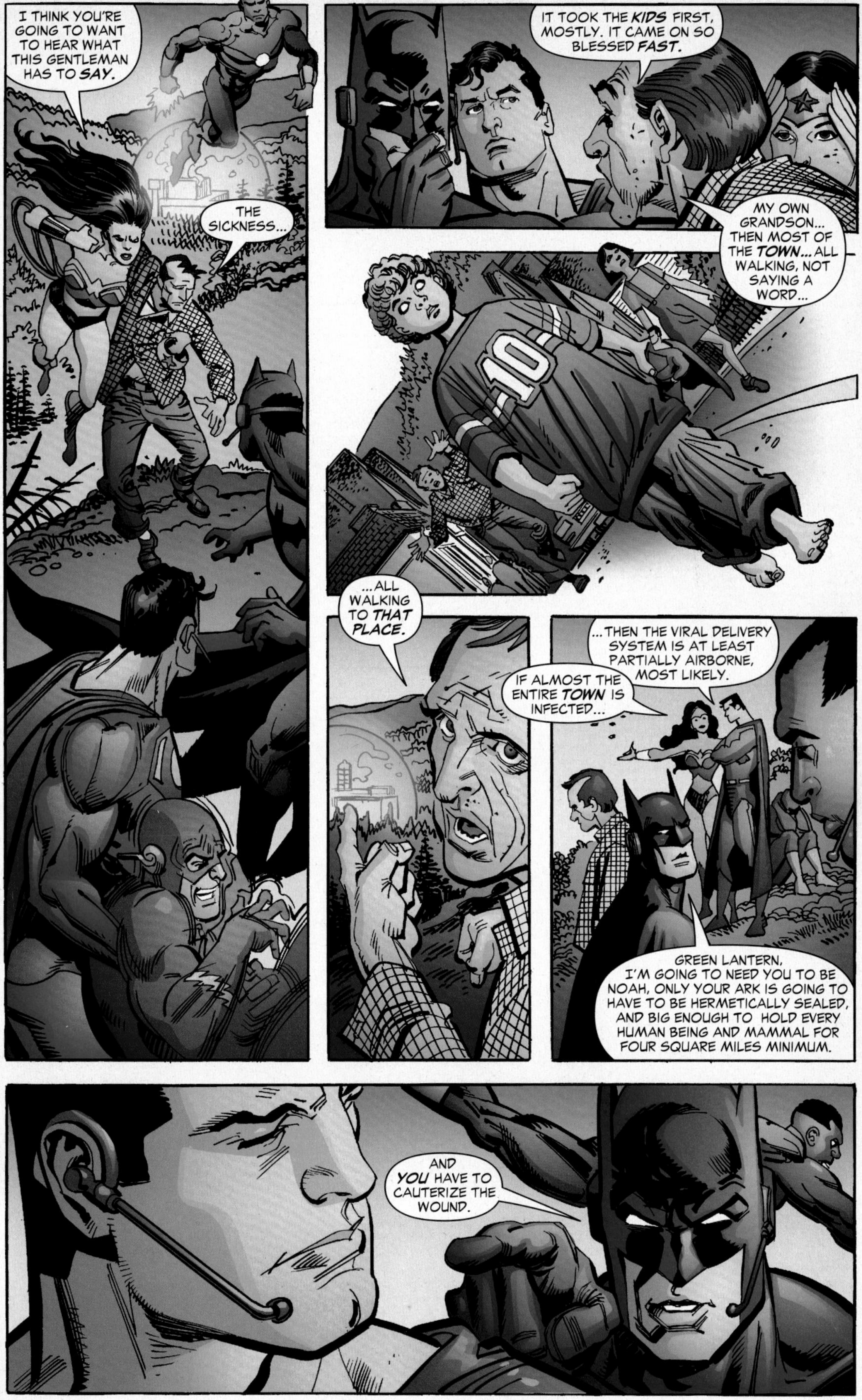
I THINK YOU'RE GOING TO WANT TO HEAR WHAT THIS GENTLEMAN HAS TO SAY.
THE SICKNESS...
IT TOOK THE KIDS FIRST, MOSTLY. IT CAME ON SO BLESSED FAST.
MY OWN GRANDSON... THEN MOST OF THE TOWN... ALL WALKING, NOT SAYING A WORD...
...ALL WALKING TO THAT PLACE.
IF ALMOST THE ENTIRE TOWN IS INFECTED...
...THEN THE VIRAL DELIVERY SYSTEM IS AT LEAST PARTIALLY AIRBORNE, MOST LIKELY.
GREEN LANTERN, I'M GOING TO NEED YOU TO BE NOAH, ONLY YOUR ARK IS GOING TO HAVE TO BE HERMETICALLY SEALED, AND BIG ENOUGH TO HOLD EVERY HUMAN BEING AND MAMMAL FOR FOUR SQUARE MILES MINIMUM.
AND YOU HAVE TO CAUTERIZE THE WOUND.

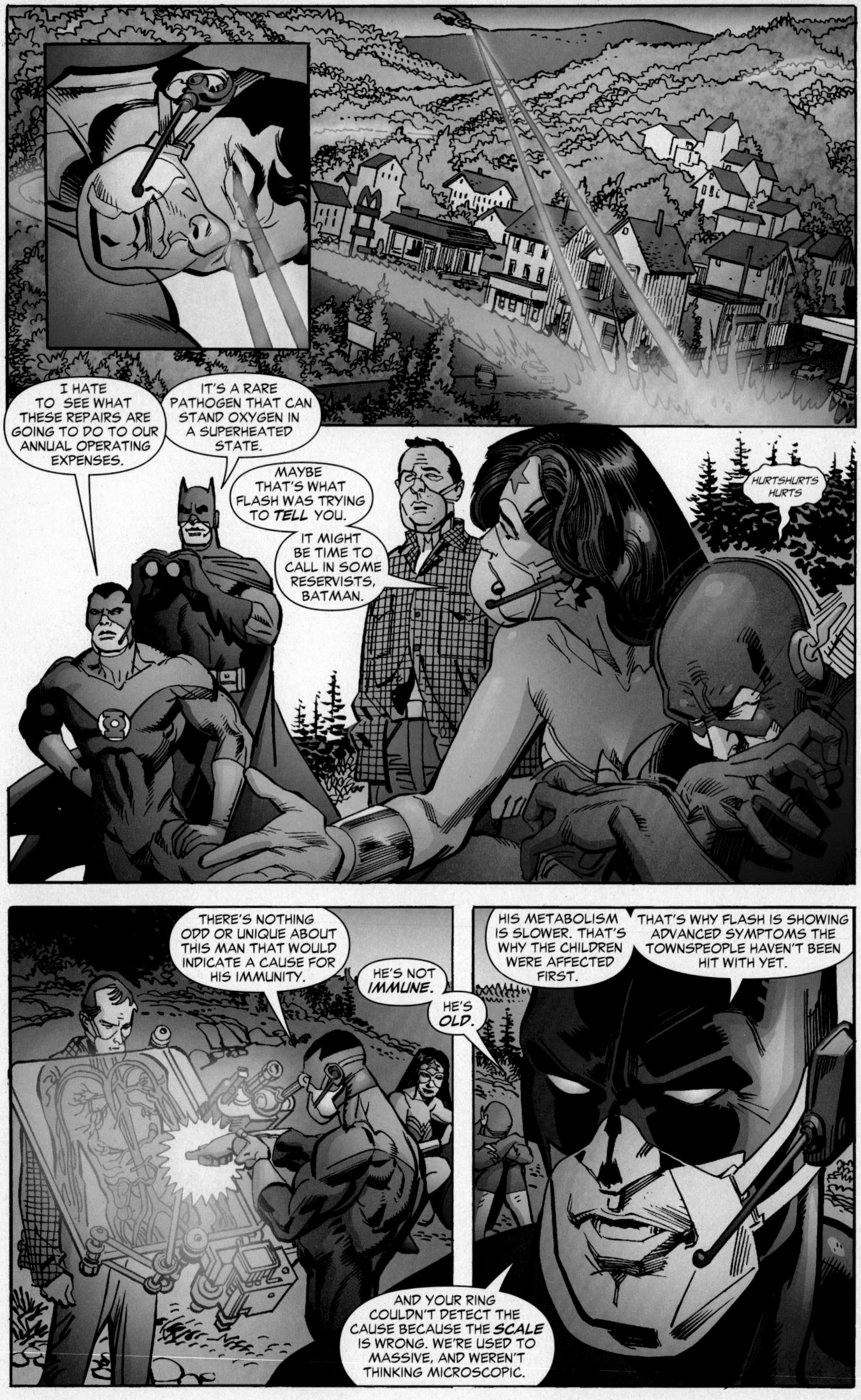
I HATE TO SEE WHAT THESE REPAIRS ARE GOING TO DO TO OUR ANNUAL OPERATING EXPENSES.
IT'S A RARE PATHOGEN THAT CAN STAND OXYGEN IN A SUPERHEATED STATE.
MAYBE THAT'S WHAT FLASH WAS TRYING TO TELL YOU.
IT MIGHT BE TIME TO CALL IN SOME RESERVISTS, BATMAN.
HURTSHURTS HURTS
THERE'S NOTHING ODD OR UNIQUE ABOUT THIS MAN THAT WOULD INDICATE A CAUSE FOR HIS IMMUNITY.
HE'S NOT IMMUNE.
HE'S OLD.
HIS METABOLISM IS SLOWER. THAT'S WHY THE CHILDREN WERE AFFECTED FIRST.
THAT'S WHY FLASH IS SHOWING ADVANCED SYMPTOMS THE TOWNSPEOPLE HAVEN'T BEEN HIT WITH YET.
AND YOUR RING COULDN'T DETECT THE CAUSE BECAUSE THE SCALE IS WRONG. WE'RE USED TO MASSIVE, AND WEREN'T THINKING MICROSCOPIC.

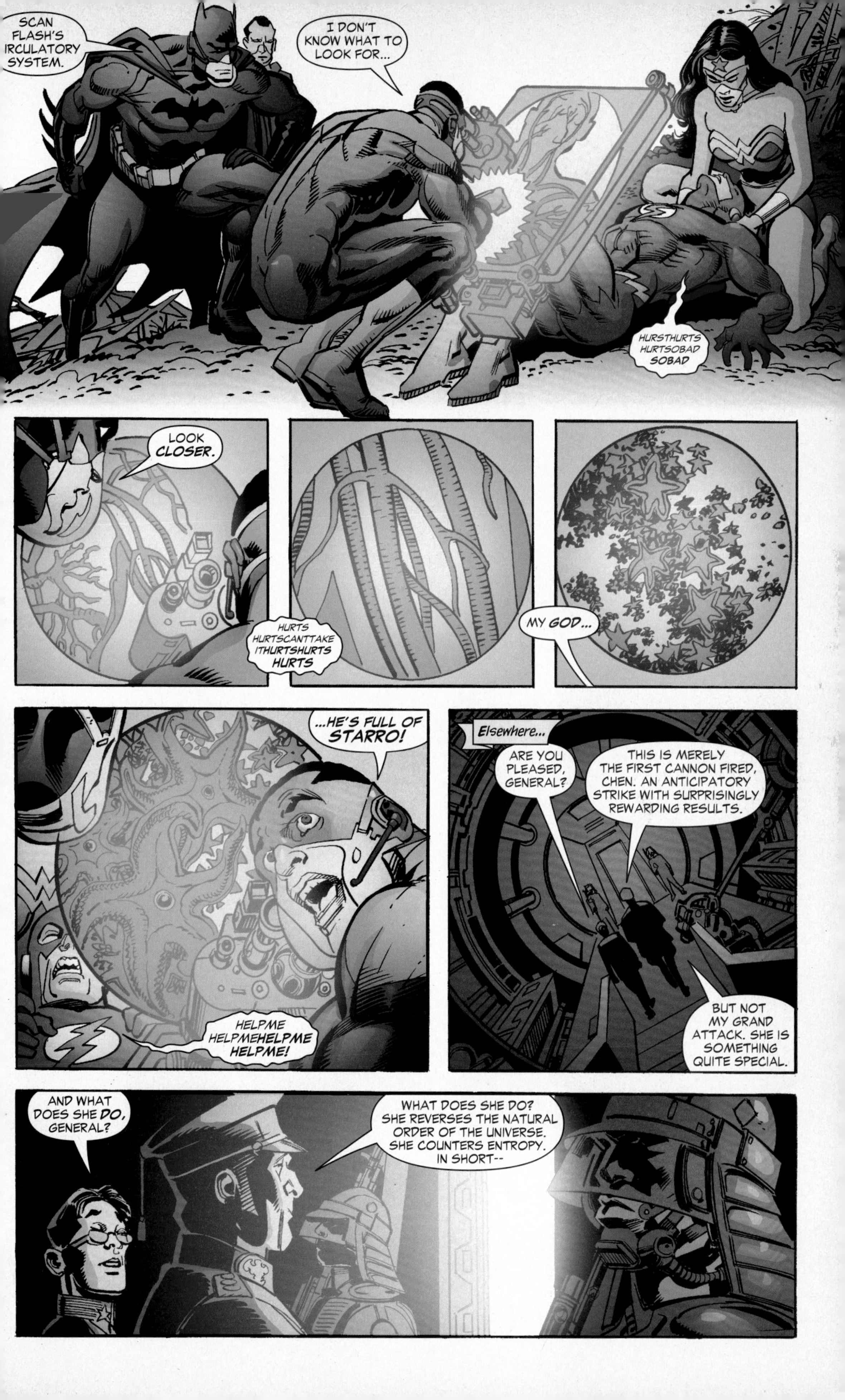
SCAN FLASH'S IRCULATORY SYSTEM.
I DON'T KNOW WHAT TO LOOK FOR...
HURSTHURTS HURTSOBAD SOBAD
LOOK CLOSER.
HURTS HURTSCANTTAKE ITHURTSHURTS HURTS
MY GOD...
...HE'S FULL OF STARRO!
HELPME HELPMEHELPME HELPME!
Elsewhere...
ARE YOU PLEASED, GENERAL?
THIS IS MERELY THE FIRST CANNON FIRED, CHEN. AN ANTICIPATORY STRIKE WITH SURPRISINGLY REWARDING RESULTS.
BUT NOT MY GRAND ATTACK. SHE IS SOMETHING QUITE SPECIAL.
AND WHAT DOES SHE DO, GENERAL?
WHAT DOES SHE DO? SHE REVERSES THE NATURAL ORDER OF THE UNIVERSE. SHE COUNTERS ENTROPY. IN SHORT--

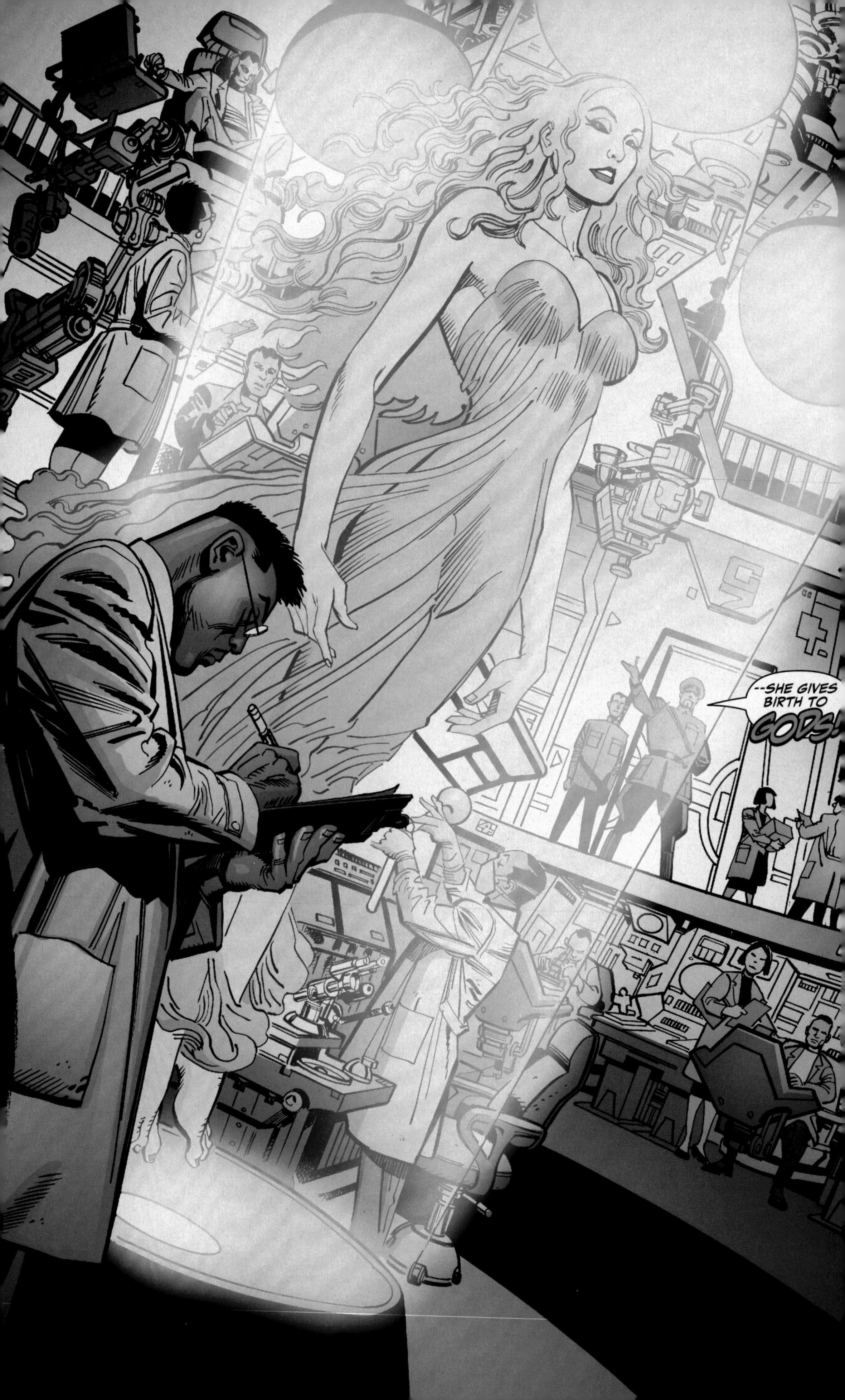
--SHE GIVES BIRTH TO GODS!

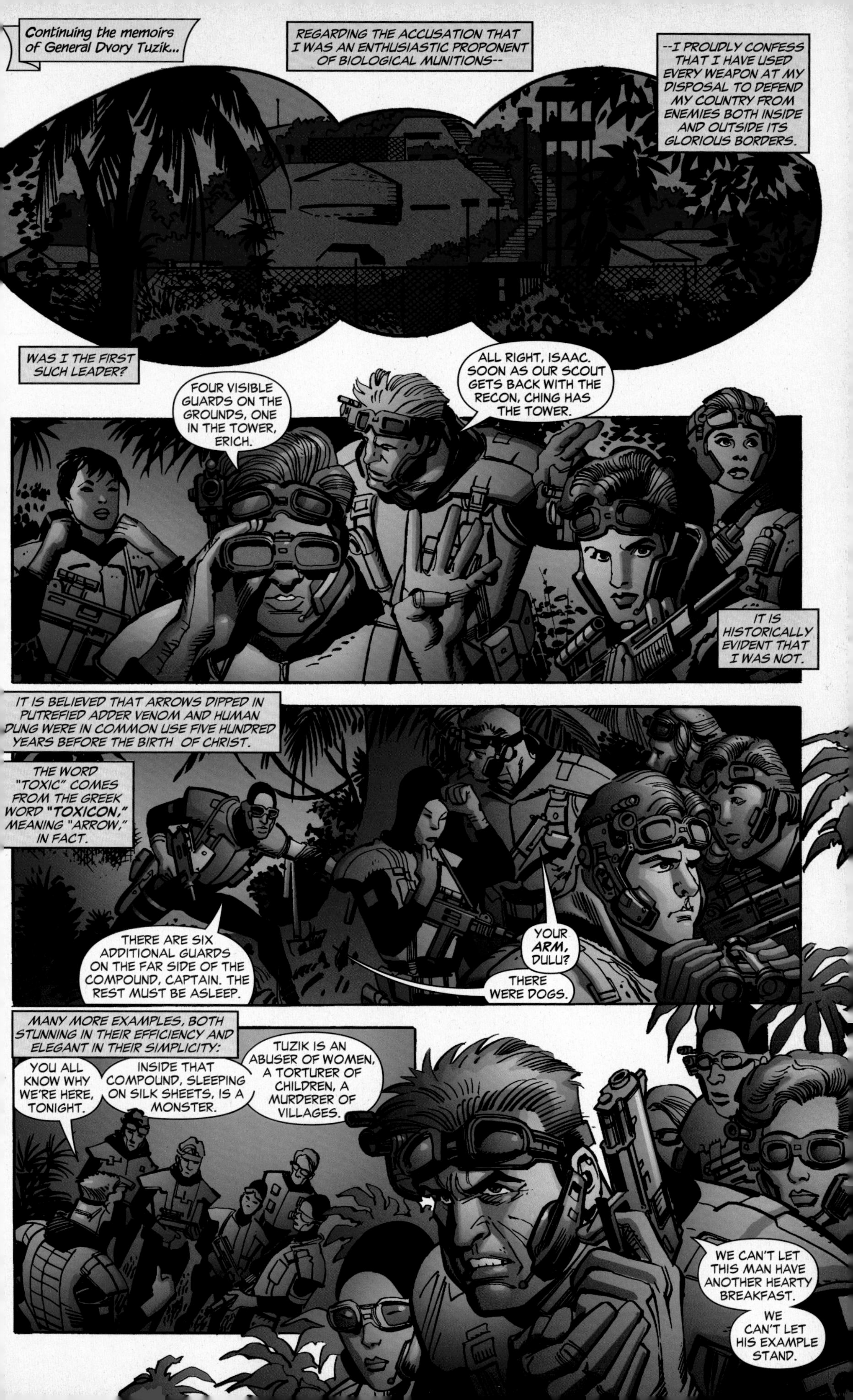
Continuing the memoirs of General Dvory Tuzik...
REGARDING THE ACCUSATION THAT I WAS AN ENTHUSIASTIC PROPONENT OF BIOLOGICAL MUNITIONS--
--I PROUDLY CONFESS THAT I HAVE USED EVERY WEAPON AT MY DISPOSAL TO DEFEND MY COUNTRY FROM ENEMIES BOTH INSIDE AND OUTSIDE ITS GLORIOUS BORDERS.
WAS I THE FIRST SUCH LEADER?
FOUR VISIBLE GUARDS ON THE GROUNDS, ONE IN THE TOWER, ERICH.
ALL RIGHT, ISAAC. SOON AS OUR SCOUT GETS BACK WITH THE RECON, CHING HAS THE TOWER.
IT IS HISTORICALLY EVIDENT THAT I WAS NOT.
IT IS BELIEVED THAT ARROWS DIPPED IN PUTREFIED ADDER VENOM AND HUMAN DUNG WERE IN COMMON USE FIVE HUNDRED YEARS BEFORE THE BIRTH OF CHRIST.
THE WORD "TOXIC" COMES FROM THE GREEK WORD "TOXICON," MEANING "ARROW," IN FACT.
THERE ARE SIX ADDITIONAL GUARDS ON THE FAR SIDE OF THE COMPOUND, CAPTAIN. THE REST MUST BE ASLEEP.
YOUR ARM, DULU?
THERE WERE DOGS.
MANY MORE EXAMPLES, BOTH STUNNING IN THEIR EFFICIENCY AND ELEGANT IN THEIR SIMPLICITY:
YOU ALL KNOW WHY WE'RE HERE, TONIGHT.
INSIDE THAT COMPOUND, SLEEPING ON SILK SHEETS, IS A MONSTER.
TUZIK IS AN ABUSER OF WOMEN, A TORTURER OF CHILDREN, A MURDERER OF VILLAGES.
WE CAN'T LET THIS MAN HAVE ANOTHER HEARTY BREAKFAST.
WE CAN'T LET HIS EXAMPLE STAND.

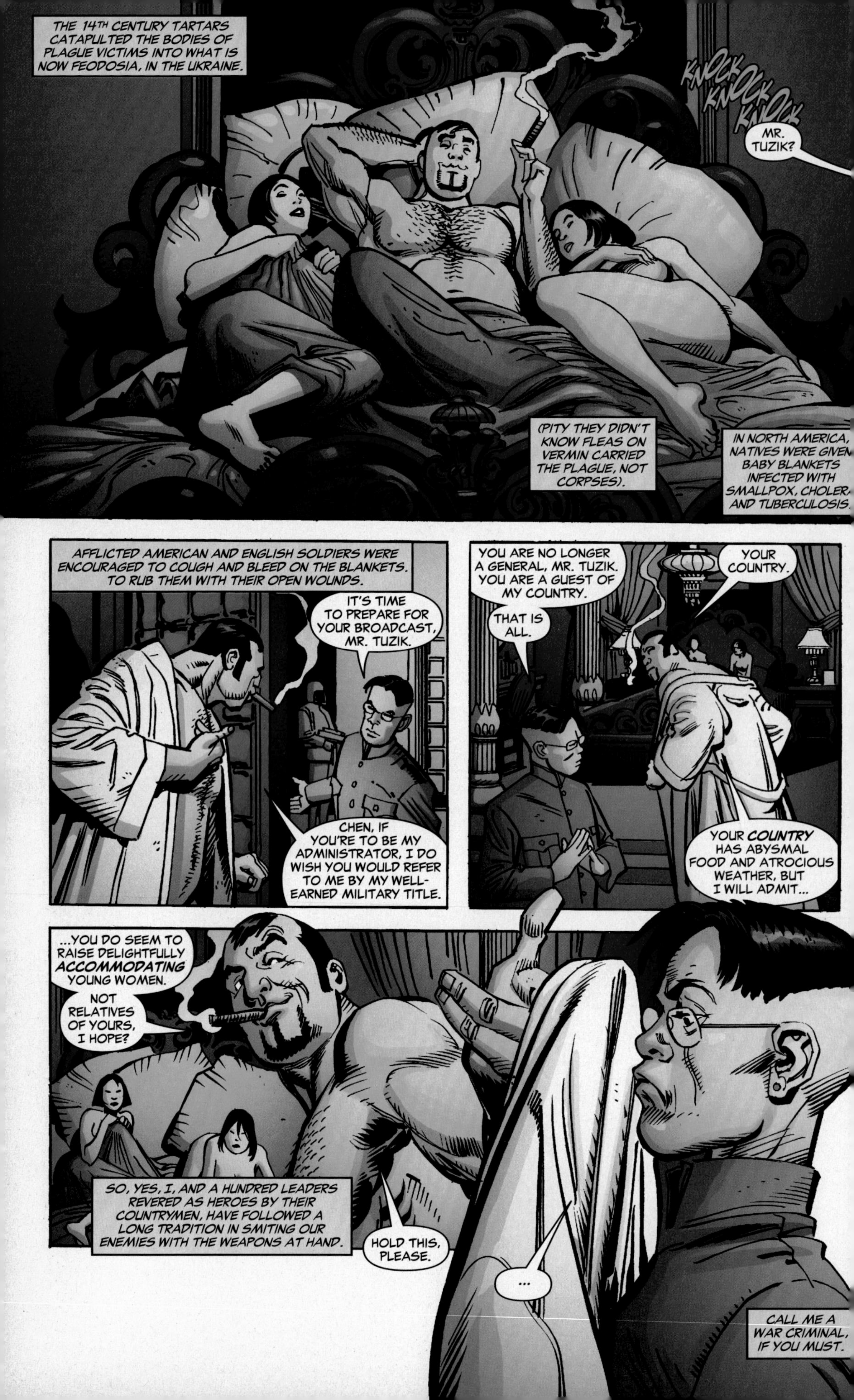
THE 14TH CENTURY TARTARS CATAPULTED THE BODIES OF PLAGUE VICTIMS INTO WHAT IS NOW FEODOSIA, IN THE UKRAINE.
KNOCK KNOCK KNOCK
MR. TUZIK?
(PITY THEY DIDN'T KNOW FLEAS ON VERMIN CARRIED THE PLAGUE, NOT CORPSES).
IN NORTH AMERICA, NATIVES WERE GIVEN BABY BLANKETS INFECTED WITH SMALLPOX, CHOLERA AND TUBERCULOSIS.
AFFLICTED AMERICAN AND ENGLISH SOLDIERS WERE ENCOURAGED TO COUGH AND BLEED ON THE BLANKETS. TO RUB THEM WITH THEIR OPEN WOUNDS.
IT'S TIME TO PREPARE FOR YOUR BROADCAST, MR. TUZIK.
CHEN, IF YOU'RE TO BE MY ADMINISTRATOR, I DO WISH YOU WOULD REFER TO ME BY MY WELL-EARNED MILITARY TITLE.
YOU ARE NO LONGER A GENERAL, MR. TUZIK. YOU ARE A GUEST OF MY COUNTRY.
THAT IS ALL.
YOUR COUNTRY.
YOUR COUNTRY HAS ABYSMAL FOOD AND ATROCIOUS WEATHER, BUT I WILL ADMIT...
...YOU DO SEEM TO RAISE DELIGHTFULLY ACCOMMODATING YOUNG WOMEN.
NOT RELATIVES OF YOURS, I HOPE?
SO, YES, I, AND A HUNDRED LEADERS REVERED AS HEROES BY THEIR COUNTRYMEN, HAVE FOLLOWED A LONG TRADITION IN SMITING OUR ENEMIES WITH THE WEAPONS AT HAND.
HOLD THIS, PLEASE.
...
CALL ME A WAR CRIMINAL, IF YOU MUST.

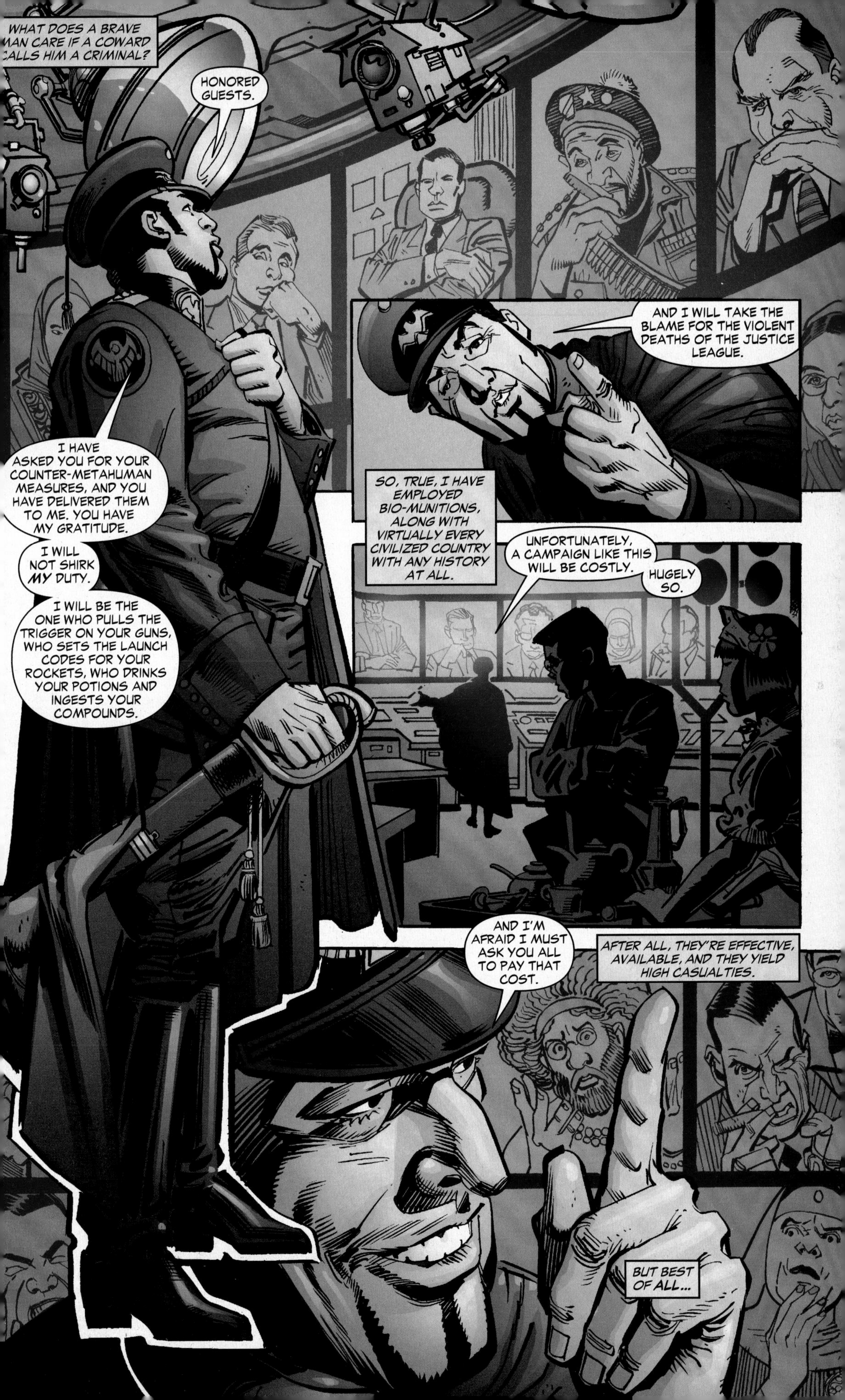
WHAT DOES A BRAVE MAN CARE IF A COWARD CALLS HIM A CRIMINAL?
HONORED GUESTS.
I HAVE ASKED YOU FOR YOUR COUNTER-METAHUMAN MEASURES, AND YOU HAVE DELIVERED THEM TO ME. YOU HAVE MY GRATITUDE.
I WILL NOT SHIRK MY DUTY.
I WILL BE THE ONE WHO PULLS THE TRIGGER ON YOUR GUNS, WHO SETS THE LAUNCH CODES FOR YOUR ROCKETS, WHO DRINKS YOUR POTIONS AND INGESTS YOUR COMPOUNDS.
AND I WILL TAKE THE BLAME FOR THE VIOLENT DEATHS OF THE JUSTICE LEAGUE.
SO, TRUE, I HAVE EMPLOYED BIO-MUNITIONS, ALONG WITH VIRTUALLY EVERY CIVILIZED COUNTRY WITH ANY HISTORY AT ALL.
UNFORTUNATELY, A CAMPAIGN LIKE THIS WILL BE COSTLY.
HUGELY SO.
AND I'M AFRAID I MUST ASK YOU ALL TO PAY THAT COST.
AFTER ALL, THEY'RE EFFECTIVE, AVAILABLE, AND THEY YIELD HIGH CASUALTIES.
BUT BEST OF ALL...

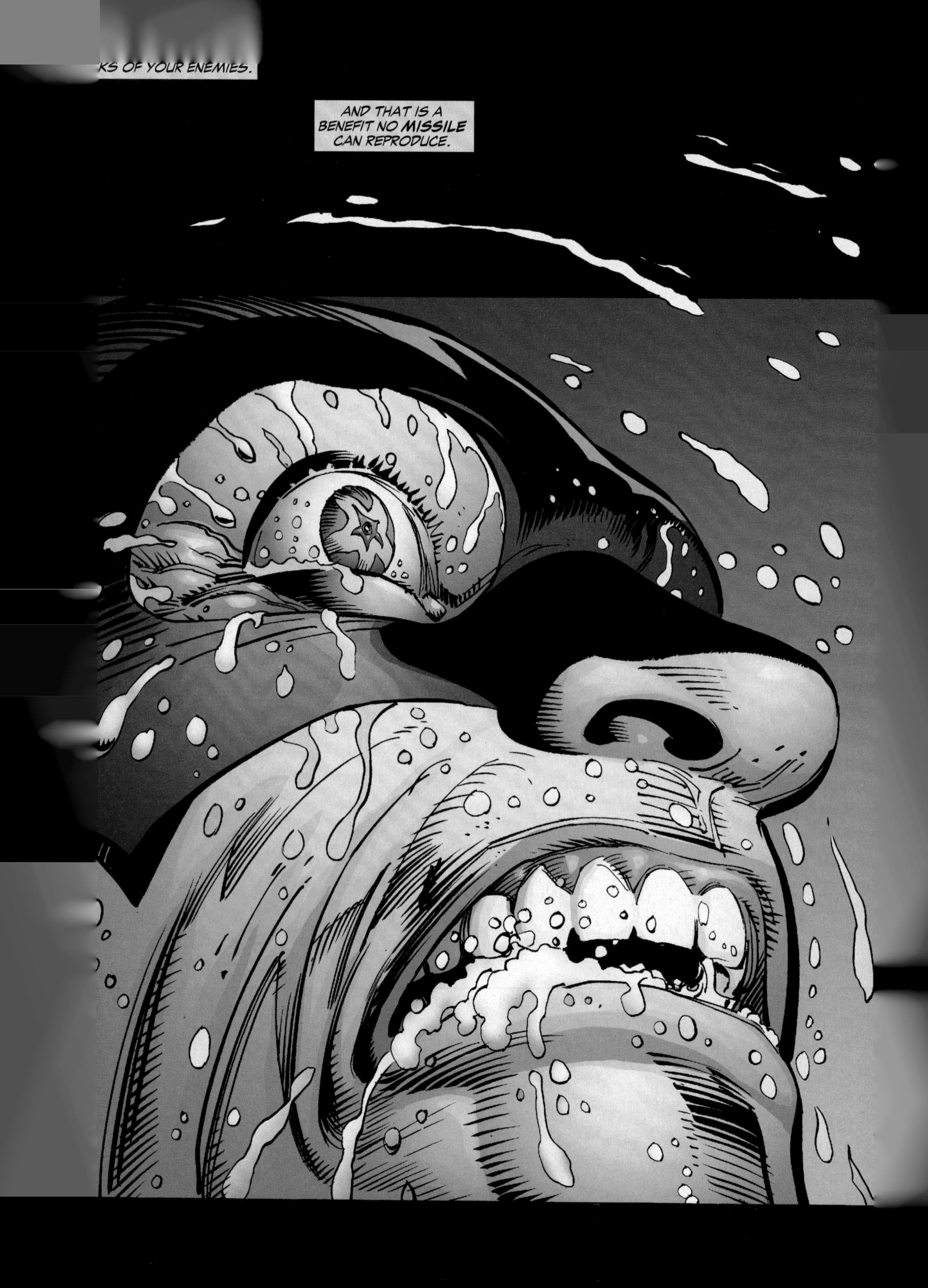

BLOOD IS NOT ENOUGH

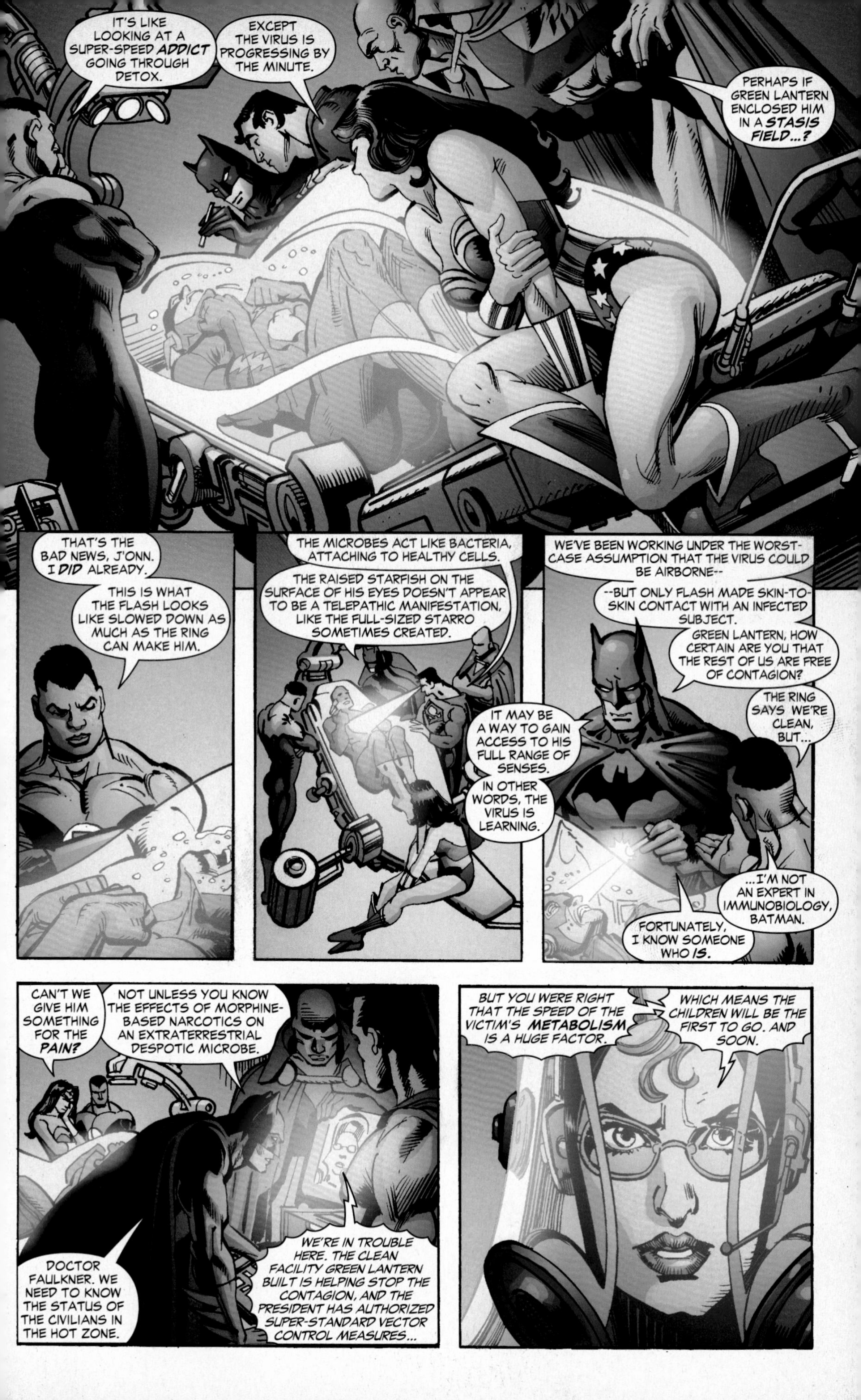
IT'S LIKE LOOKING AT A SUPER-SPEED ADDICT GOING THROUGH DETOX.
EXCEPT THE VIRUS IS PROGRESSING BY THE MINUTE.
PERHAPS IF GREEN LANTERN ENCLOSED HIM IN A STASIS FIELD...?
THAT'S THE BAD NEWS, J'ONN. I DID ALREADY.
THIS IS WHAT THE FLASH LOOKS LIKE SLOWED DOWN AS MUCH AS THE RING CAN MAKE HIM.
THE MICROBES ACT LIKE BACTERIA, ATTACHING TO HEALTHY CELLS.
THE RAISED STARFISH ON THE SURFACE OF HIS EYES DOESN'T APPEAR TO BE A TELEPATHIC MANIFESTATION, LIKE THE FULL-SIZED STARRO SOMETIMES CREATED.
IT MAY BE A WAY TO GAIN ACCESS TO HIS FULL RANGE OF SENSES.
IN OTHER WORDS, THE VIRUS IS LEARNING.
WE'VE BEEN WORKING UNDER THE WORST-CASE ASSUMPTION THAT THE VIRUS COULD BE AIRBORNE--
--BUT ONLY FLASH MADE SKIN-TO-SKIN CONTACT WITH AN INFECTED SUBJECT.
GREEN LANTERN, HOW CERTAIN ARE YOU THAT THE REST OF US ARE FREE OF CONTAGION?
THE RING SAYS WE'RE CLEAN, BUT...
...I'M NOT AN EXPERT IN IMMUNOBIOLOGY, BATMAN.
FORTUNATELY, I KNOW SOMEONE WHO IS.
CAN'T WE GIVE HIM SOMETHING FOR THE PAIN?
NOT UNLESS YOU KNOW THE EFFECTS OF MORPHINE-BASED NARCOTICS ON AN EXTRATERRESTRIAL DESPOTIC MICROBE.
DOCTOR FAULKNER. WE NEED TO KNOW THE STATUS OF THE CIVILIANS IN THE HOT ZONE.
WE'RE IN TROUBLE HERE. THE CLEAN FACILITY GREEN LANTERN BUILT IS HELPING STOP THE CONTAGION, AND THE PRESIDENT HAS AUTHORIZED SUPER-STANDARD VECTOR CONTROL MEASURES...
BUT YOU WERE RIGHT THAT THE SPEED OF THE VICTIM'S METABOLISM IS A HUGE FACTOR.
WHICH MEANS THE CHILDREN WILL BE THE FIRST TO GO. AND SOON.

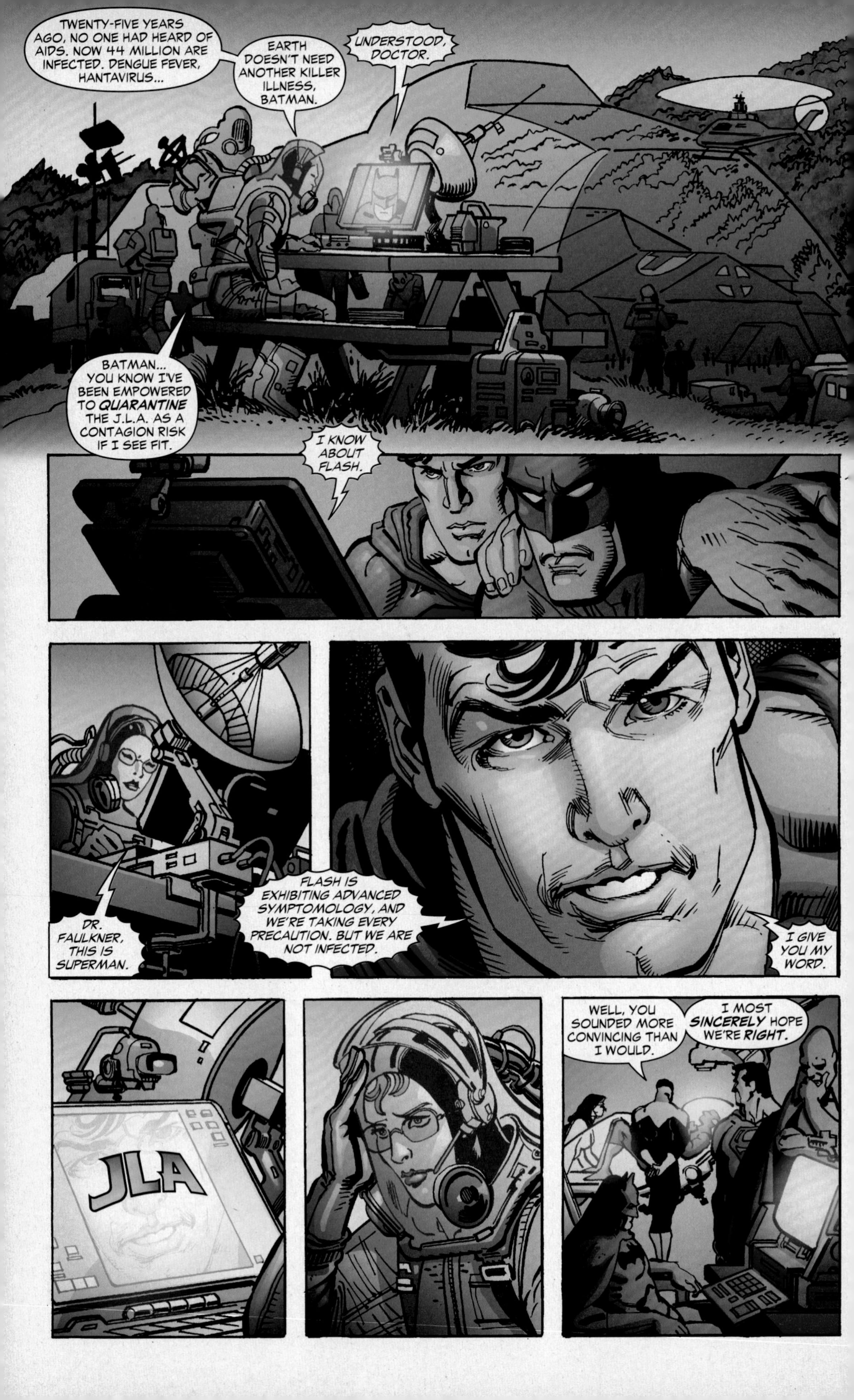
TWENTY-FIVE YEARS AGO, NO ONE HAD HEARD OF AIDS. NOW 44 MILLION ARE INFECTED. DENGUE FEVER, HANTAVIRUS...
EARTH DOESN'T NEED ANOTHER KILLER ILLNESS, BATMAN.
UNDERSTOOD, DOCTOR.
BATMAN... YOU KNOW I'VE BEEN EMPOWERED TO QUARANTINE THE J.L.A. AS A CONTAGION RISK IF I SEE FIT.
I KNOW ABOUT FLASH.
DR. FAULKNER, THIS IS SUPERMAN.
FLASH IS EXHIBITING ADVANCED SYMPTOMOLOGY, AND WE'RE TAKING EVERY PRECAUTION. BUT WE ARE NOT INFECTED.
I GIVE YOU MY WORD.
JLA
WELL, YOU SOUNDED MORE CONVINCING THAN I WOULD.
I MOST SINCERELY HOPE WE'RE RIGHT.

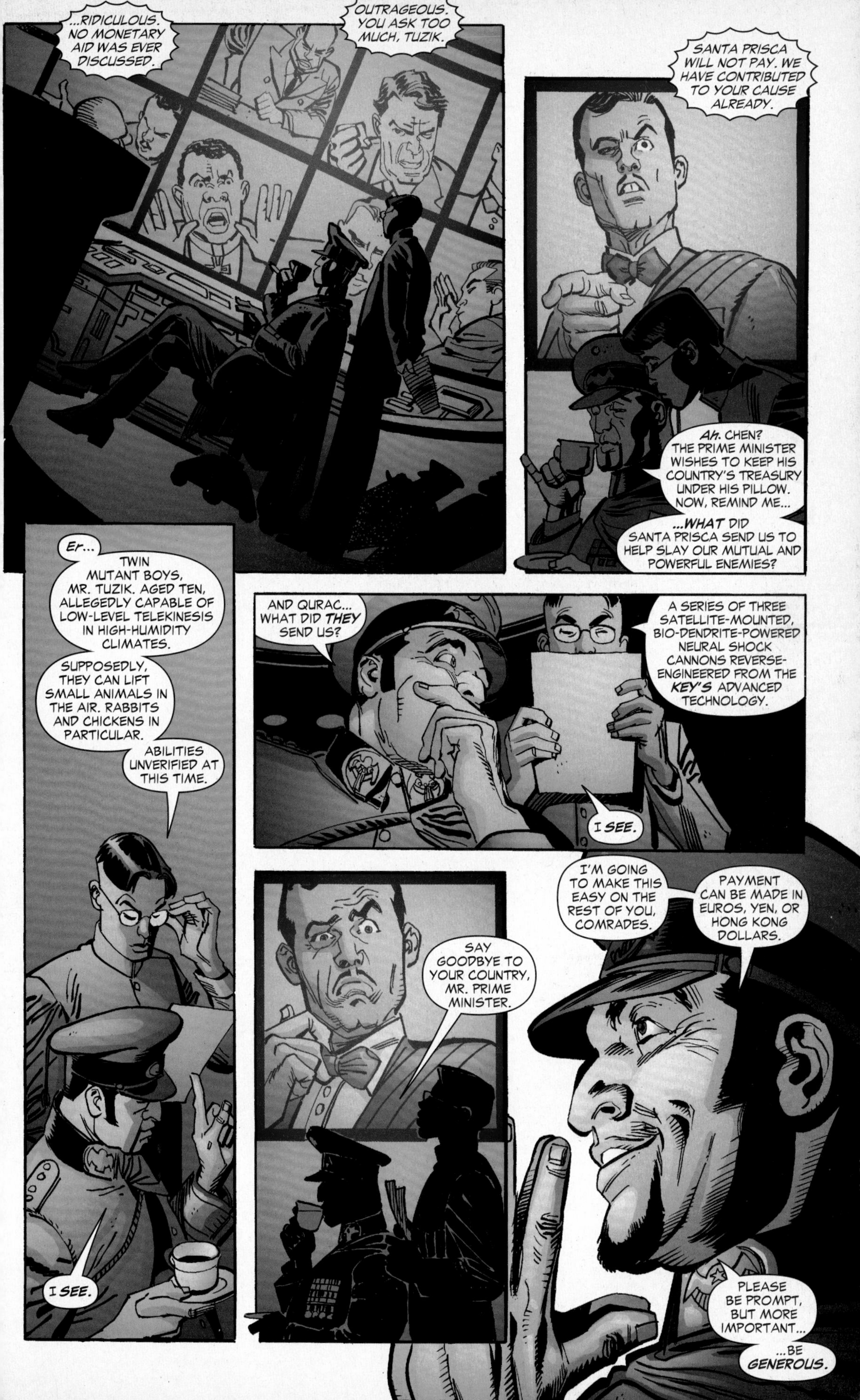
...RIDICULOUS. NO MONETARY AID WAS EVER DISCUSSED.
OUTRAGEOUS. YOU ASK TOO MUCH, TUZIK.
SANTA PRISCA WILL NOT PAY. WE HAVE CONTRIBUTED TO YOUR CAUSE ALREADY.
Ah. CHEN? THE PRIME MINISTER WISHES TO KEEP HIS COUNTRY'S TREASURY UNDER HIS PILLOW. NOW, REMIND ME...
...*WHAT* DID SANTA PRISCA SEND US TO HELP SLAY OUR MUTUAL AND POWERFUL ENEMIES?
Er...
TWIN MUTANT BOYS, MR. TUZIK. AGED TEN, ALLEGEDLY CAPABLE OF LOW-LEVEL TELEKINESIS IN HIGH-HUMIDITY CLIMATES.
SUPPOSEDLY, THEY CAN LIFT SMALL ANIMALS IN THE AIR. RABBITS AND CHICKENS IN PARTICULAR.
ABILITIES UNVERIFIED AT THIS TIME.
I *SEE.*
AND QURAC... WHAT DID *THEY* SEND US?
A SERIES OF THREE SATELLITE-MOUNTED, BIO-DENDRITE-POWERED NEURAL SHOCK CANNONS REVERSE-ENGINEERED FROM THE *KEY'S* ADVANCED TECHNOLOGY.
I *SEE.*
SAY GOODBYE TO YOUR COUNTRY, MR. PRIME MINISTER.
I'M GOING TO MAKE THIS EASY ON THE REST OF YOU, COMRADES.
PAYMENT CAN BE MADE IN EUROS, YEN, OR HONG KONG DOLLARS.
PLEASE BE PROMPT, BUT MORE IMPORTANT...
...BE *GENEROUS.*

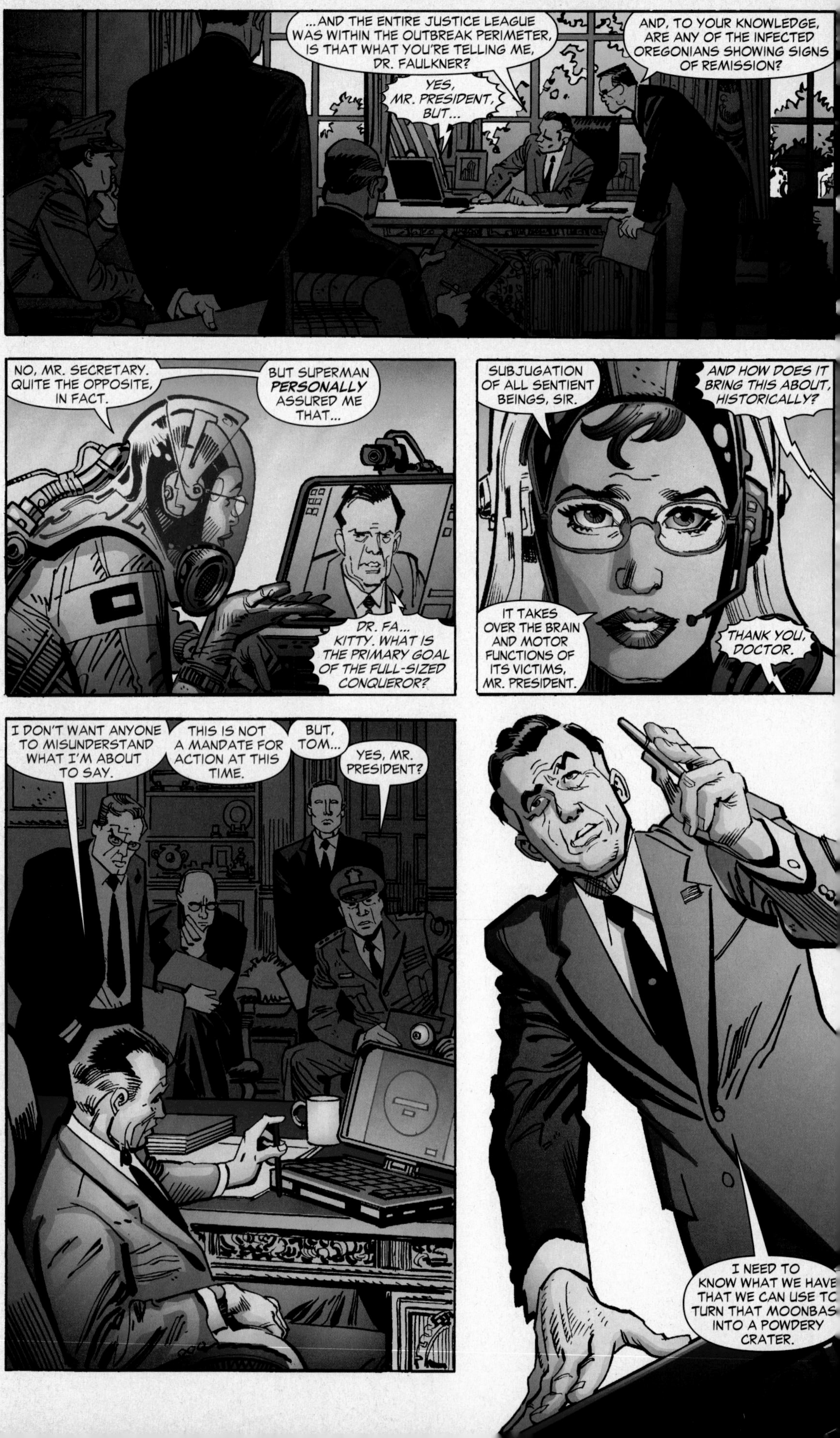
...AND THE ENTIRE JUSTICE LEAGUE WAS WITHIN THE OUTBREAK PERIMETER, IS THAT WHAT YOU'RE TELLING ME, DR. FAULKNER?
YES, MR. PRESIDENT, BUT...
AND, TO YOUR KNOWLEDGE, ARE ANY OF THE INFECTED OREGONIANS SHOWING SIGNS OF REMISSION?
NO, MR. SECRETARY. QUITE THE OPPOSITE, IN FACT.
BUT SUPERMAN PERSONALLY ASSURED ME THAT...
DR. FA... KITTY. WHAT IS THE PRIMARY GOAL OF THE FULL-SIZED CONQUEROR?
SUBJUGATION OF ALL SENTIENT BEINGS, SIR.
AND HOW DOES IT BRING THIS ABOUT, HISTORICALLY?
IT TAKES OVER THE BRAIN AND MOTOR FUNCTIONS OF ITS VICTIMS, MR. PRESIDENT.
THANK YOU, DOCTOR.
I DON'T WANT ANYONE TO MISUNDERSTAND WHAT I'M ABOUT TO SAY.
THIS IS NOT A MANDATE FOR ACTION AT THIS TIME.
BUT, TOM...
YES, MR. PRESIDENT?
I NEED TO KNOW WHAT WE HAVE THAT WE CAN USE TO TURN THAT MOONBAS INTO A POWDERY CRATER.

HATE TO ADD TO OUR PROBLEMS, BUT...

PEOPLE ALREADY THINK WE'RE CARRIERS.

...WHEN OUR **NEWS 4** CHOPPER BRAVELY CAUGHT THIS GBS EXCLUSIVE FOOTAGE...

...A GLOWING STRUCTURE LOOKING FOR ALL THE WORLD LIKE A TEMPORARY PRISON CAMP...

CITYWIDE DISASTER

...THE FRIGHTENING POSSIBILITY THE MEMBERS OF THE JUSTICE LEAGUE ARE IN FACT ALREADY INFECTED...

...BREAKING STORY, AS THE TINY COUNTRY OF SANTA PRISCA IS EXPERIENCING WHAT SEEMS TO BE AN EPIDEMIC OF SEIZURES...

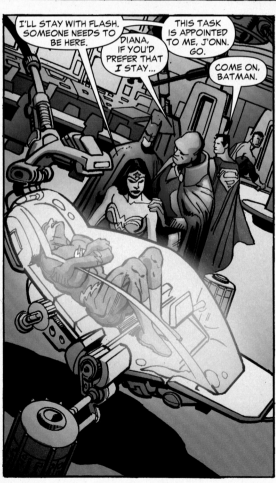

I'LL STAY WITH FLASH. SOMEONE NEEDS TO BE HERE.

DIANA, IF YOU'D PREFER THAT I STAY...

THIS TASK IS APPOINTED TO ME, J'ONN. GO.

COME ON, BATMAN.

HE'LL BE ALL RIGHT.

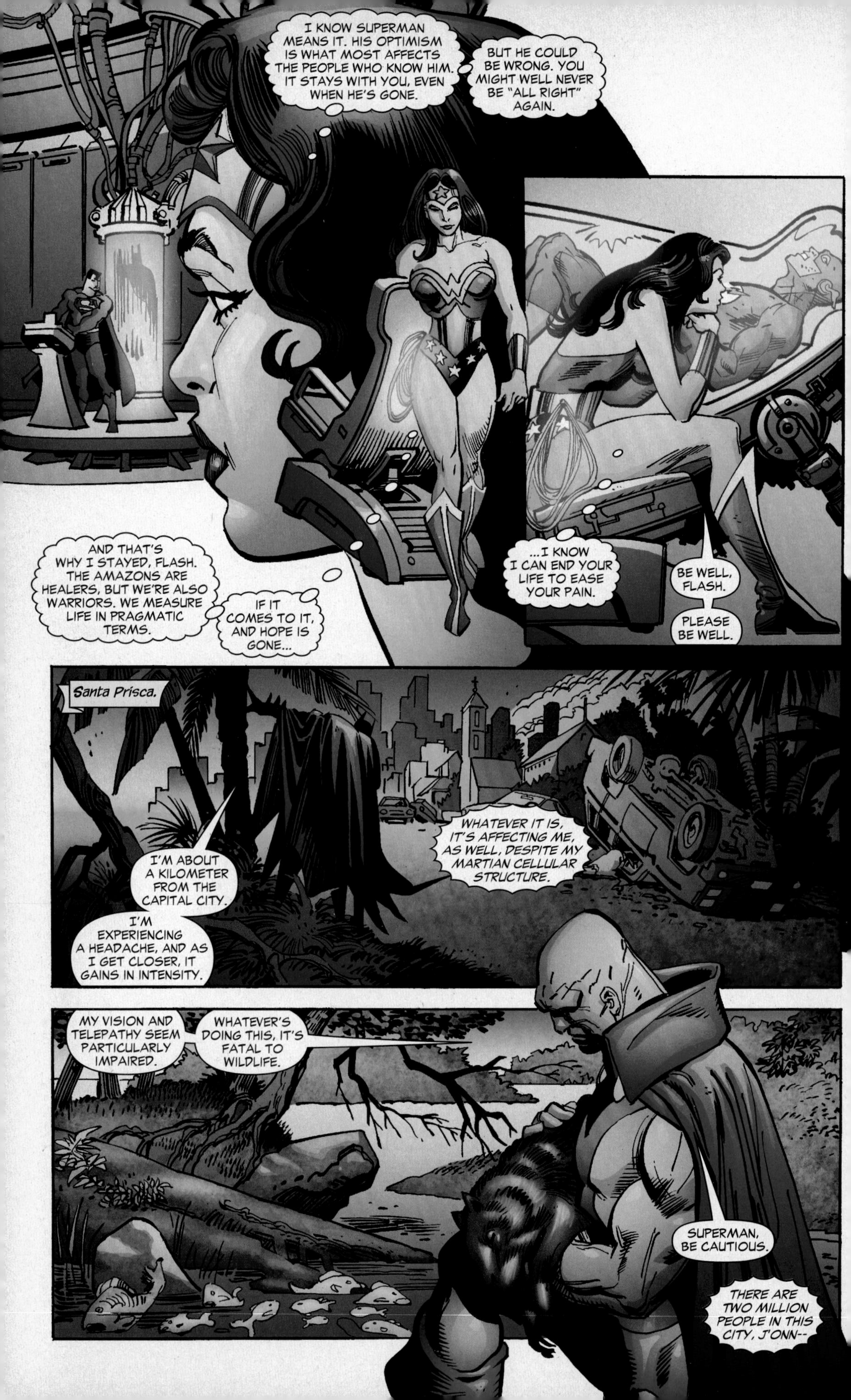
I KNOW SUPERMAN MEANS IT. HIS OPTIMISM IS WHAT MOST AFFECTS THE PEOPLE WHO KNOW HIM. IT STAYS WITH YOU, EVEN WHEN HE'S GONE.
BUT HE COULD BE WRONG. YOU MIGHT WELL NEVER BE "ALL RIGHT" AGAIN.
AND THAT'S WHY I STAYED, FLASH. THE AMAZONS ARE HEALERS, BUT WE'RE ALSO WARRIORS. WE MEASURE LIFE IN PRAGMATIC TERMS.
IF IT COMES TO IT, AND HOPE IS GONE...
...I KNOW I CAN END YOUR LIFE TO EASE YOUR PAIN.
BE WELL, FLASH.
PLEASE BE WELL.
Santa Prisca.
I'M ABOUT A KILOMETER FROM THE CAPITAL CITY.
I'M EXPERIENCING A HEADACHE, AND AS I GET CLOSER, IT GAINS IN INTENSITY.
WHATEVER IT IS, IT'S AFFECTING ME, AS WELL, DESPITE MY MARTIAN CELLULAR STRUCTURE.
MY VISION AND TELEPATHY SEEM PARTICULARLY IMPAIRED.
WHATEVER'S DOING THIS, IT'S FATAL TO WILDLIFE.
SUPERMAN, BE CAUTIOUS.
THERE ARE TWO MILLION PEOPLE IN THIS CITY, J'ONN--

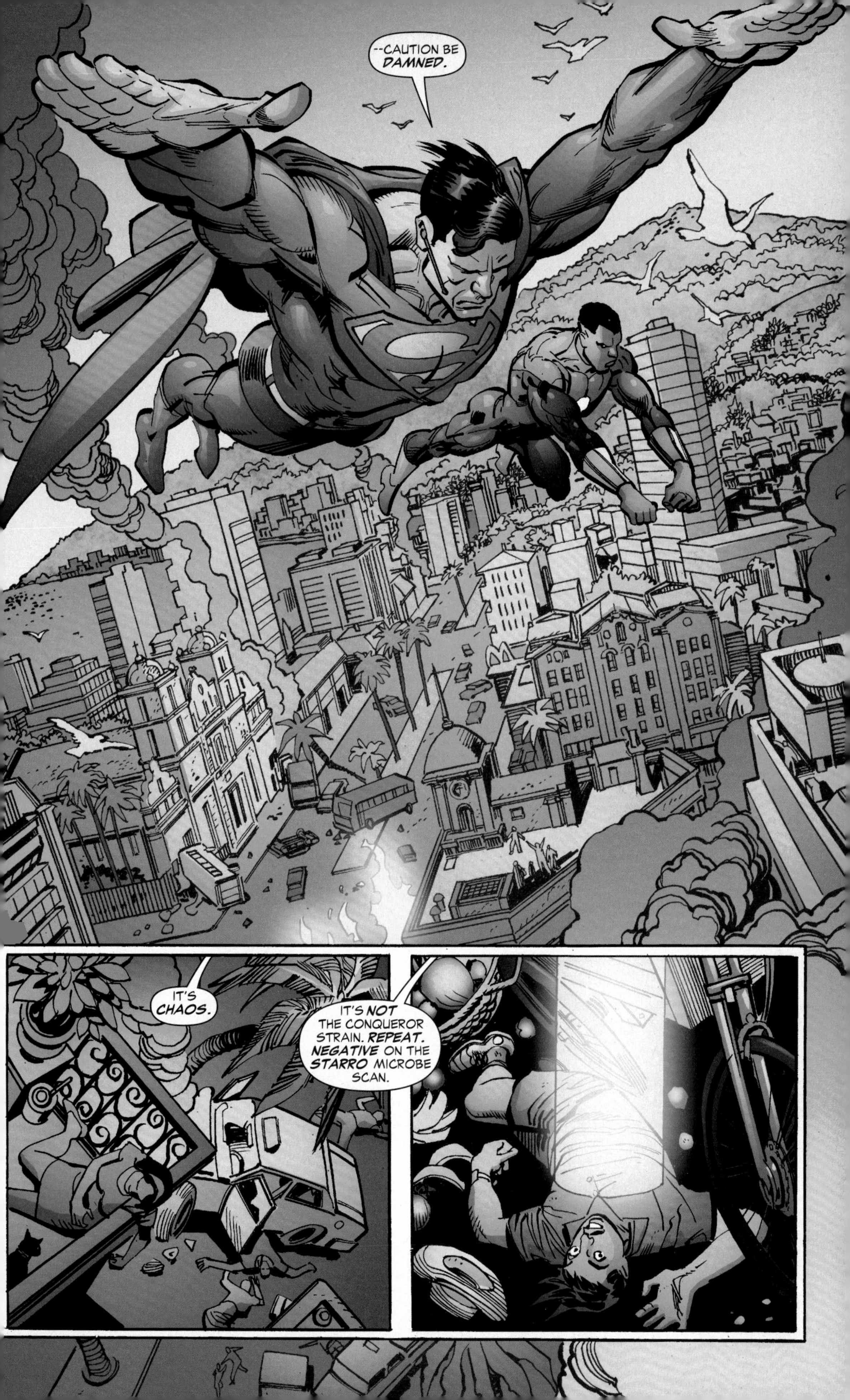
--CAUTION BE DAMNED.
IT'S CHAOS.
IT'S NOT THE CONQUEROR STRAIN. REPEAT. NEGATIVE ON THE STARRO MICROBE SCAN.

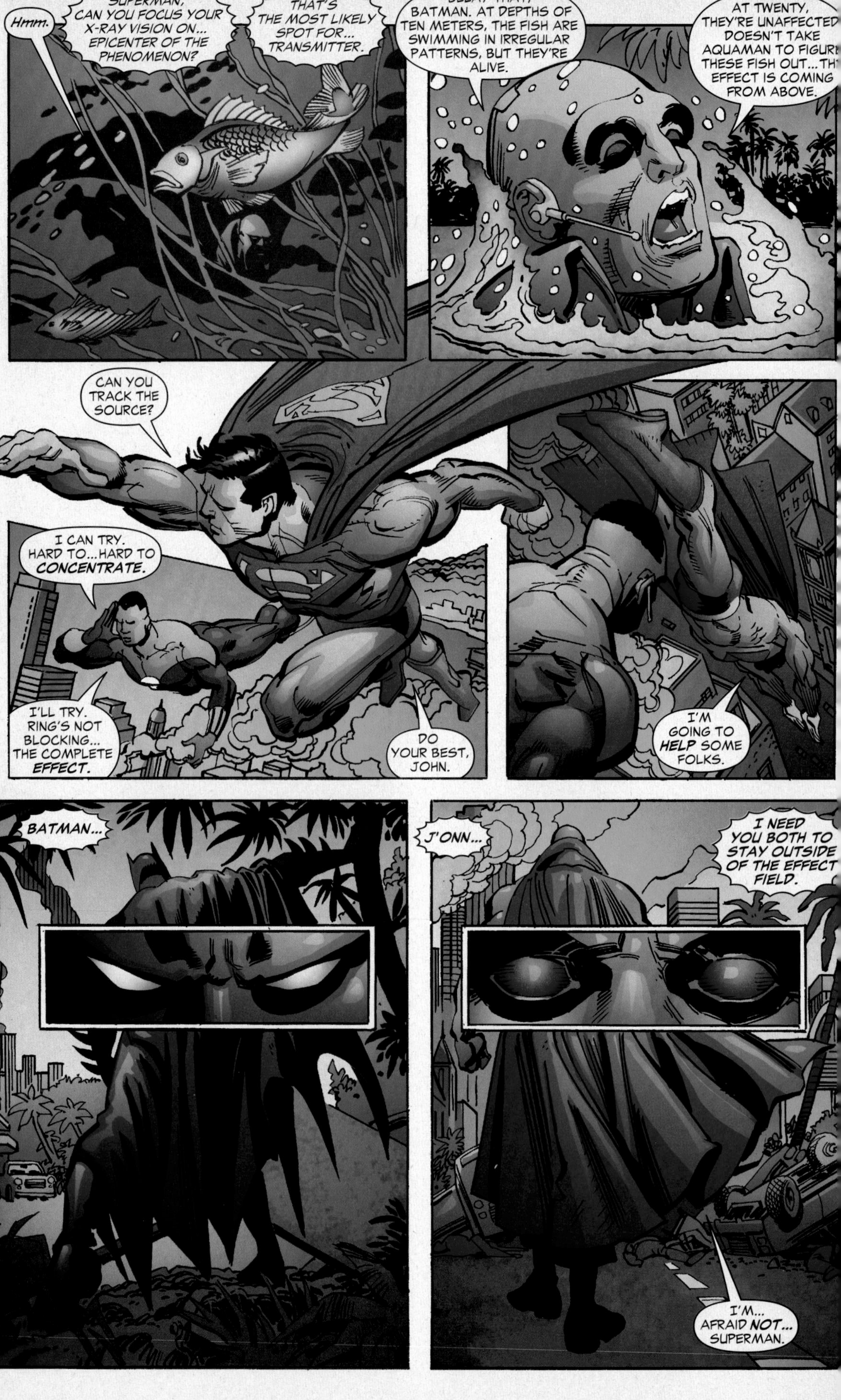
Hmm.
SUPERMAN, CAN YOU FOCUS YOUR X-RAY VISION ON... EPICENTER OF THE PHENOMENON?
THAT'S THE MOST LIKELY SPOT FOR... TRANSMITTER.
BELAY THAT, BATMAN. AT DEPTHS OF TEN METERS, THE FISH ARE SWIMMING IN IRREGULAR PATTERNS, BUT THEY'RE ALIVE.
AT TWENTY, THEY'RE UNAFFECTED DOESN'T TAKE AQUAMAN TO FIGURE THESE FISH OUT...TH EFFECT IS COMING FROM ABOVE.
CAN YOU TRACK THE SOURCE?
I CAN TRY. HARD TO...HARD TO CONCENTRATE.
I'LL TRY. RING'S NOT BLOCKING... THE COMPLETE EFFECT.
DO YOUR BEST, JOHN.
I'M GOING TO HELP SOME FOLKS.
BATMAN...
J'ONN...
I NEED YOU BOTH TO STAY OUTSIDE OF THE EFFECT FIELD.
I'M... AFRAID NOT... SUPERMAN.

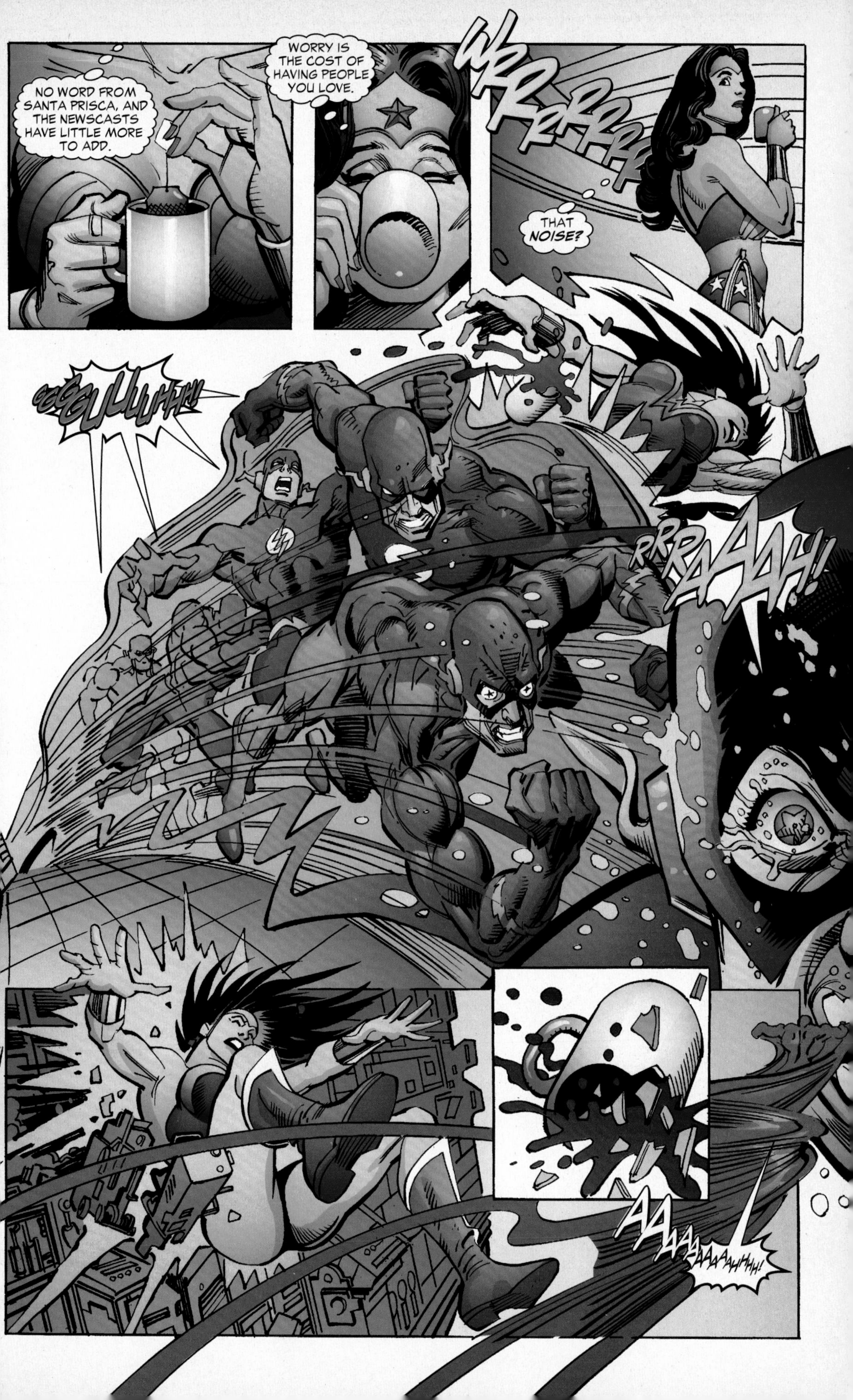

NO WORD FROM SANTA PRISCA, AND THE NEWSCASTS HAVE LITTLE MORE TO ADD.
WORRY IS THE COST OF HAVING PEOPLE YOU LOVE.
WRRRRRRR
THAT NOISE?
GGGGUUUUHH!!
RRRAAAAH!
AAAAAAAAAHHHH!

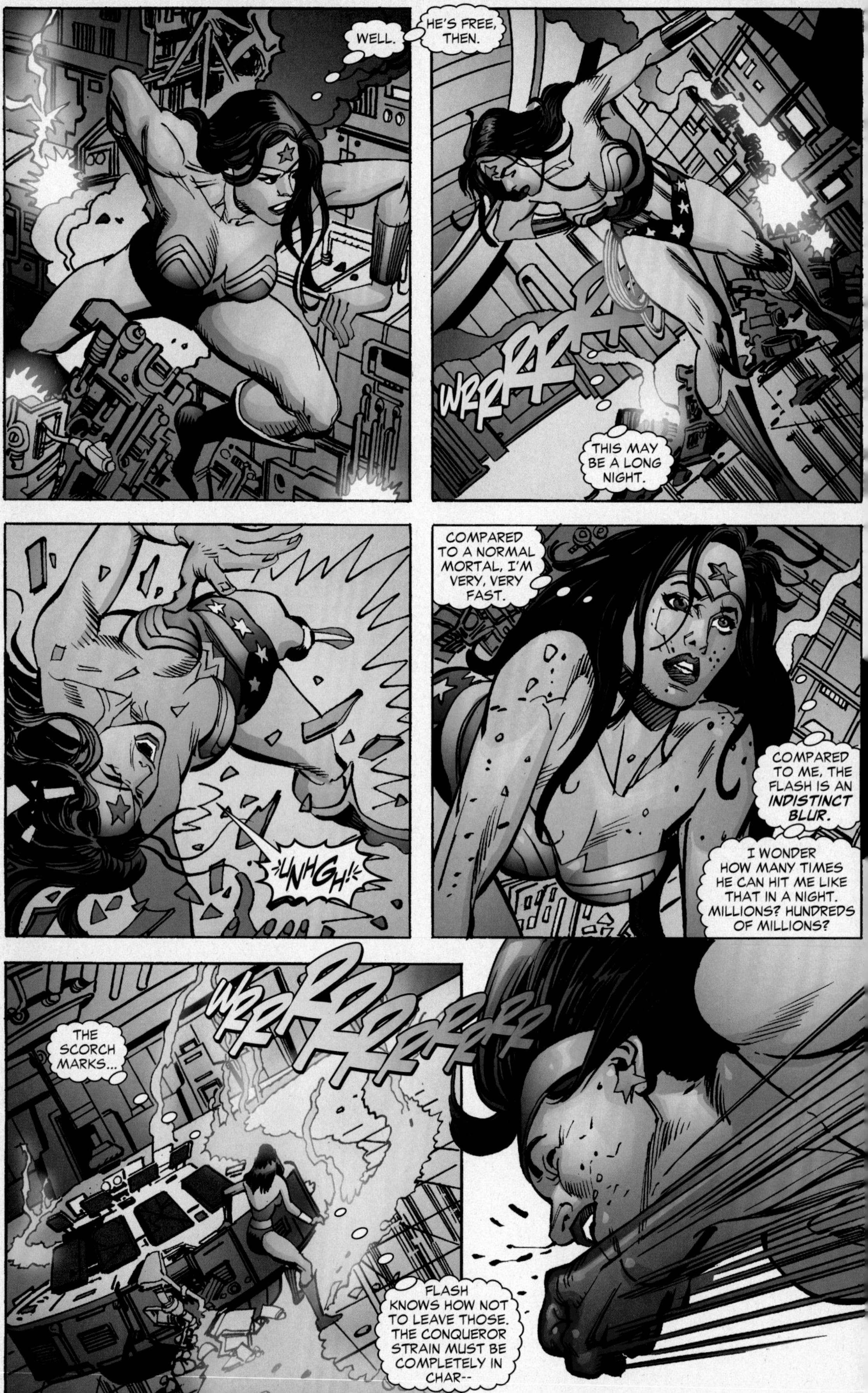
WELL.
HE'S FREE, THEN.
WRRRR
THIS MAY BE A LONG NIGHT.
UNHGH
COMPARED TO A NORMAL MORTAL, I'M VERY, VERY FAST.
COMPARED TO ME, THE FLASH IS AN INDISTINCT BLUR.
I WONDER HOW MANY TIMES HE CAN HIT ME LIKE THAT IN A NIGHT. MILLIONS? HUNDREDS OF MILLIONS?
WRRRRRRRRRRR
THE SCORCH MARKS...
FLASH KNOWS HOW NOT TO LEAVE THOSE. THE CONQUEROR STRAIN MUST BE COMPLETELY IN CHAR--

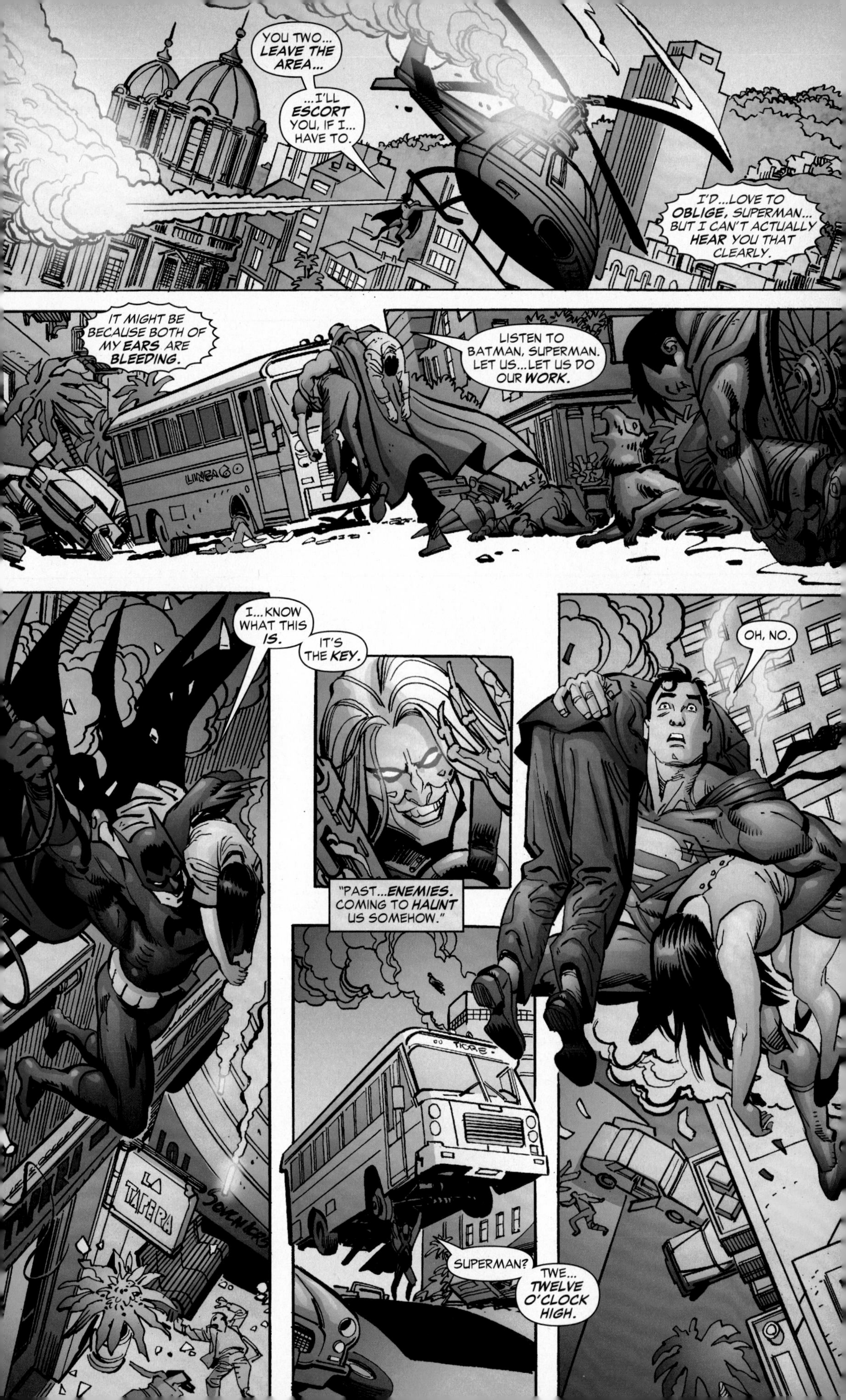
YOU TWO... LEAVE THE AREA...
...I'LL ESCORT YOU, IF I... HAVE TO.
I'D...LOVE TO OBLIGE, SUPERMAN... BUT I CAN'T ACTUALLY HEAR YOU THAT CLEARLY.
IT MIGHT BE BECAUSE BOTH OF MY EARS ARE BLEEDING.
LISTEN TO BATMAN, SUPERMAN. LET US...LET US DO OUR WORK.
LINEA 60
I...KNOW WHAT THIS IS.
IT'S THE KEY.
"PAST...ENEMIES. COMING TO HAUNT US SOMEHOW."
OH, NO.
TIGRE
LA TAPERA
SUPERMAN?
TWE... TWELVE O'CLOCK HIGH.

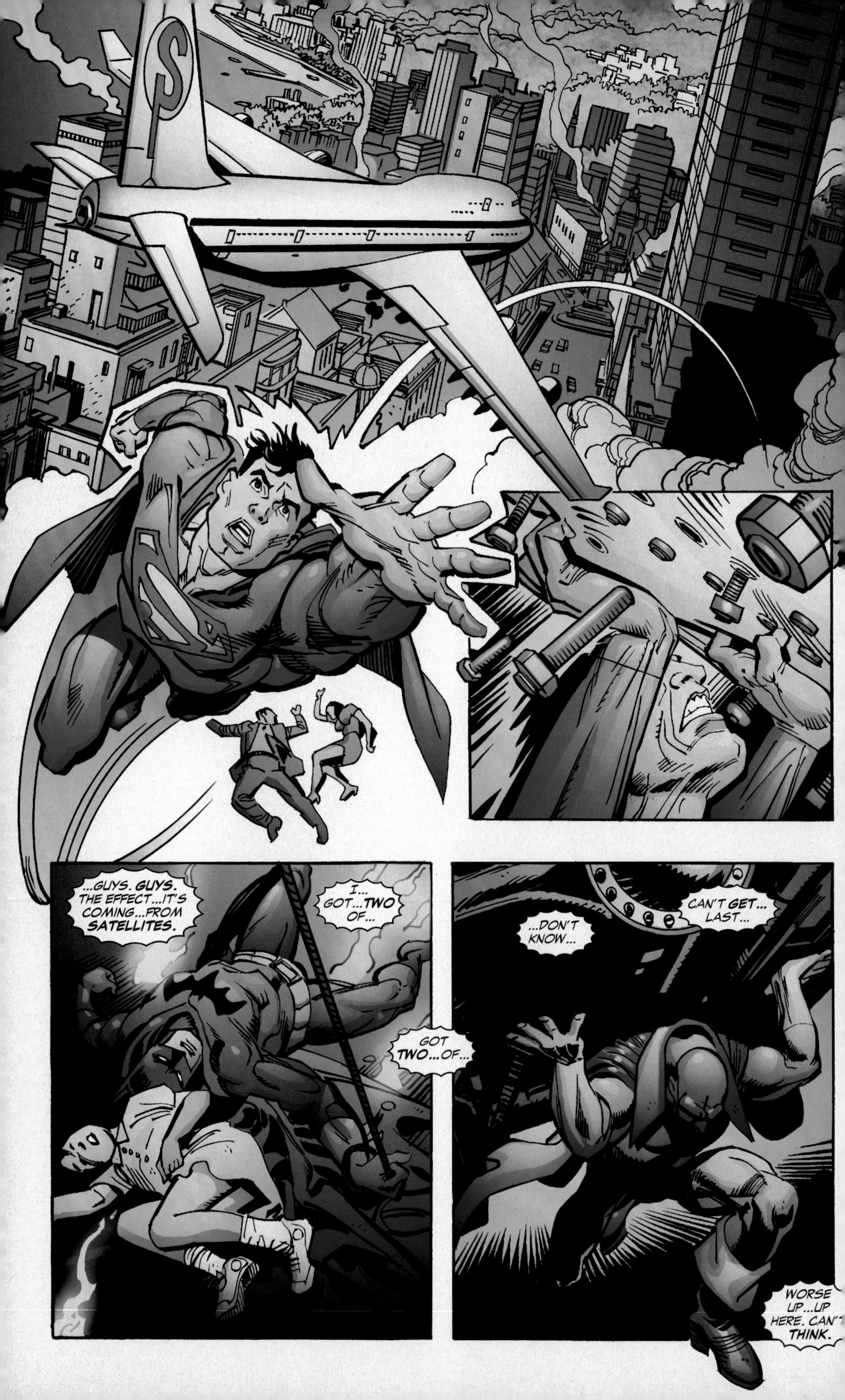
...GUYS. GUYS. THE EFFECT...IT'S COMING...FROM SATELLITES.
I... GOT...TWO OF...
GOT TWO...OF...
...DON'T KNOW...
CAN'T GET... LAST...
WORSE UP...UP HERE. CAN'T THINK.

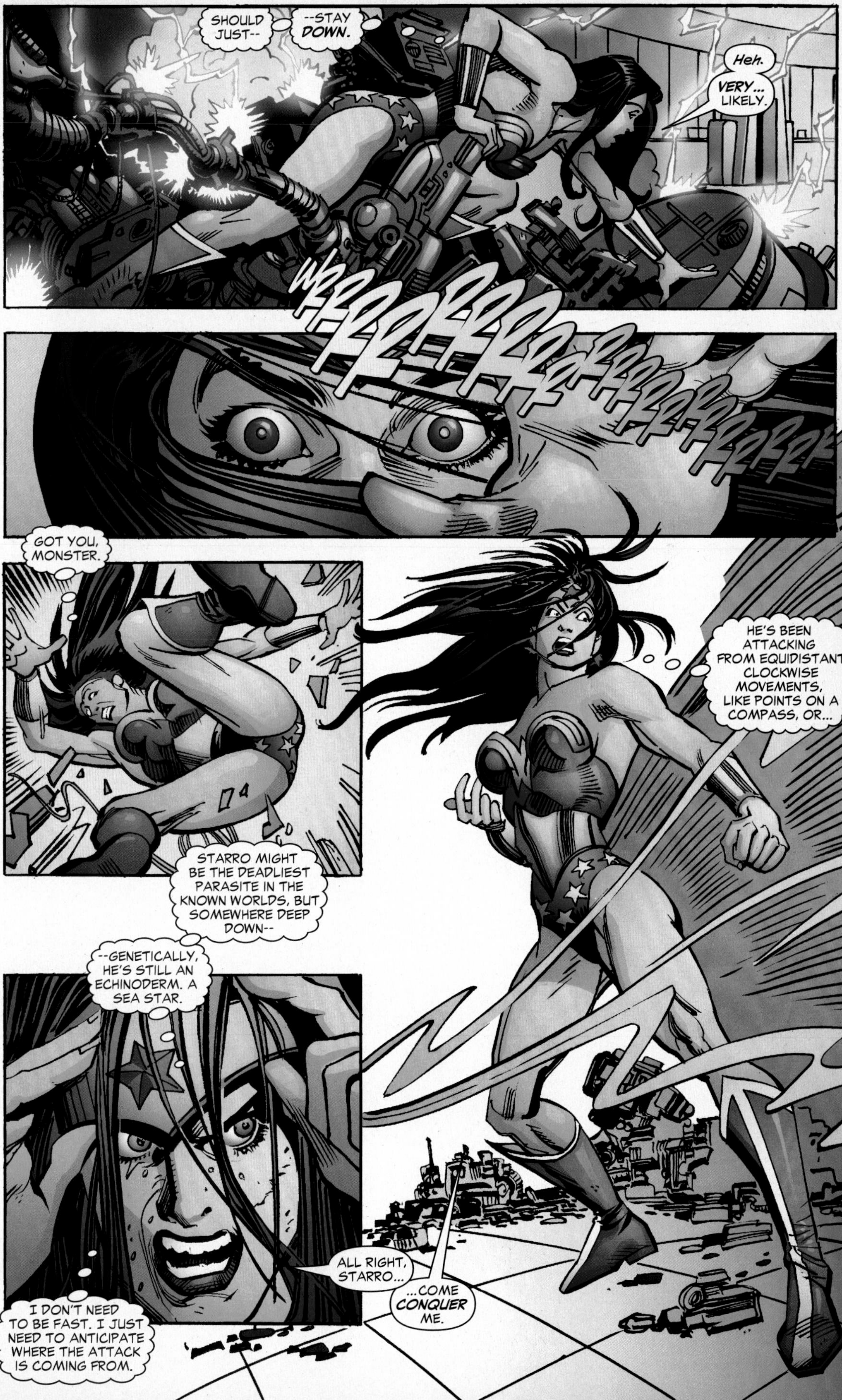
SHOULD JUST--
--STAY DOWN.
Heh.
VERY... LIKELY.
WRRRRRRRRRRRRRRRRRRRRRRRRR
GOT YOU, MONSTER.
HE'S BEEN ATTACKING FROM EQUIDISTANT CLOCKWISE MOVEMENTS, LIKE POINTS ON A COMPASS, OR...
STARRO MIGHT BE THE DEADLIEST PARASITE IN THE KNOWN WORLDS, BUT SOMEWHERE DEEP DOWN--
--GENETICALLY, HE'S STILL AN ECHINODERM. A SEA STAR.
I DON'T NEED TO BE FAST. I JUST NEED TO ANTICIPATE WHERE THE ATTACK IS COMING FROM.
ALL RIGHT, STARRO...
...COME CONQUER ME.

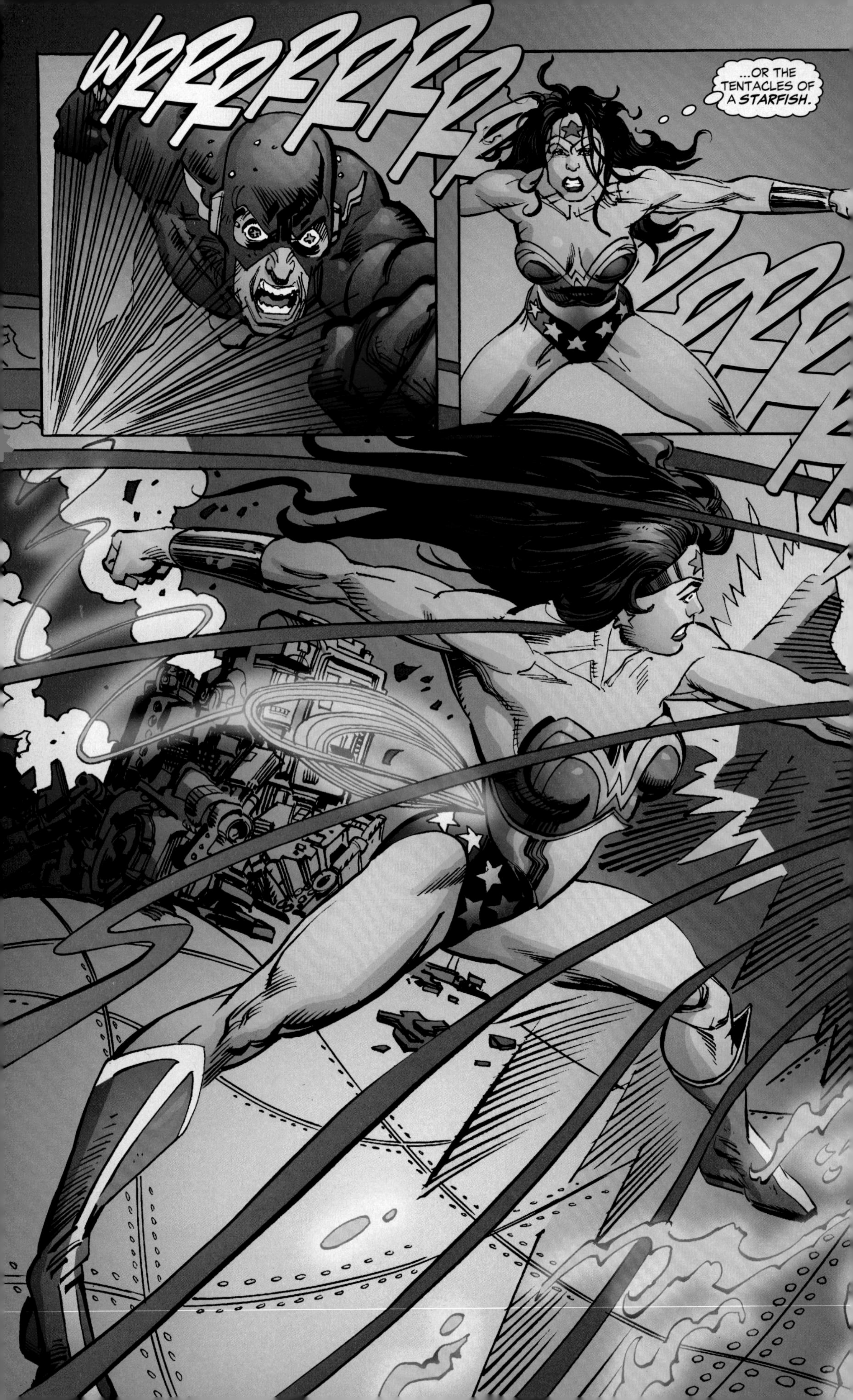

WRRRRRRRRRR
...OR THE TENTACLES OF A STARFISH.

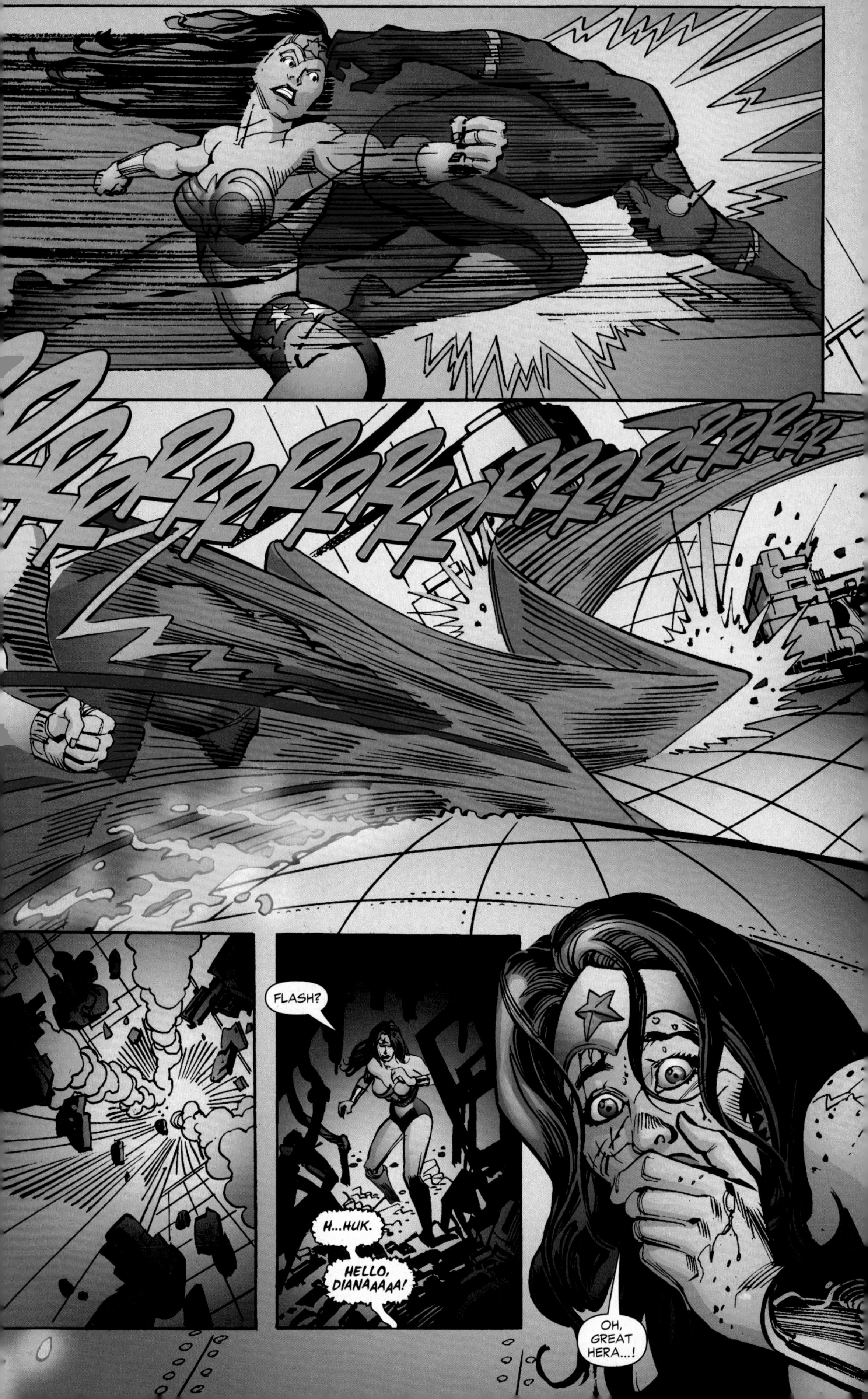

FLASH?
H...HUK.
HELLO, DIANAAAAA!
OH, GREAT HERA...!

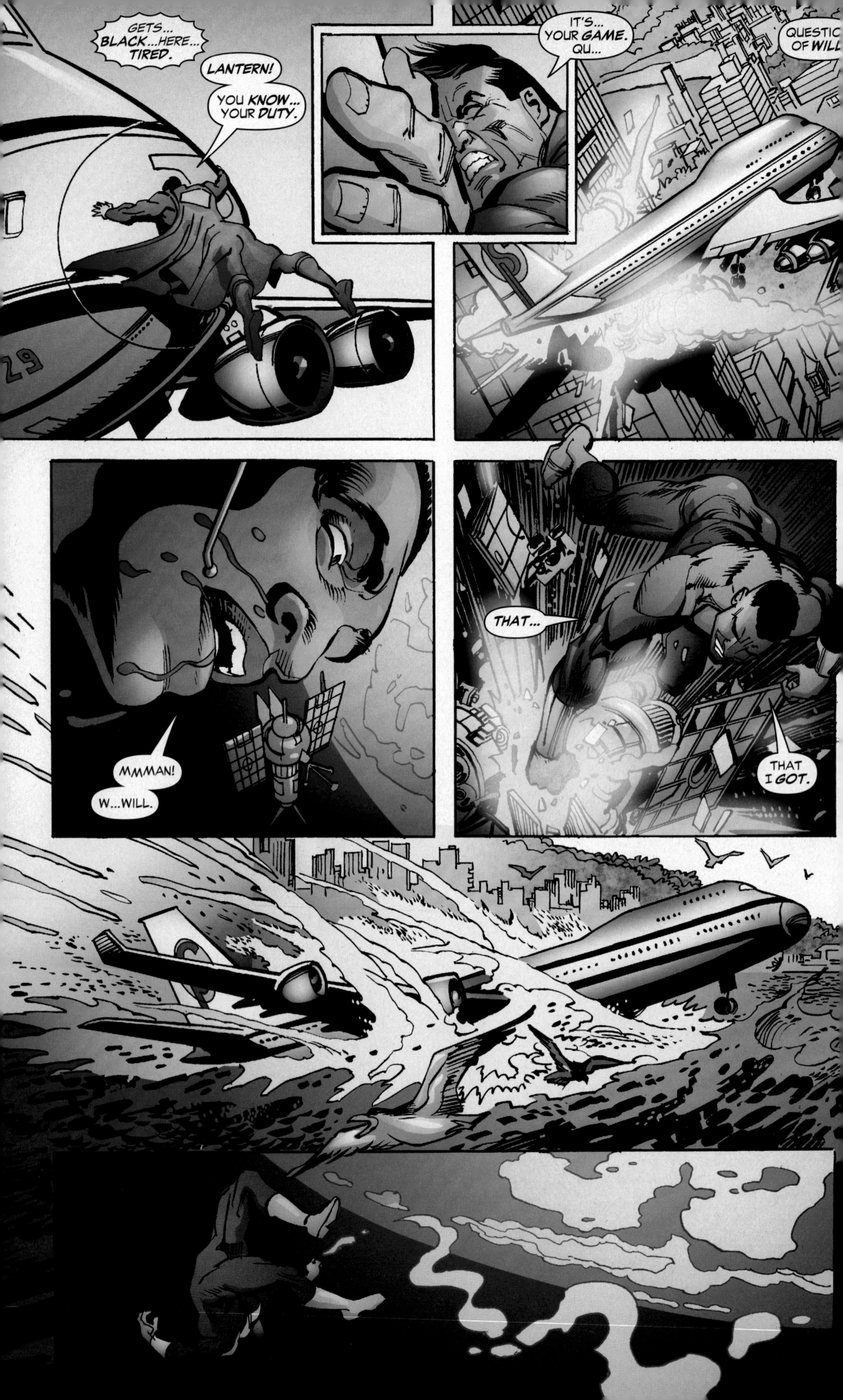
GETS... BLACK...HERE... TIRED.
LANTERN!
YOU KNOW... YOUR DUTY.
IT'S... YOUR GAME. QU...
QUESTIC OF WILL
MMMAN!
W...WILL.
THAT...
THAT I GOT.

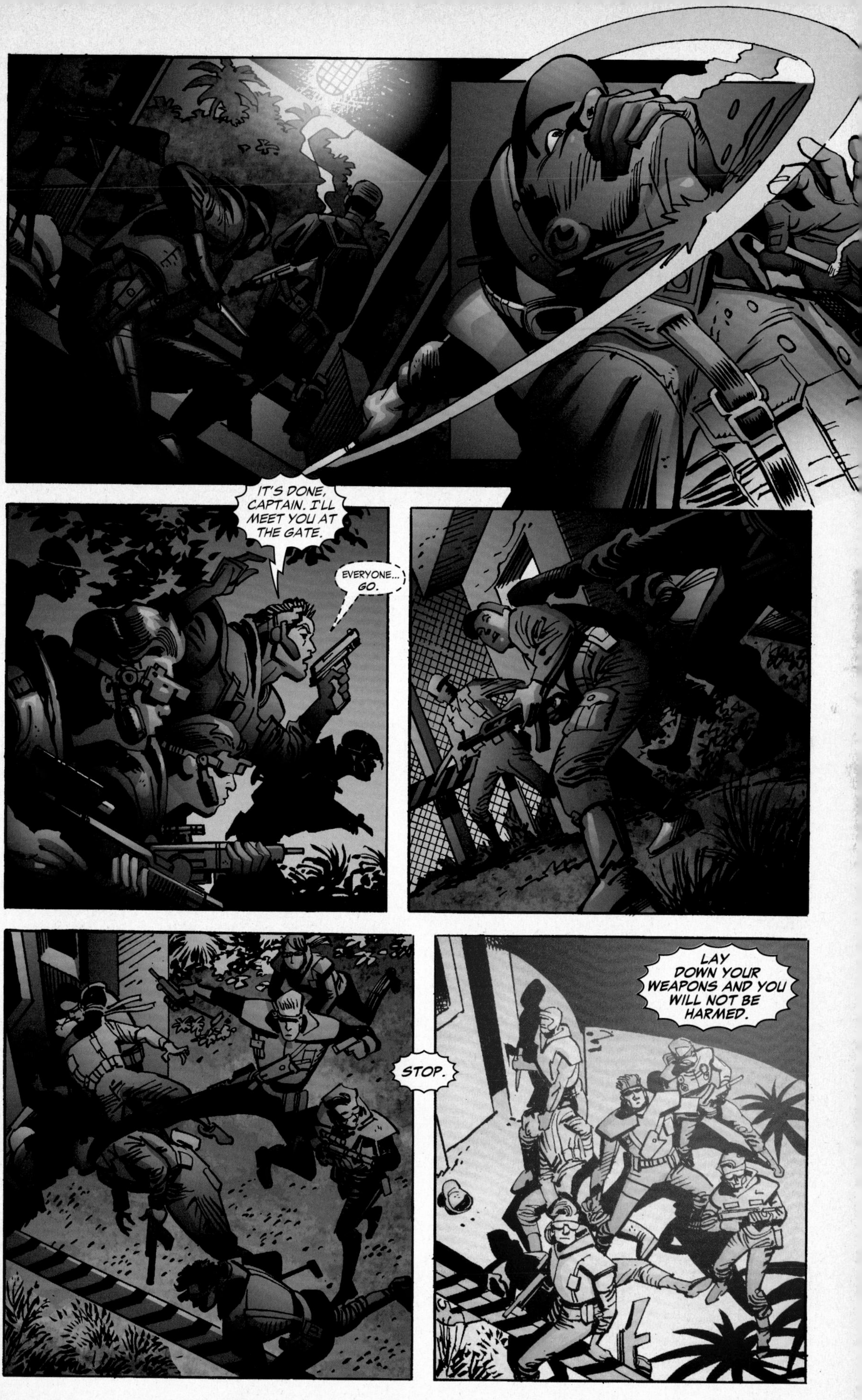
IT'S DONE, CAPTAIN. I'LL MEET YOU AT THE GATE.
EVERYONE... GO.
STOP.
LAY DOWN YOUR WEAPONS AND YOU WILL NOT BE HARMED.

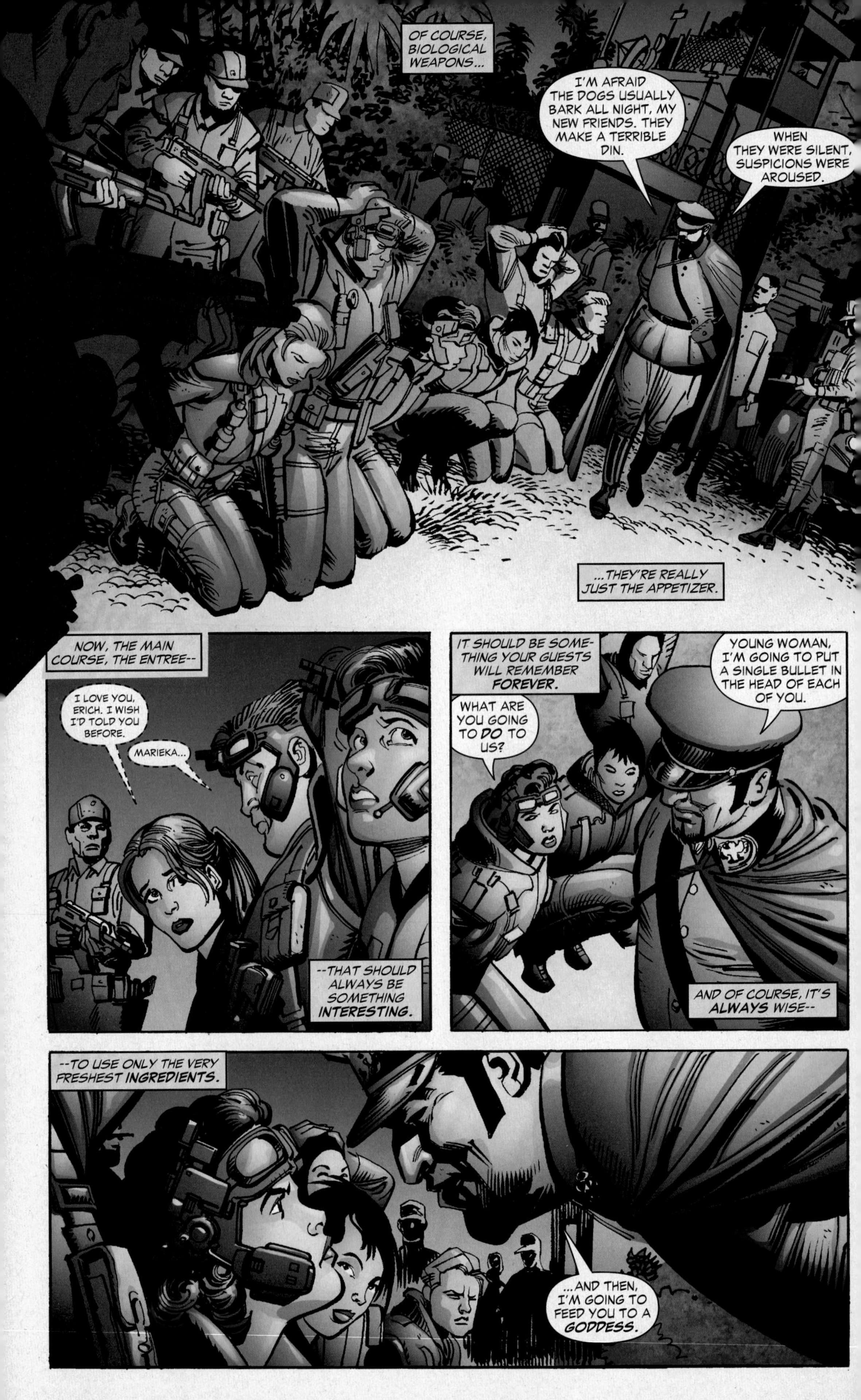
OF COURSE, BIOLOGICAL WEAPONS...
I'M AFRAID THE DOGS USUALLY BARK ALL NIGHT, MY NEW FRIENDS. THEY MAKE A TERRIBLE DIN.
WHEN THEY WERE SILENT, SUSPICIONS WERE AROUSED.
...THEY'RE REALLY JUST THE APPETIZER.
NOW, THE MAIN COURSE, THE ENTREE--
I LOVE YOU, ERICH. I WISH I'D TOLD YOU BEFORE.
MARIEKA...
--THAT SHOULD ALWAYS BE SOMETHING INTERESTING.
IT SHOULD BE SOME-THING YOUR GUESTS WILL REMEMBER FOREVER.
WHAT ARE YOU GOING TO DO TO US?
YOUNG WOMAN, I'M GOING TO PUT A SINGLE BULLET IN THE HEAD OF EACH OF YOU.
AND OF COURSE, IT'S ALWAYS WISE--
--TO USE ONLY THE VERY FRESHEST INGREDIENTS.
...AND THEN, I'M GOING TO FEED YOU TO A GODDESS.

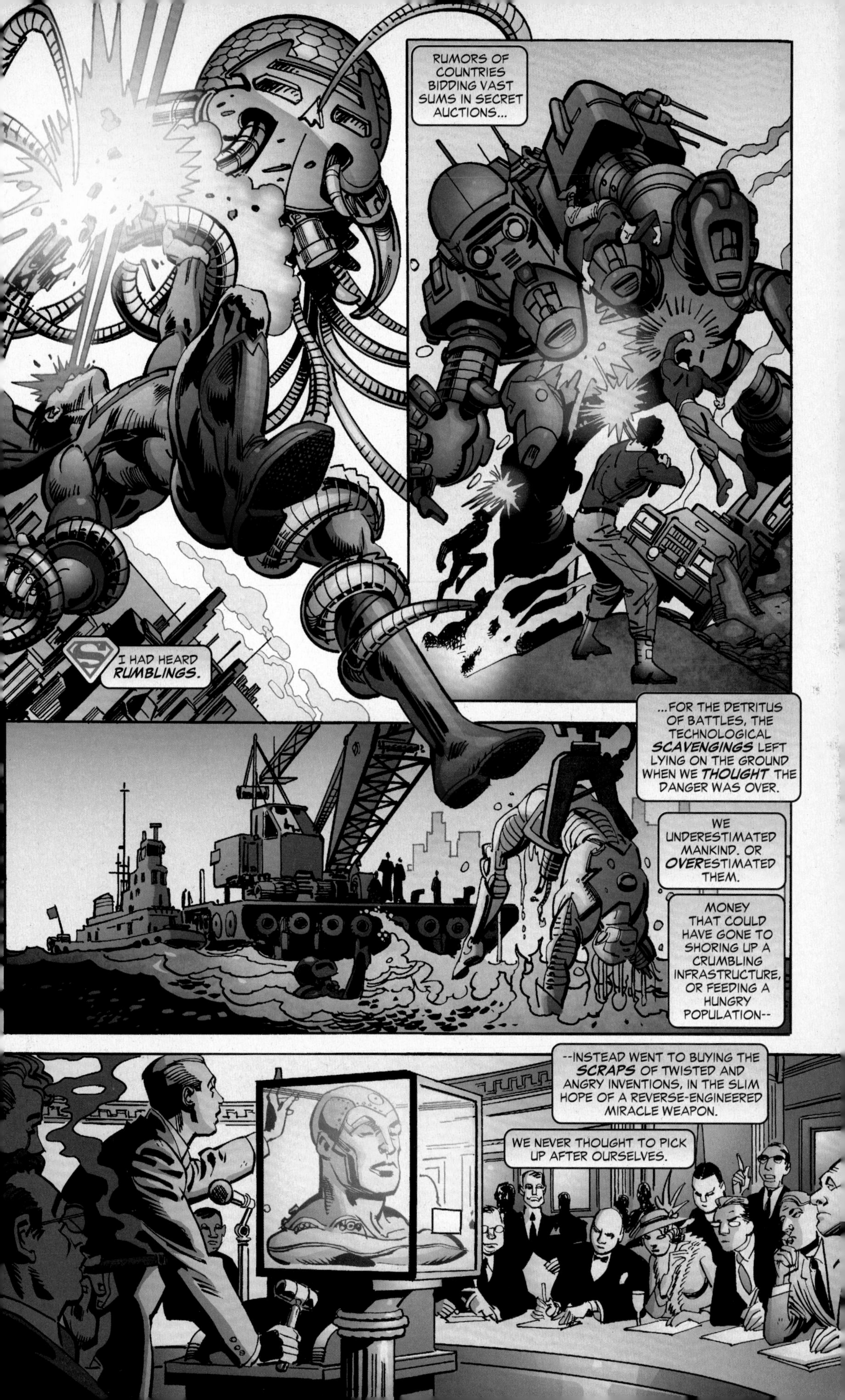
I HAD HEARD RUMBLINGS.
RUMORS OF COUNTRIES BIDDING VAST SUMS IN SECRET AUCTIONS...
...FOR THE DETRITUS OF BATTLES, THE TECHNOLOGICAL SCAVENGINGS LEFT LYING ON THE GROUND WHEN WE THOUGHT THE DANGER WAS OVER.
WE UNDERESTIMATED MANKIND. OR OVERESTIMATED THEM.
MONEY THAT COULD HAVE GONE TO SHORING UP A CRUMBLING INFRASTRUCTURE, OR FEEDING A HUNGRY POPULATION--
--INSTEAD WENT TO BUYING THE SCRAPS OF TWISTED AND ANGRY INVENTIONS, IN THE SLIM HOPE OF A REVERSE-ENGINEERED MIRACLE WEAPON.
WE NEVER THOUGHT TO PICK UP AFTER OURSELVES.

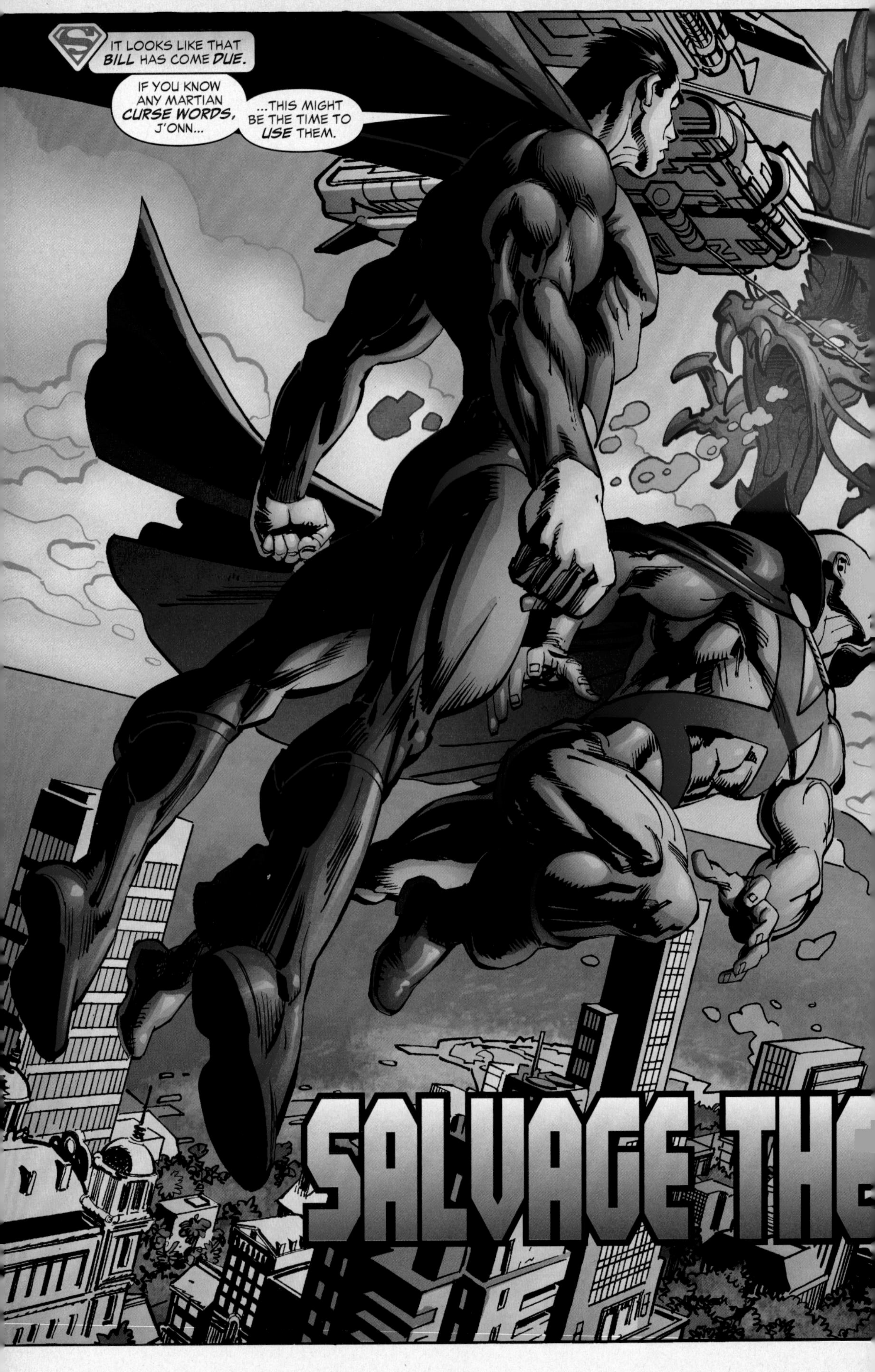
IT LOOKS LIKE THAT BILL HAS COME DUE.
IF YOU KNOW ANY MARTIAN CURSE WORDS, J'ONN...
...THIS MIGHT BE THE TIME TO USE THEM.
SALVAGE THE

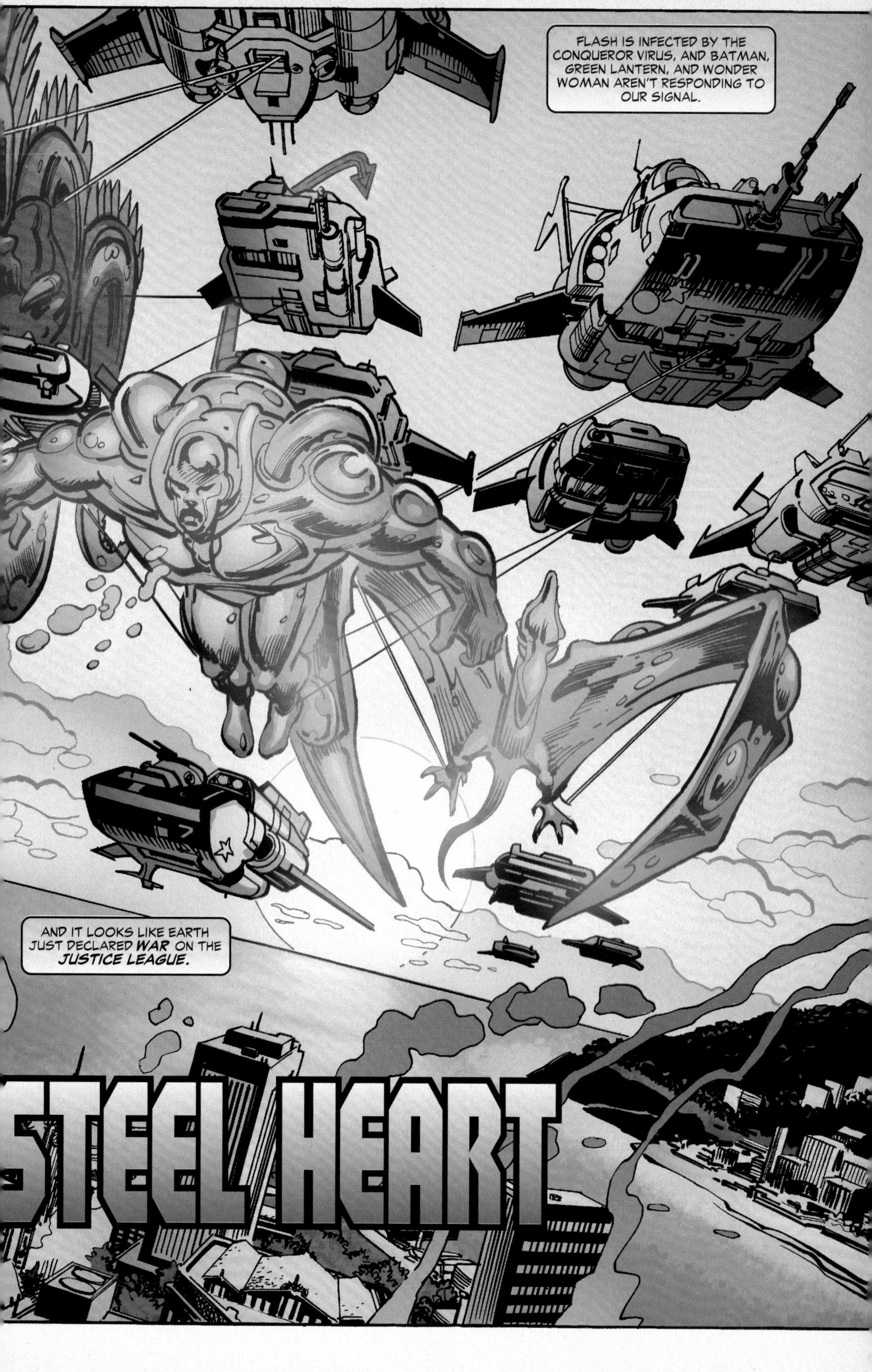
FLASH IS INFECTED BY THE CONQUEROR VIRUS, AND BATMAN, GREEN LANTERN, AND WONDER WOMAN AREN'T RESPONDING TO OUR SIGNAL.
AND IT LOOKS LIKE EARTH JUST DECLARED WAR ON THE JUSTICE LEAGUE.
STEEL HEART

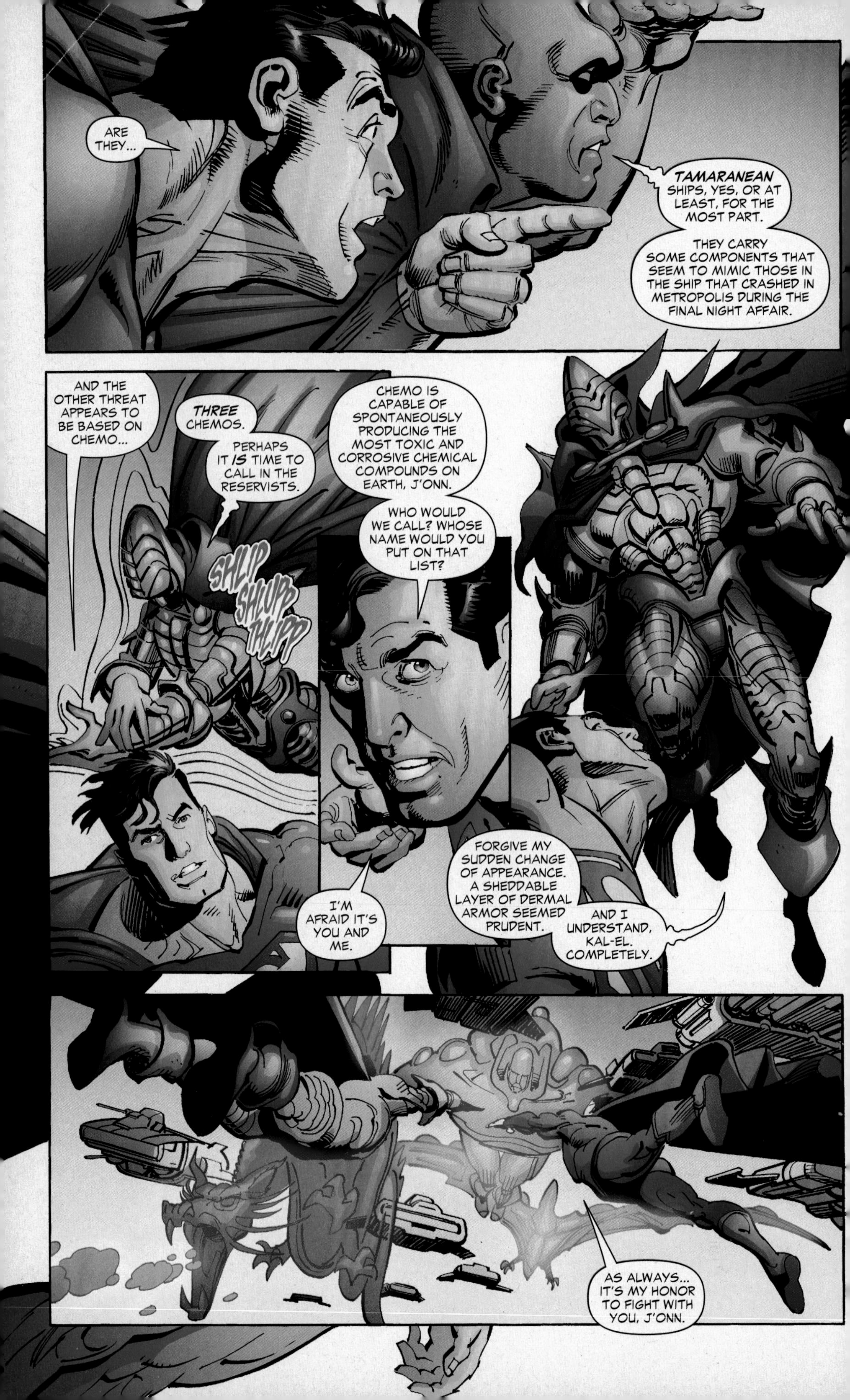
ARE THEY...
TAMARANEAN SHIPS, YES, OR AT LEAST, FOR THE MOST PART.
THEY CARRY SOME COMPONENTS THAT SEEM TO MIMIC THOSE IN THE SHIP THAT CRASHED IN METROPOLIS DURING THE FINAL NIGHT AFFAIR.
AND THE OTHER THREAT APPEARS TO BE BASED ON CHEMO...
THREE CHEMOS.
PERHAPS IT IS TIME TO CALL IN THE RESERVISTS.
SHLIP SHLUPP THLIPP
CHEMO IS CAPABLE OF SPONTANEOUSLY PRODUCING THE MOST TOXIC AND CORROSIVE CHEMICAL COMPOUNDS ON EARTH, J'ONN.
WHO WOULD WE CALL? WHOSE NAME WOULD YOU PUT ON THAT LIST?
I'M AFRAID IT'S YOU AND ME.
FORGIVE MY SUDDEN CHANGE OF APPEARANCE. A SHEDDABLE LAYER OF DERMAL ARMOR SEEMED PRUDENT.
AND I UNDERSTAND, KAL-EL. COMPLETELY.
AS ALWAYS... IT'S MY HONOR TO FIGHT WITH YOU, J'ONN.

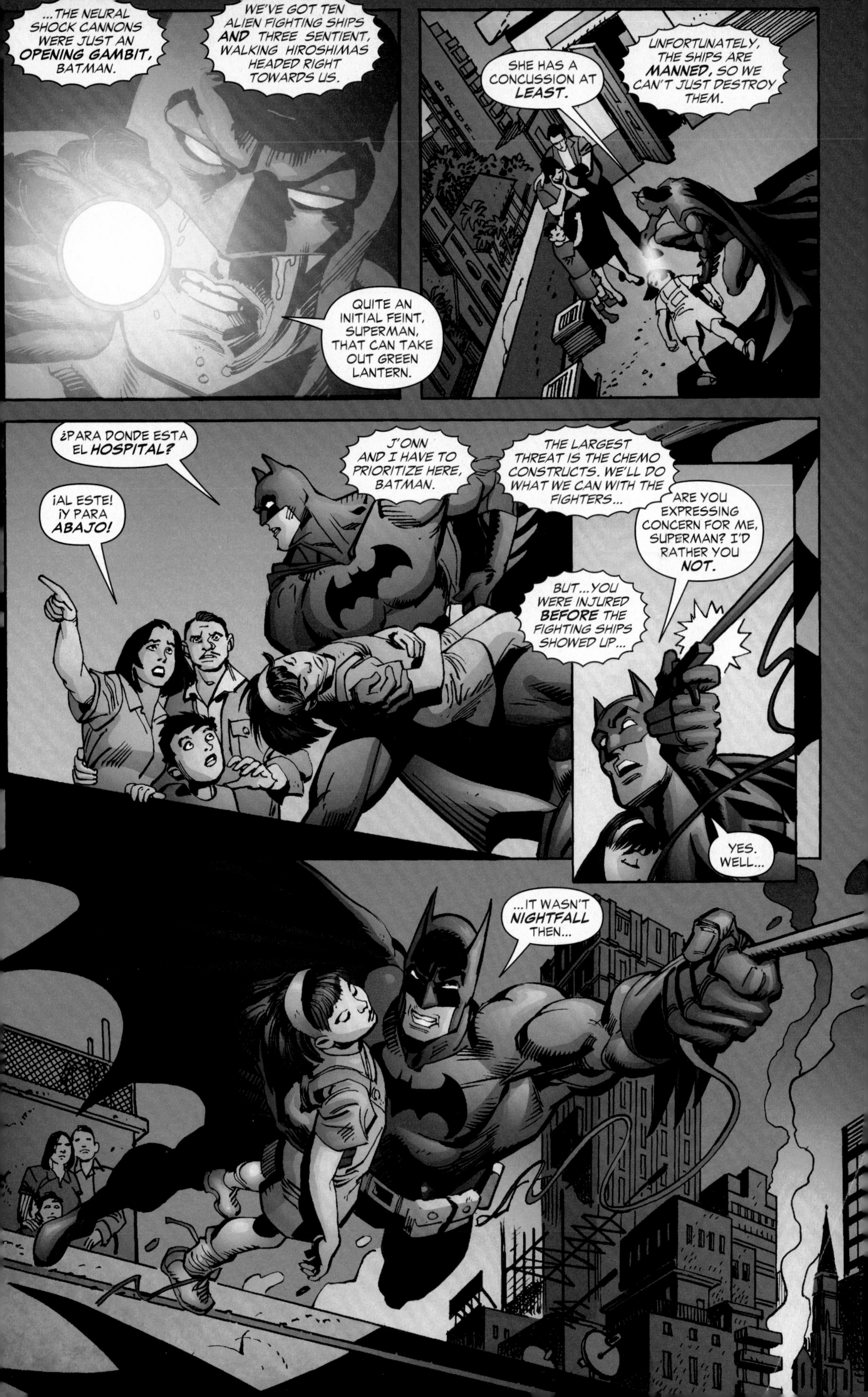
...THE NEURAL SHOCK CANNONS WERE JUST AN OPENING GAMBIT, BATMAN.
WE'VE GOT TEN ALIEN FIGHTING SHIPS AND THREE SENTIENT, WALKING HIROSHIMAS HEADED RIGHT TOWARDS US.
QUITE AN INITIAL FEINT, SUPERMAN, THAT CAN TAKE OUT GREEN LANTERN.
SHE HAS A CONCUSSION AT LEAST.
UNFORTUNATELY, THE SHIPS ARE MANNED, SO WE CAN'T JUST DESTROY THEM.
¿PARA DONDE ESTA EL HOSPITAL?
¡AL ESTE! ¡Y PARA ABAJO!
J'ONN AND I HAVE TO PRIORITIZE HERE, BATMAN.
THE LARGEST THREAT IS THE CHEMO CONSTRUCTS. WE'LL DO WHAT WE CAN WITH THE FIGHTERS...
ARE YOU EXPRESSING CONCERN FOR ME, SUPERMAN? I'D RATHER YOU NOT.
BUT...YOU WERE INJURED BEFORE THE FIGHTING SHIPS SHOWED UP...
YES. WELL...
...IT WASN'T NIGHTFALL THEN...

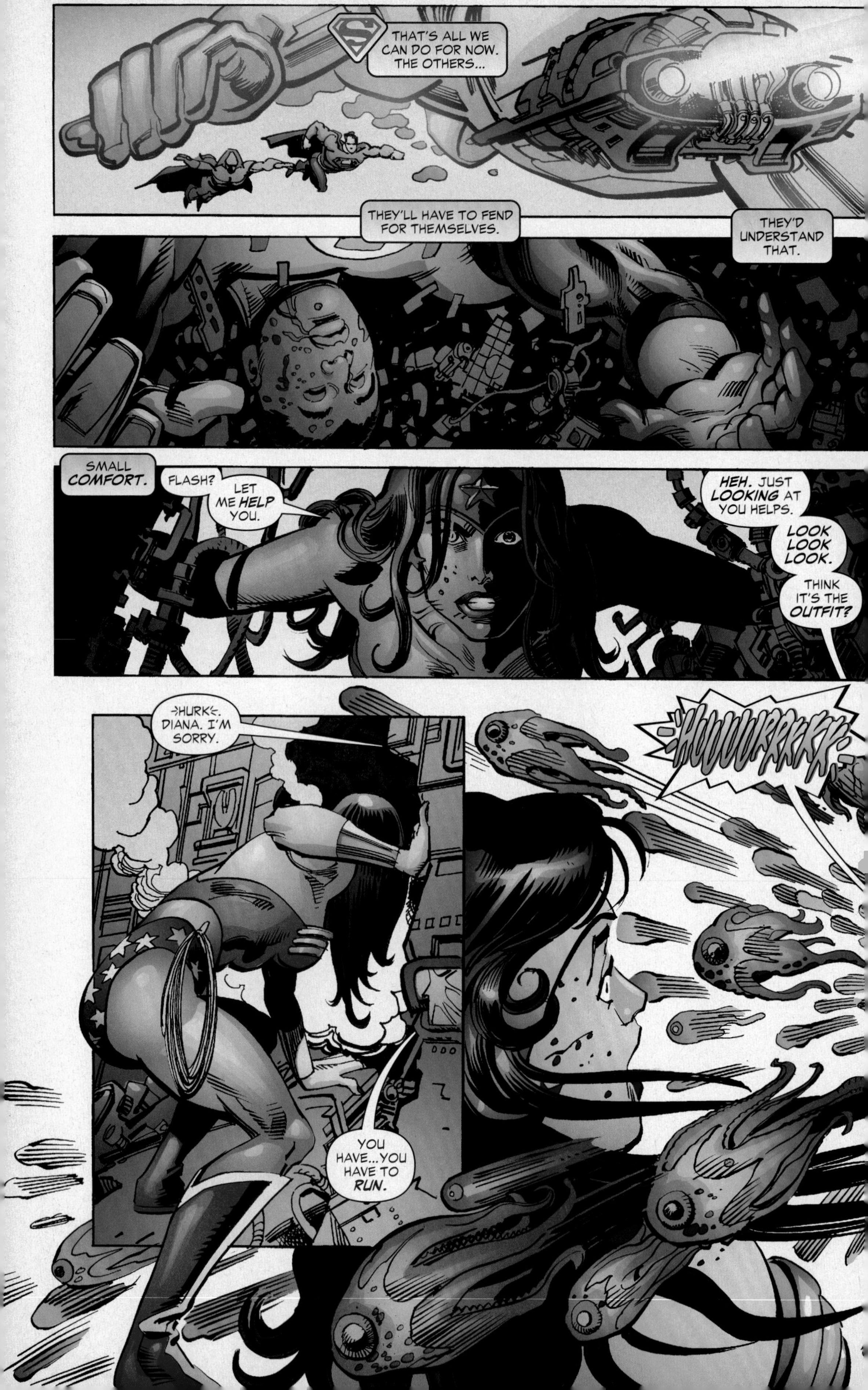
THAT'S ALL WE CAN DO FOR NOW. THE OTHERS...
THEY'LL HAVE TO FEND FOR THEMSELVES.
THEY'D UNDERSTAND THAT.
SMALL COMFORT.
FLASH?
LET ME HELP YOU.
HEH. JUST LOOKING AT YOU HELPS.
LOOK LOOK LOOK.
THINK IT'S THE OUTFIT?
HURK. DIANA. I'M SORRY.
HUUUURRKKK
YOU HAVE...YOU HAVE TO RUN.

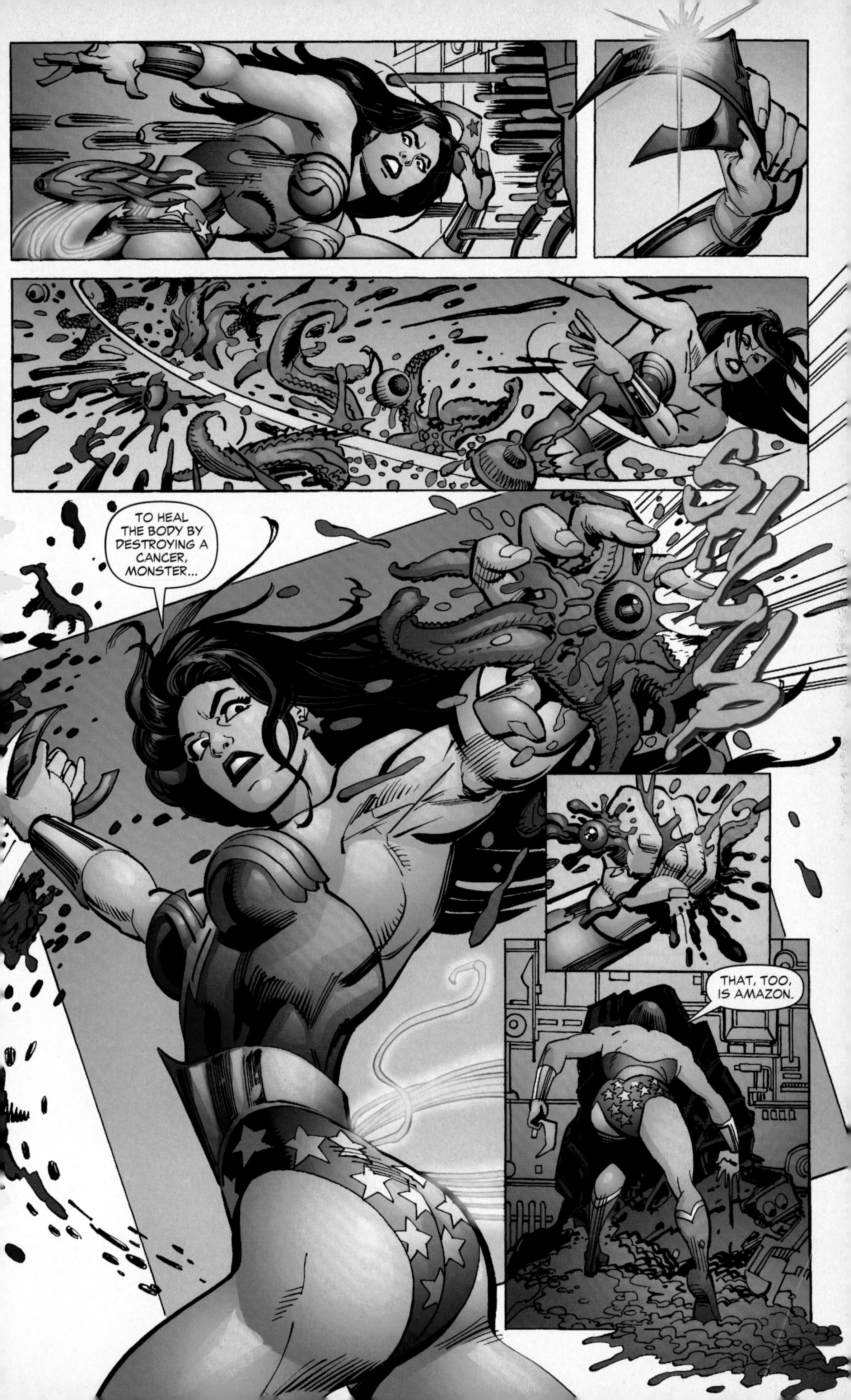
SHLUK
TO HEAL THE BODY BY DESTROYING A CANCER, MONSTER...
THAT, TOO, IS AMAZON.

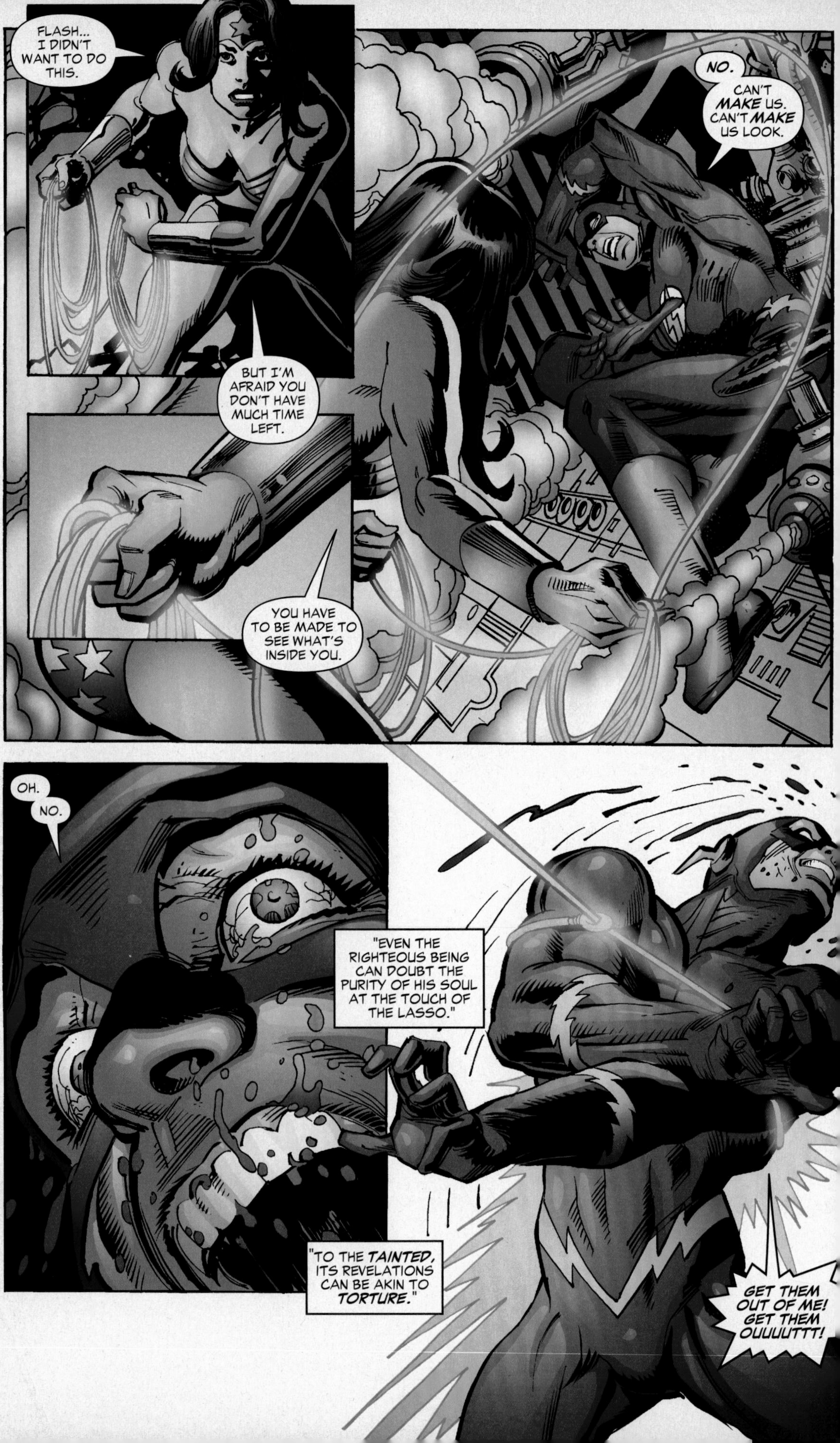

FLASH... I DIDN'T WANT TO DO THIS.
NO.
CAN'T *MAKE* US. CAN'T *MAKE* US LOOK.
BUT I'M AFRAID YOU DON'T HAVE MUCH TIME LEFT.
YOU HAVE TO BE MADE TO SEE WHAT'S INSIDE YOU.
OH. NO.
"EVEN THE RIGHTEOUS BEING CAN DOUBT THE PURITY OF HIS SOUL AT THE TOUCH OF THE LASSO."
"TO THE *TAINTED*, ITS REVELATIONS CAN BE AKIN TO *TORTURE*."
GET THEM OUT OF ME! GET THEM OUUUUTTT!

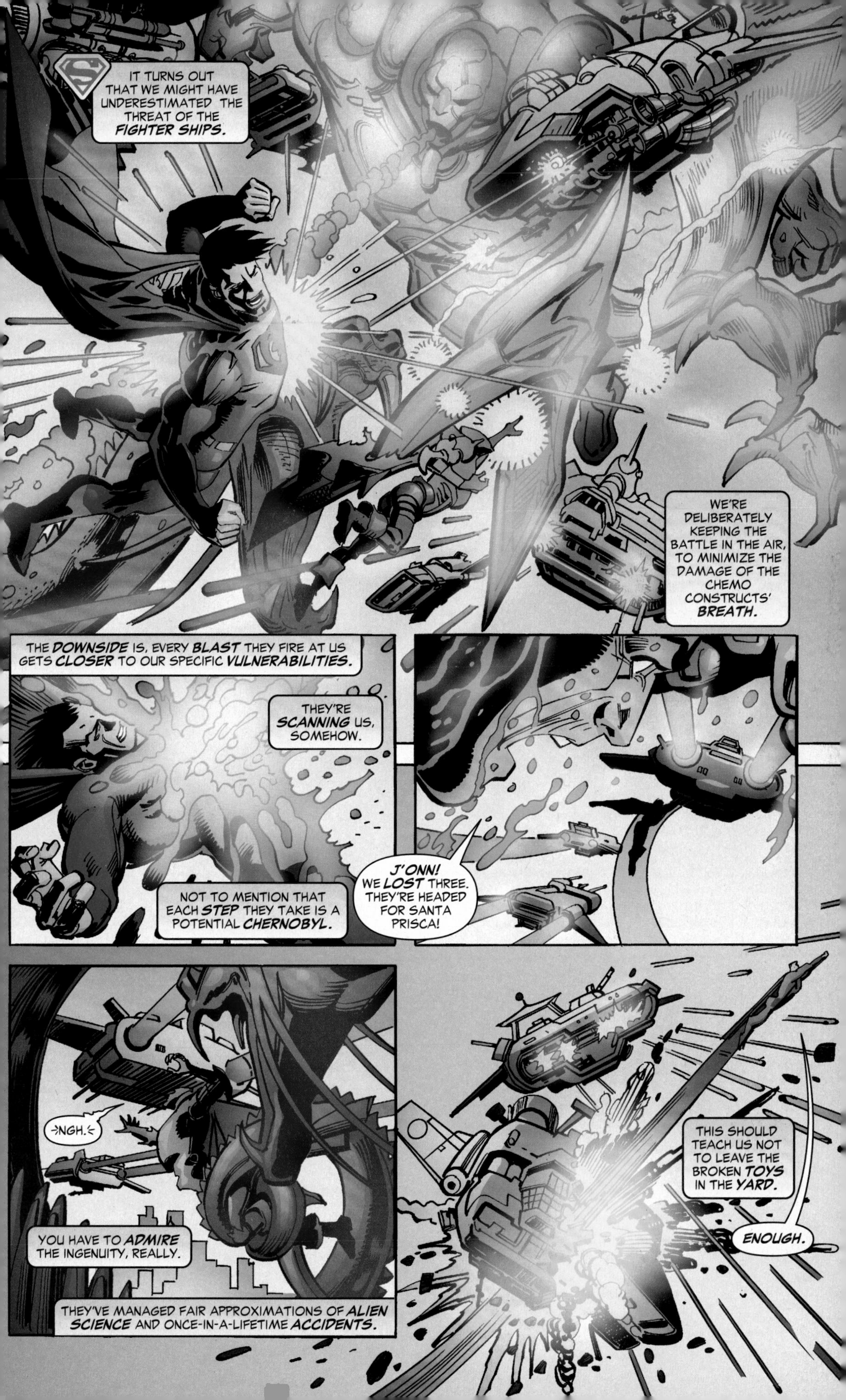
IT TURNS OUT THAT WE MIGHT HAVE UNDERESTIMATED THE THREAT OF THE FIGHTER SHIPS.
WE'RE DELIBERATELY KEEPING THE BATTLE IN THE AIR, TO MINIMIZE THE DAMAGE OF THE CHEMO CONSTRUCTS' BREATH.
THE DOWNSIDE IS, EVERY BLAST THEY FIRE AT US GETS CLOSER TO OUR SPECIFIC VULNERABILITIES.
THEY'RE SCANNING US, SOMEHOW.
NOT TO MENTION THAT EACH STEP THEY TAKE IS A POTENTIAL CHERNOBYL.
J'ONN! WE LOST THREE. THEY'RE HEADED FOR SANTA PRISCA!
NGH.
YOU HAVE TO ADMIRE THE INGENUITY, REALLY.
THEY'VE MANAGED FAIR APPROXIMATIONS OF ALIEN SCIENCE AND ONCE-IN-A-LIFETIME ACCIDENTS.
THIS SHOULD TEACH US NOT TO LEAVE THE BROKEN TOYS IN THE YARD.
ENOUGH.

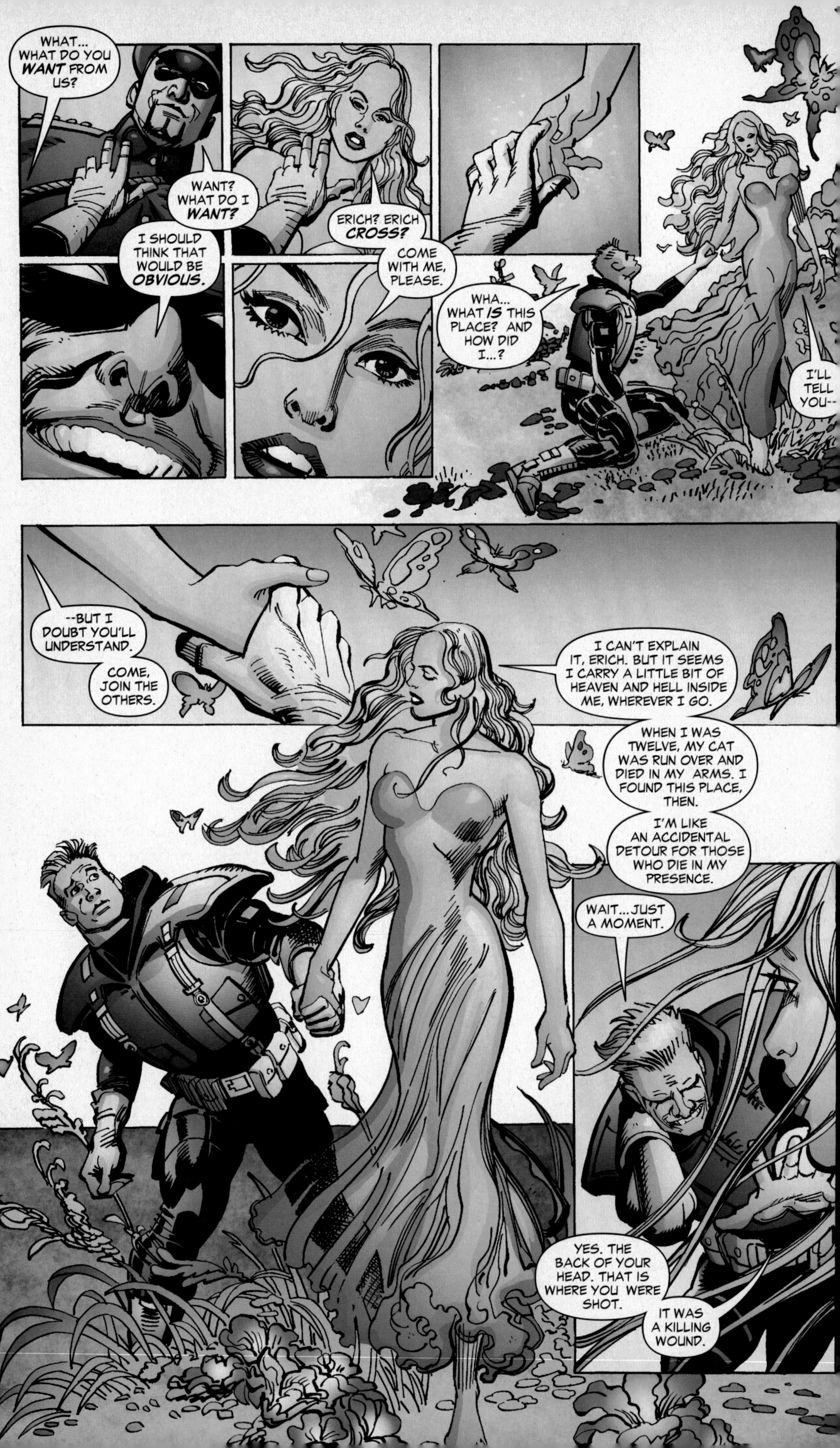

WHAT... WHAT DO YOU WANT FROM US?
WANT? WHAT DO I WANT?
I SHOULD THINK THAT WOULD BE OBVIOUS.
ERICH? ERICH CROSS?
COME WITH ME, PLEASE.
WHA... WHAT IS THIS PLACE? AND HOW DID I...?
I'LL TELL YOU--
--BUT I DOUBT YOU'LL UNDERSTAND.
COME, JOIN THE OTHERS.
I CAN'T EXPLAIN IT, ERICH. BUT IT SEEMS I CARRY A LITTLE BIT OF HEAVEN AND HELL INSIDE ME, WHEREVER I GO.
WHEN I WAS TWELVE, MY CAT WAS RUN OVER AND DIED IN MY ARMS. I FOUND THIS PLACE, THEN.
I'M LIKE AN ACCIDENTAL DETOUR FOR THOSE WHO DIE IN MY PRESENCE.
WAIT...JUST A MOMENT.
YES. THE BACK OF YOUR HEAD. THAT IS WHERE YOU WERE SHOT.
IT WAS A KILLING WOUND.

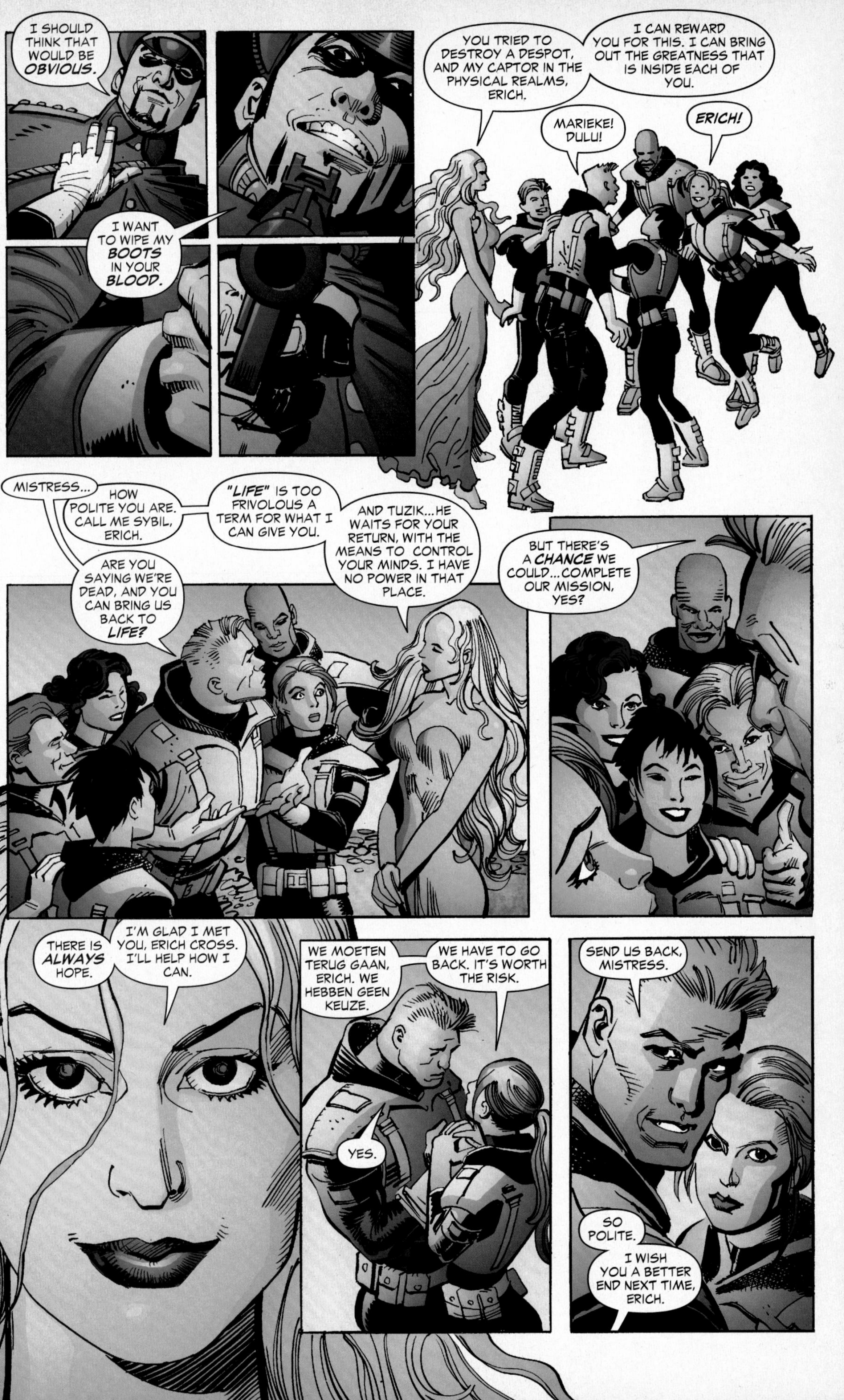
I SHOULD THINK THAT WOULD BE OBVIOUS.
I WANT TO WIPE MY BOOTS IN YOUR BLOOD.
YOU TRIED TO DESTROY A DESPOT, AND MY CAPTOR IN THE PHYSICAL REALMS, ERICH.
I CAN REWARD YOU FOR THIS. I CAN BRING OUT THE GREATNESS THAT IS INSIDE EACH OF YOU.
MARIEKE! DULU!
ERICH!
MISTRESS...
HOW POLITE YOU ARE. CALL ME SYBIL, ERICH.
ARE YOU SAYING WE'RE DEAD, AND YOU CAN BRING US BACK TO LIFE?
"LIFE" IS TOO FRIVOLOUS A TERM FOR WHAT I CAN GIVE YOU.
AND TUZIK...HE WAITS FOR YOUR RETURN, WITH THE MEANS TO CONTROL YOUR MINDS. I HAVE NO POWER IN THAT PLACE.
BUT THERE'S A CHANCE WE COULD...COMPLETE OUR MISSION, YES?
THERE IS ALWAYS HOPE.
I'M GLAD I MET YOU, ERICH CROSS. I'LL HELP HOW I CAN.
WE MOETEN TERUG GAAN, ERICH. WE HEBBEN GEEN KEUZE.
WE HAVE TO GO BACK. IT'S WORTH THE RISK.
YES.
SEND US BACK, MISTRESS.
SO POLITE.
I WISH YOU A BETTER END NEXT TIME, ERICH.

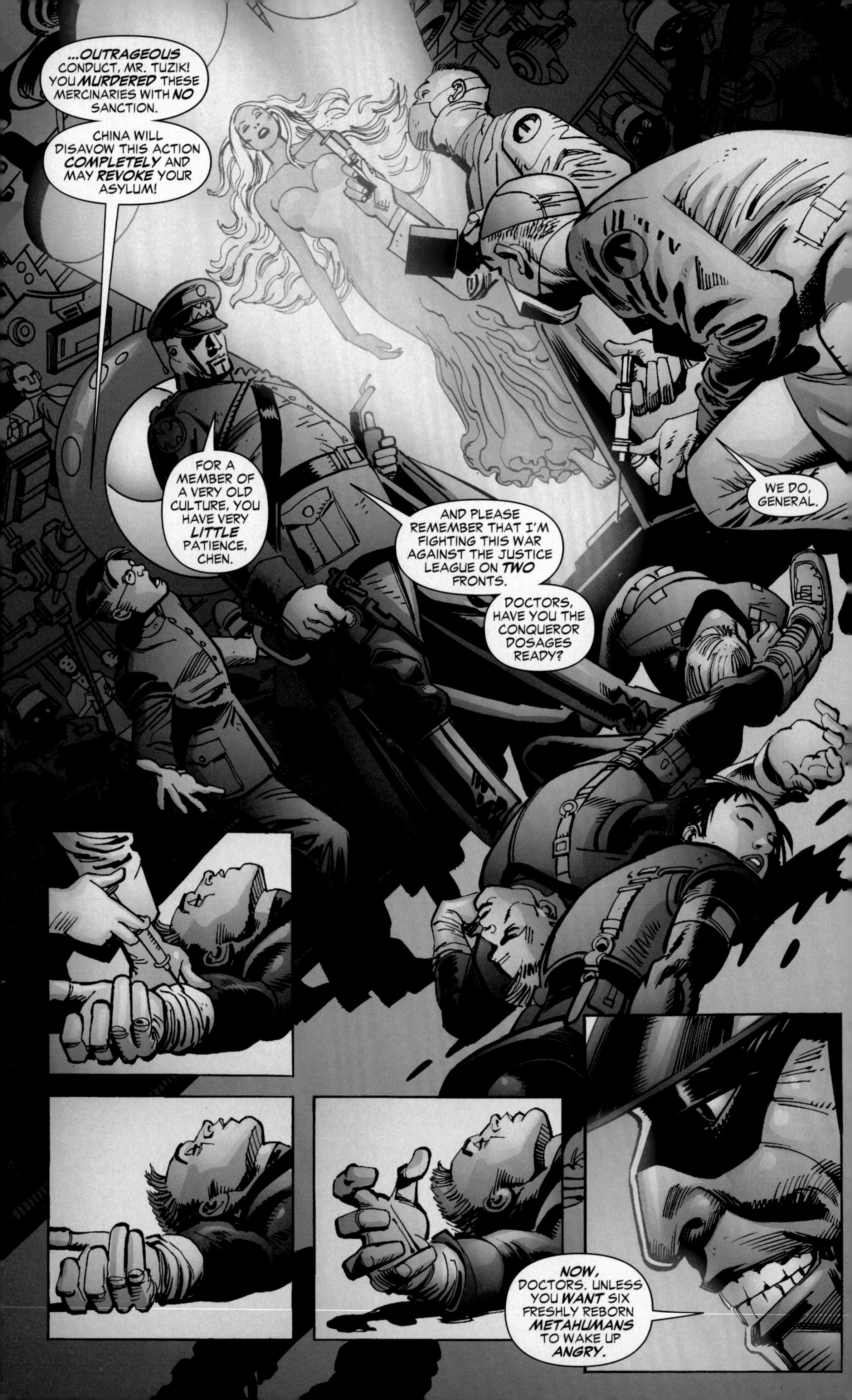
...OUTRAGEOUS CONDUCT, MR. TUZIK! YOU MURDERED THESE MERCINARIES WITH NO SANCTION.
CHINA WILL DISAVOW THIS ACTION COMPLETELY AND MAY REVOKE YOUR ASYLUM!
FOR A MEMBER OF A VERY OLD CULTURE, YOU HAVE VERY LITTLE PATIENCE, CHEN.
AND PLEASE REMEMBER THAT I'M FIGHTING THIS WAR AGAINST THE JUSTICE LEAGUE ON TWO FRONTS.
DOCTORS, HAVE YOU THE CONQUEROR DOSAGES READY?
WE DO, GENERAL.
NOW, DOCTORS. UNLESS YOU WANT SIX FRESHLY REBORN METAHUMANS TO WAKE UP ANGRY.

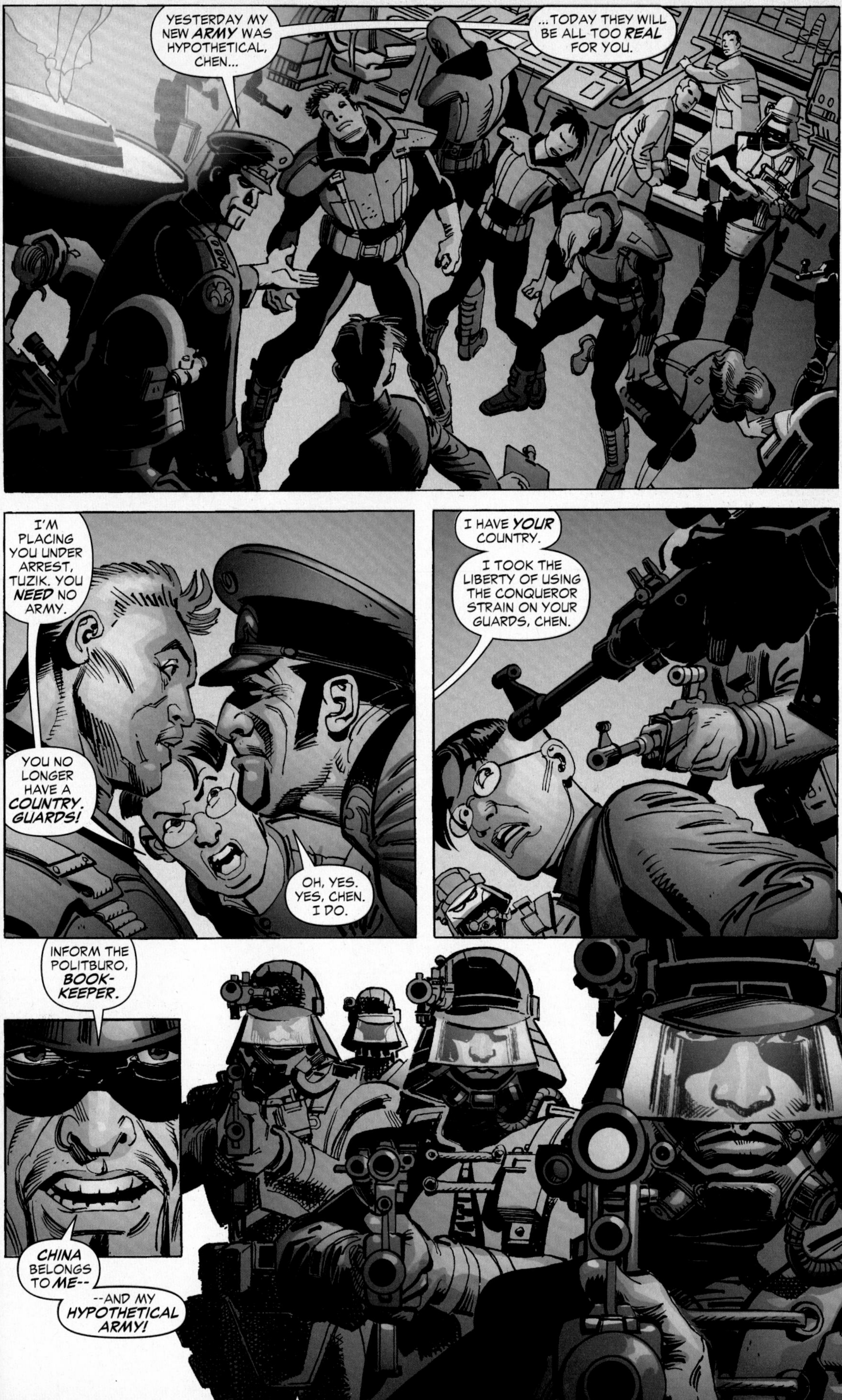
YESTERDAY MY NEW ARMY WAS HYPOTHETICAL, CHEN...
...TODAY THEY WILL BE ALL TOO REAL FOR YOU.
I'M PLACING YOU UNDER ARREST, TUZIK. YOU NEED NO ARMY.
YOU NO LONGER HAVE A COUNTRY. GUARDS!
OH, YES. YES, CHEN. I DO.
I HAVE YOUR COUNTRY.
I TOOK THE LIBERTY OF USING THE CONQUEROR STRAIN ON YOUR GUARDS, CHEN.
INFORM THE POLITBURO, BOOK-KEEPER.
CHINA BELONGS TO ME--
--AND MY HYPOTHETICAL ARMY!

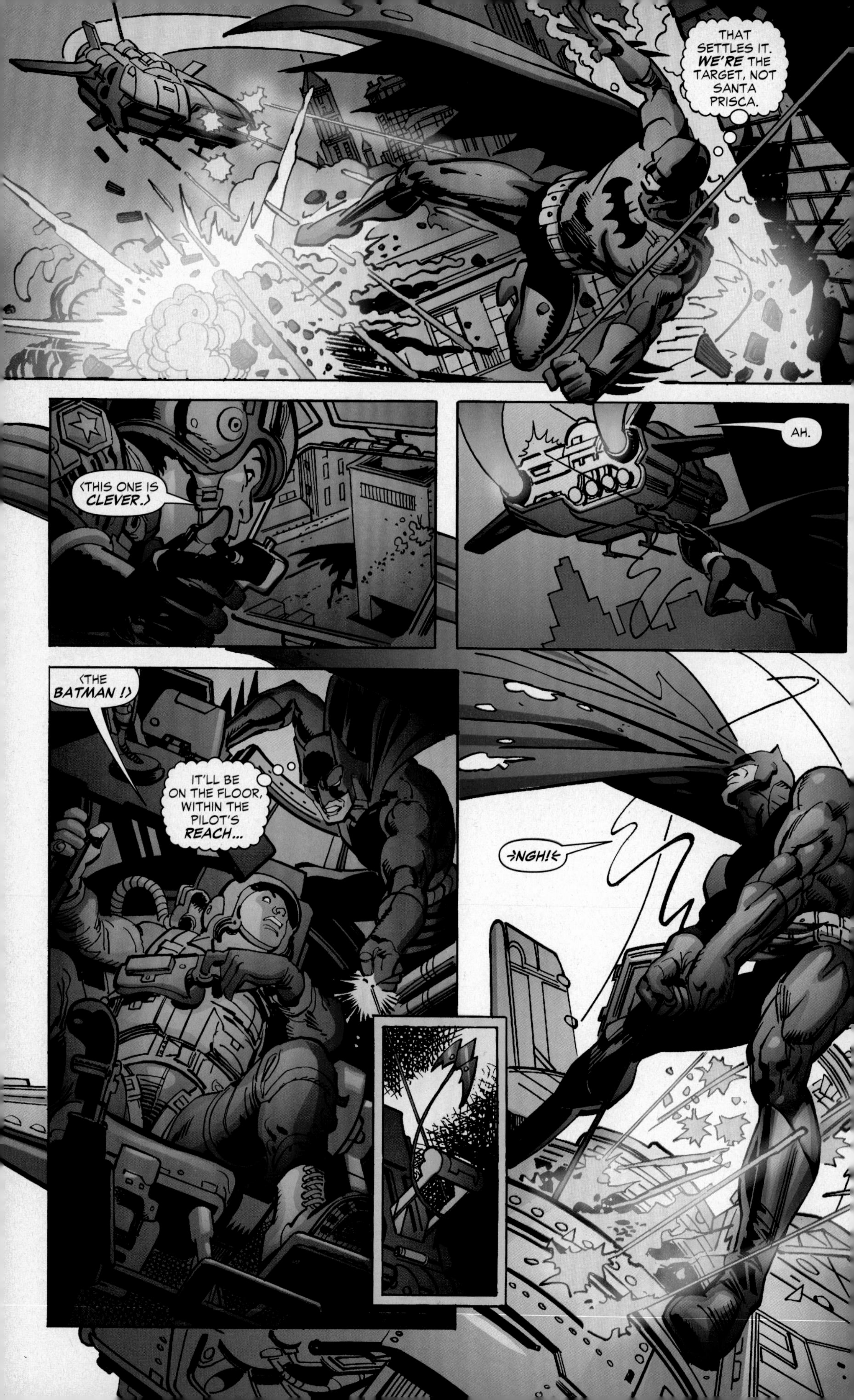

THAT SETTLES IT. WE'RE THE TARGET, NOT SANTA PRISCA.
‹THIS ONE IS CLEVER.›
AH.
‹THE BATMAN!›
IT'LL BE ON THE FLOOR, WITHIN THE PILOT'S REACH...
NGH!

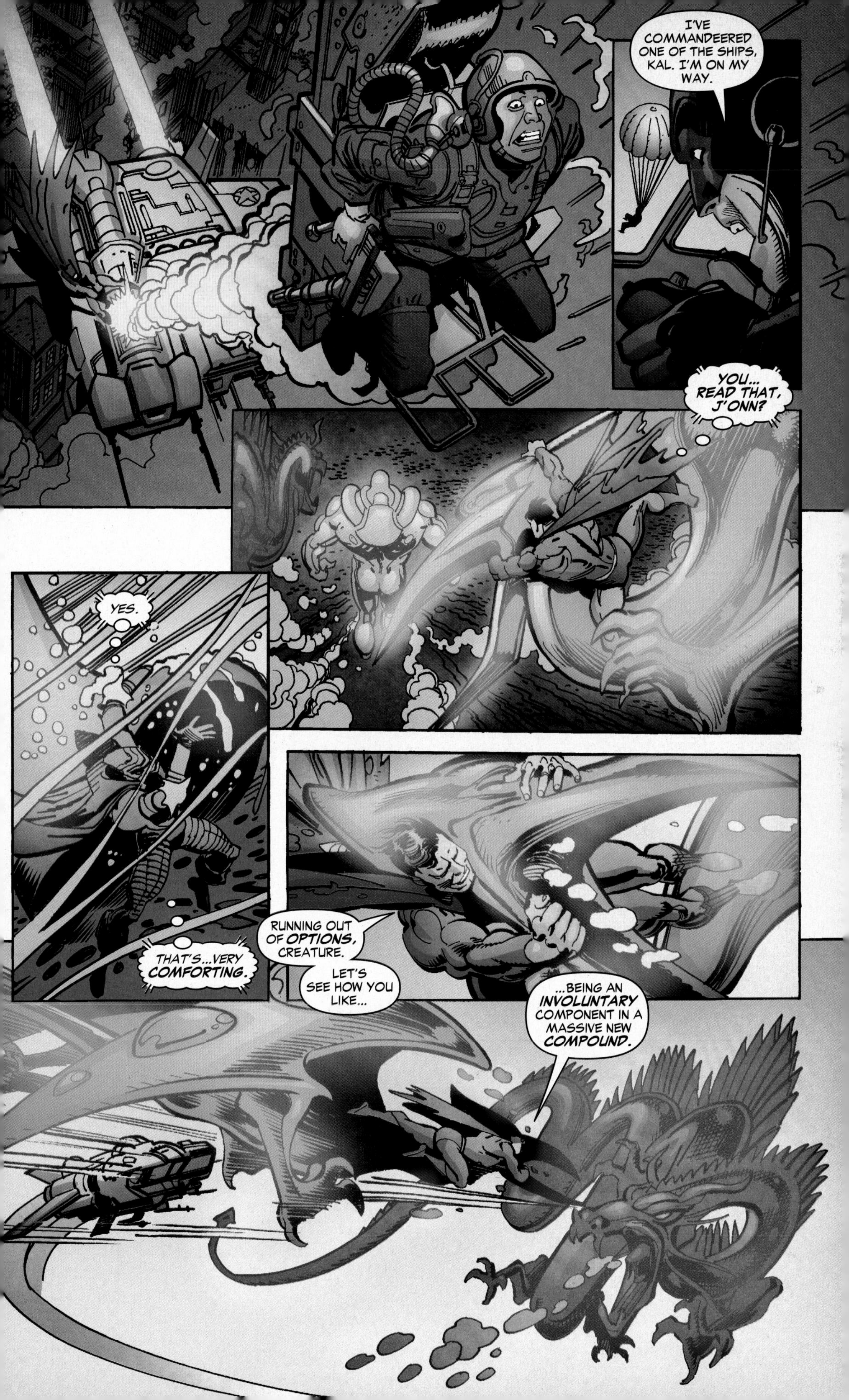

I'VE COMMANDEERED ONE OF THE SHIPS, KAL. I'M ON MY WAY.
YOU... READ THAT, J'ONN?
YES.
THAT'S...VERY COMFORTING.
RUNNING OUT OF OPTIONS, CREATURE.
LET'S SEE HOW YOU LIKE...
...BEING AN INVOLUNTARY COMPONENT IN A MASSIVE NEW COMPOUND.

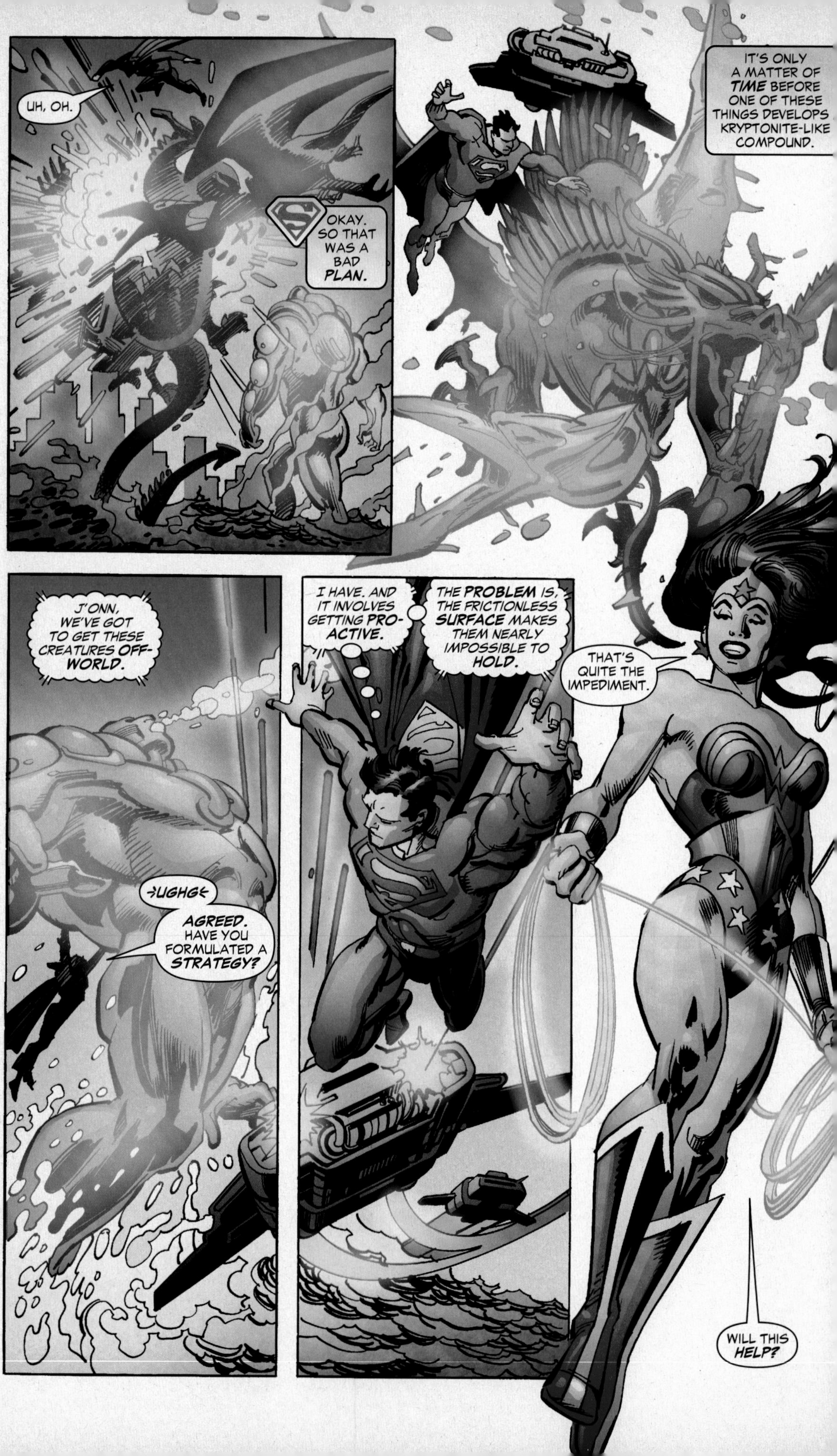
UH, OH.
OKAY. SO THAT WAS A BAD PLAN.
IT'S ONLY A MATTER OF TIME BEFORE ONE OF THESE THINGS DEVELOPS KRYPTONITE-LIKE COMPOUND.
J'ONN, WE'VE GOT TO GET THESE CREATURES OFF-WORLD.
UGHG
AGREED. HAVE YOU FORMULATED A STRATEGY?
I HAVE. AND IT INVOLVES GETTING PRO-ACTIVE.
THE PROBLEM IS, THE FRICTIONLESS SURFACE MAKES THEM NEARLY IMPOSSIBLE TO HOLD.
THAT'S QUITE THE IMPEDIMENT.
WILL THIS HELP?

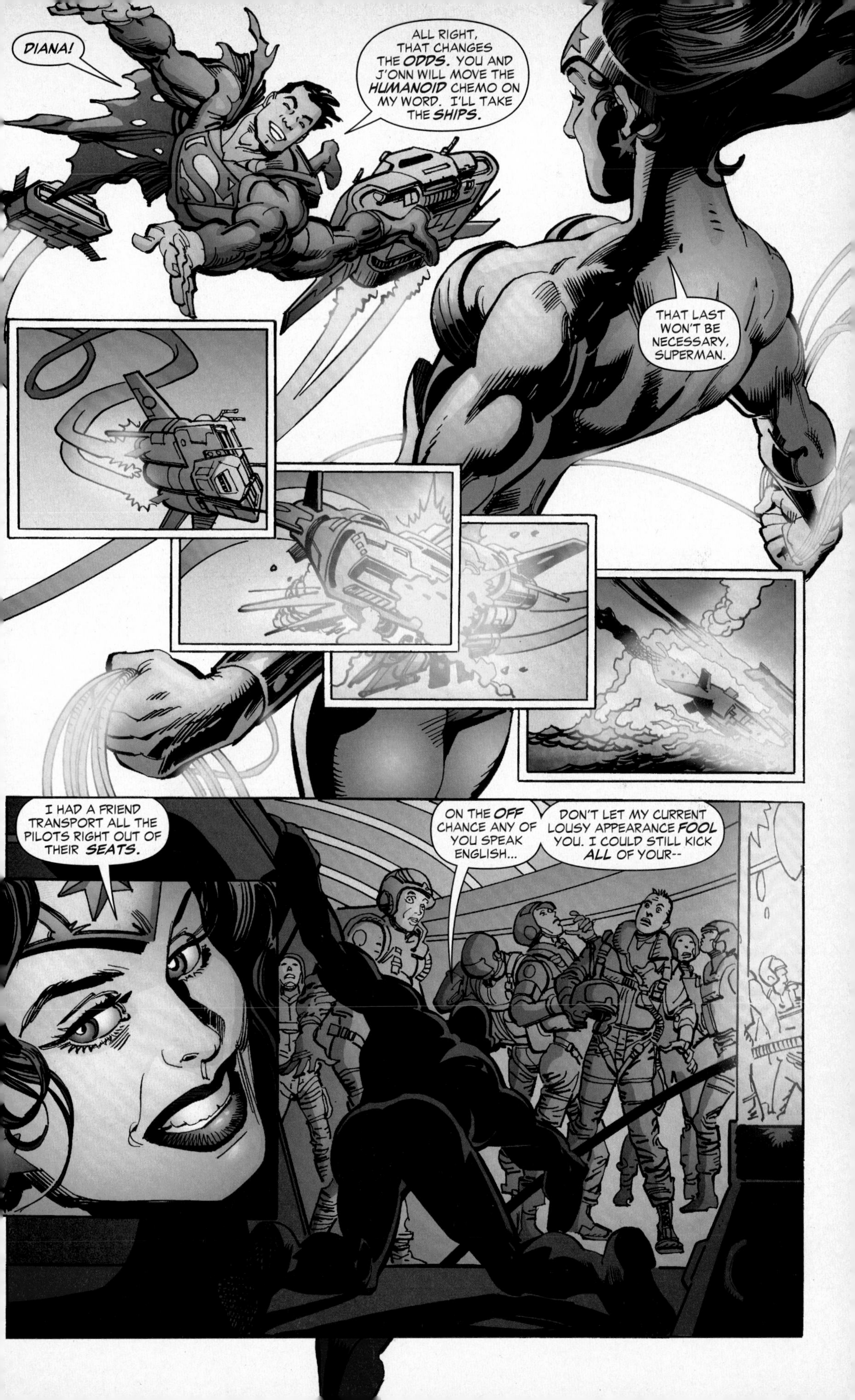
DIANA!
ALL RIGHT, THAT CHANGES THE ODDS. YOU AND J'ONN WILL MOVE THE HUMANOID CHEMO ON MY WORD. I'LL TAKE THE SHIPS.
THAT LAST WON'T BE NECESSARY, SUPERMAN.
I HAD A FRIEND TRANSPORT ALL THE PILOTS RIGHT OUT OF THEIR SEATS.
ON THE OFF CHANCE ANY OF YOU SPEAK ENGLISH...
DON'T LET MY CURRENT LOUSY APPEARANCE FOOL YOU. I COULD STILL KICK ALL OF YOUR--

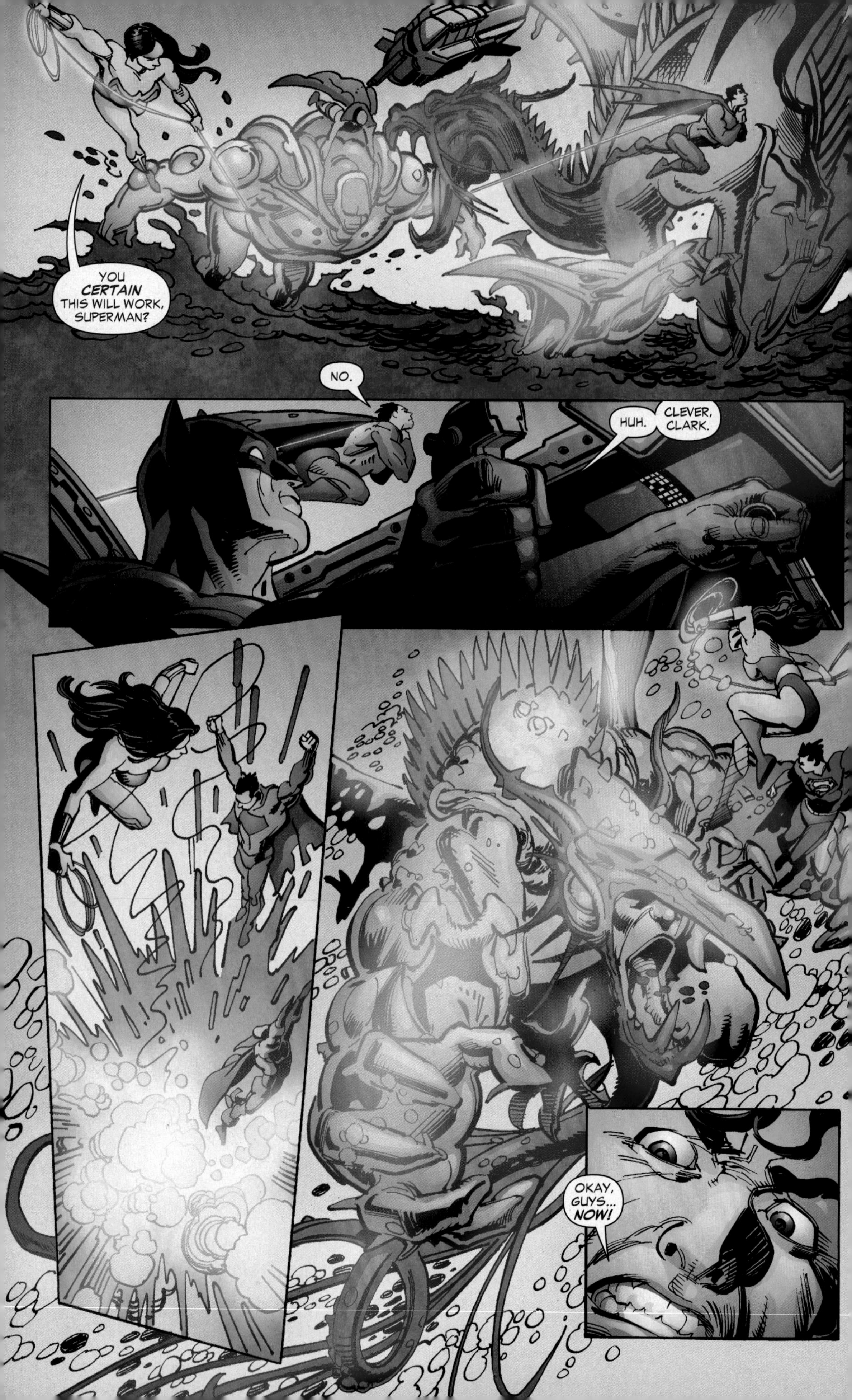
YOU CERTAIN THIS WILL WORK, SUPERMAN?
NO.
HUH.
CLEVER, CLARK.
OKAY, GUYS... NOW!

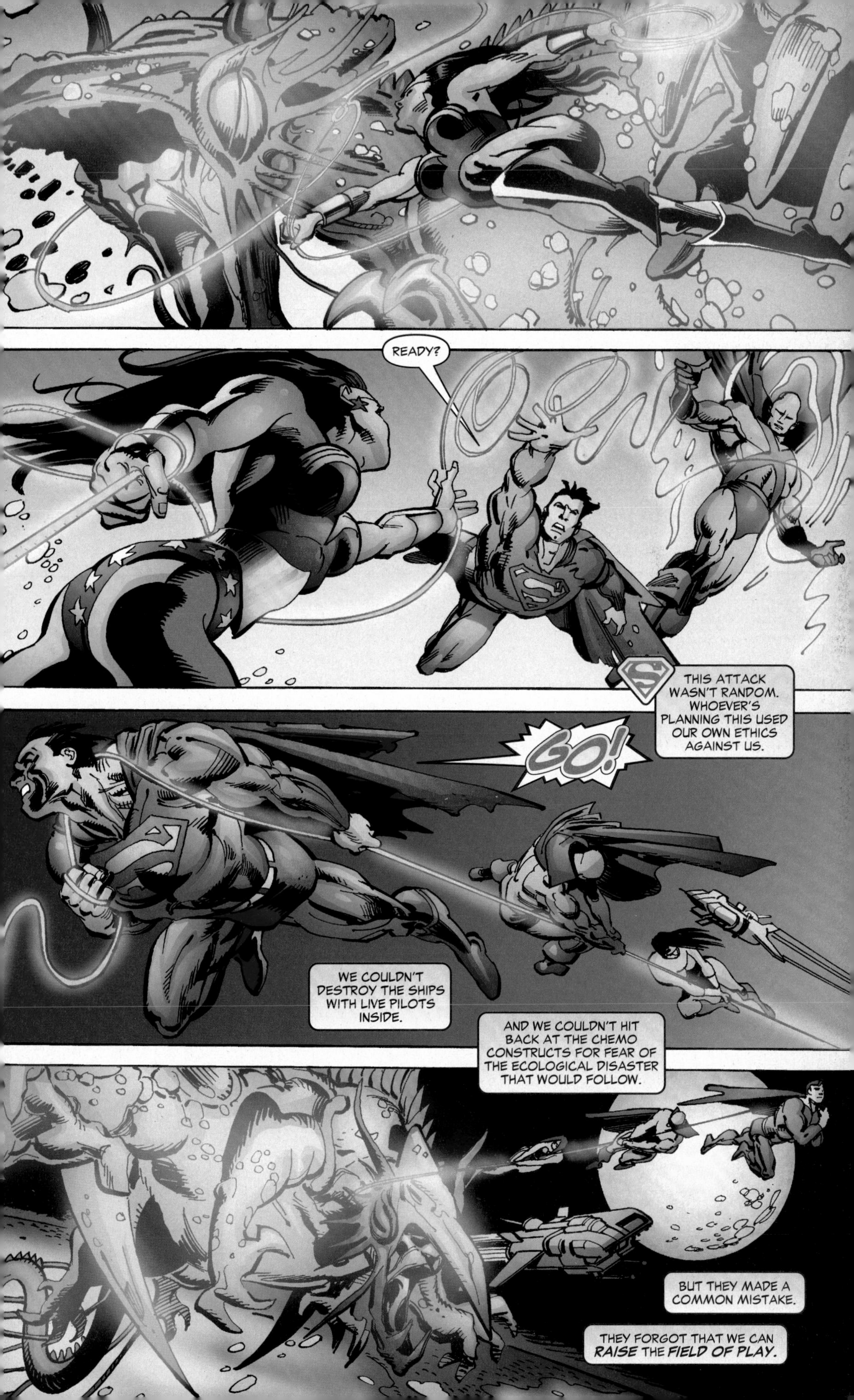
READY?
THIS ATTACK WASN'T RANDOM. WHOEVER'S PLANNING THIS USED OUR OWN ETHICS AGAINST US.
GO!
WE COULDN'T DESTROY THE SHIPS WITH LIVE PILOTS INSIDE.
AND WE COULDN'T HIT BACK AT THE CHEMO CONSTRUCTS FOR FEAR OF THE ECOLOGICAL DISASTER THAT WOULD FOLLOW.
BUT THEY MADE A COMMON MISTAKE.
THEY FORGOT THAT WE CAN RAISE THE FIELD OF PLAY.

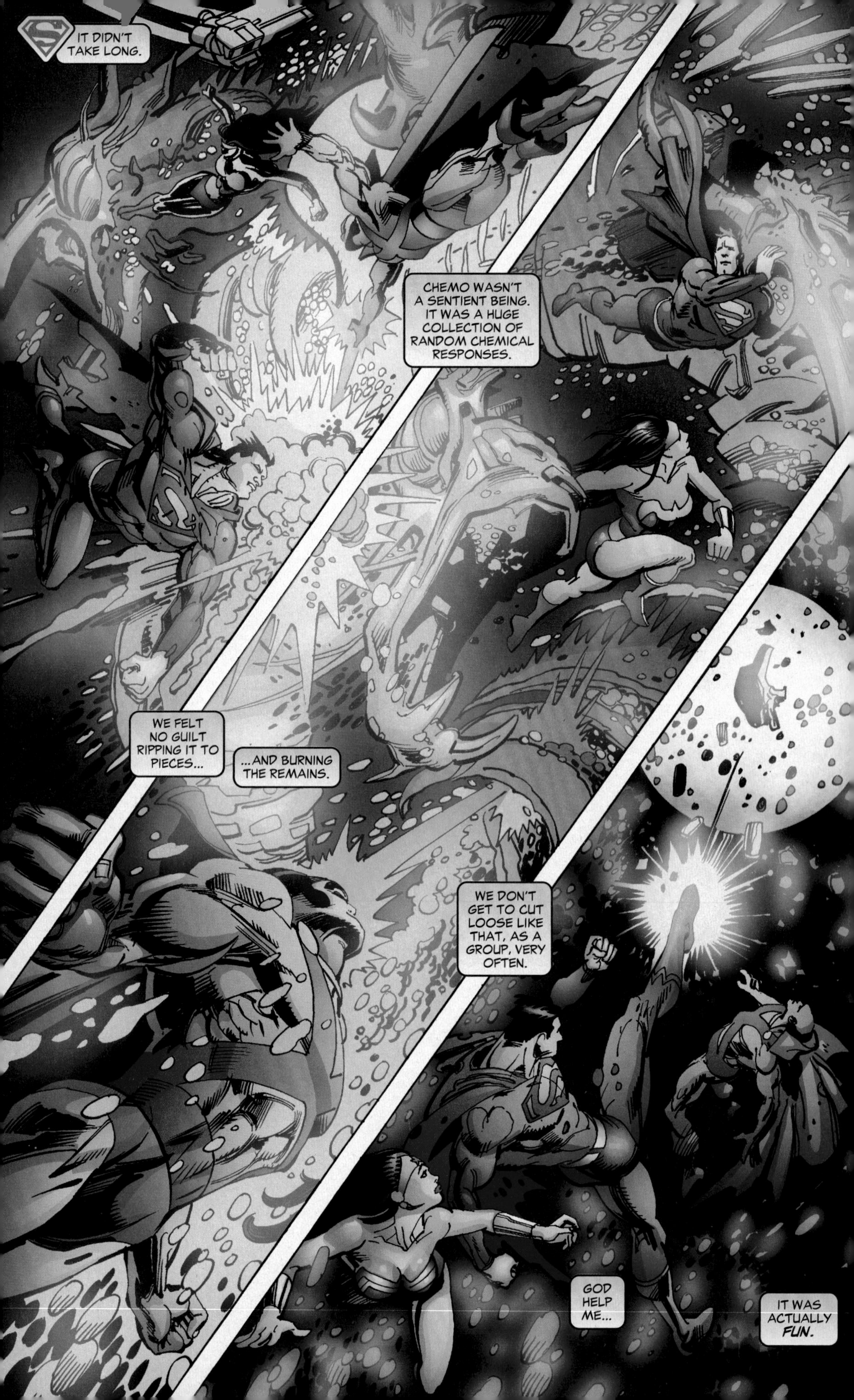
IT DIDN'T TAKE LONG.
CHEMO WASN'T A SENTIENT BEING. IT WAS A HUGE COLLECTION OF RANDOM CHEMICAL RESPONSES.
WE FELT NO GUILT RIPPING IT TO PIECES...
...AND BURNING THE REMAINS.
WE DON'T GET TO CUT LOOSE LIKE THAT, AS A GROUP, VERY OFTEN.
GOD HELP ME...
IT WAS ACTUALLY *FUN*.

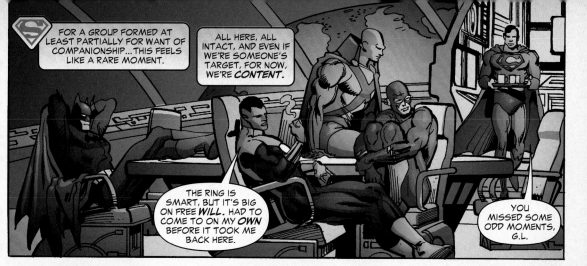

FOR A GROUP FORMED AT LEAST PARTIALLY FOR WANT OF COMPANIONSHIP...THIS FEELS LIKE A RARE MOMENT.

ALL HERE, ALL INTACT, AND EVEN IF WE'RE SOMEONE'S TARGET, FOR NOW, WE'RE *CONTENT.*

THE RING IS SMART, BUT IT'S BIG ON FREE *WILL.* HAD TO COME TO ON MY *OWN* BEFORE IT TOOK ME BACK HERE.

YOU MISSED SOME ODD MOMENTS, G.L.

THANKS, SUPES.

SO ANYWAY, DON'T THINK THE LI'L STARROS AREN'T *SMART.*

THEY BLOCKED MY BRAIN'S *ACCESS* TO THE VIBRATIONAL *FREQUENCY* THAT WOULD BURN THEM OUT OF MY *CELLS.*

'TIL WONDER WO--! HEY, WHERE *IS* DIANA?

I THOUGHT I'D MAKE SOME REFRESHMENTS.

IT'S A THEMYSCIRAN CONFECTION, SWEETENED WITH POMEGRANATE. MY MOTHER'S RECIPE.

WONDER WOMAN *BAKED?*

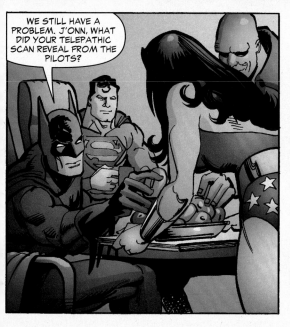

WE STILL HAVE A PROBLEM. J'ONN, WHAT DID YOUR TELEPATHIC SCAN REVEAL FROM THE PILOTS?

NOTHING. THEY'RE INFECTED BY THE CONQUEROR STRAIN, UNTIL WE FIGURE OUT HOW TO DO FLASH'S VIBRATIONAL EFFECT WITHOUT KILLING THE *HOST* BODIES.

GREEN LANTERN'S QUARANTINED THEM IN THE SICK BAY.

I'M AFRAID TO TRY IT, AND I'M AFRAID *NOT* TO TRY IT.

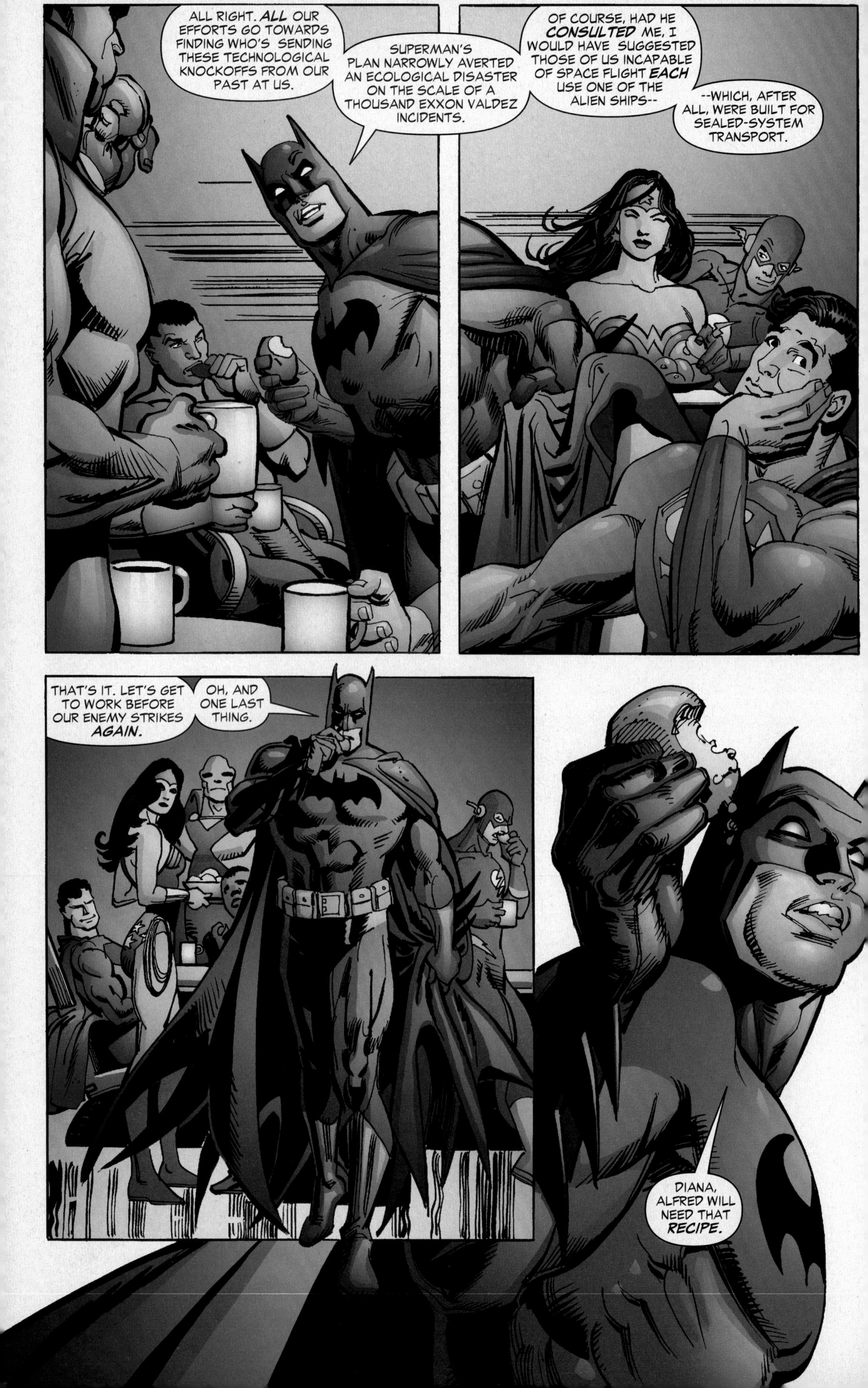
ALL RIGHT. ALL OUR EFFORTS GO TOWARDS FINDING WHO'S SENDING THESE TECHNOLOGICAL KNOCKOFFS FROM OUR PAST AT US.
SUPERMAN'S PLAN NARROWLY AVERTED AN ECOLOGICAL DISASTER ON THE SCALE OF A THOUSAND EXXON VALDEZ INCIDENTS.
OF COURSE, HAD HE CONSULTED ME, I WOULD HAVE SUGGESTED THOSE OF US INCAPABLE OF SPACE FLIGHT EACH USE ONE OF THE ALIEN SHIPS--
--WHICH, AFTER ALL, WERE BUILT FOR SEALED-SYSTEM TRANSPORT.
THAT'S IT. LET'S GET TO WORK BEFORE OUR ENEMY STRIKES AGAIN.
OH, AND ONE LAST THING.
DIANA, ALFRED WILL NEED THAT RECIPE.

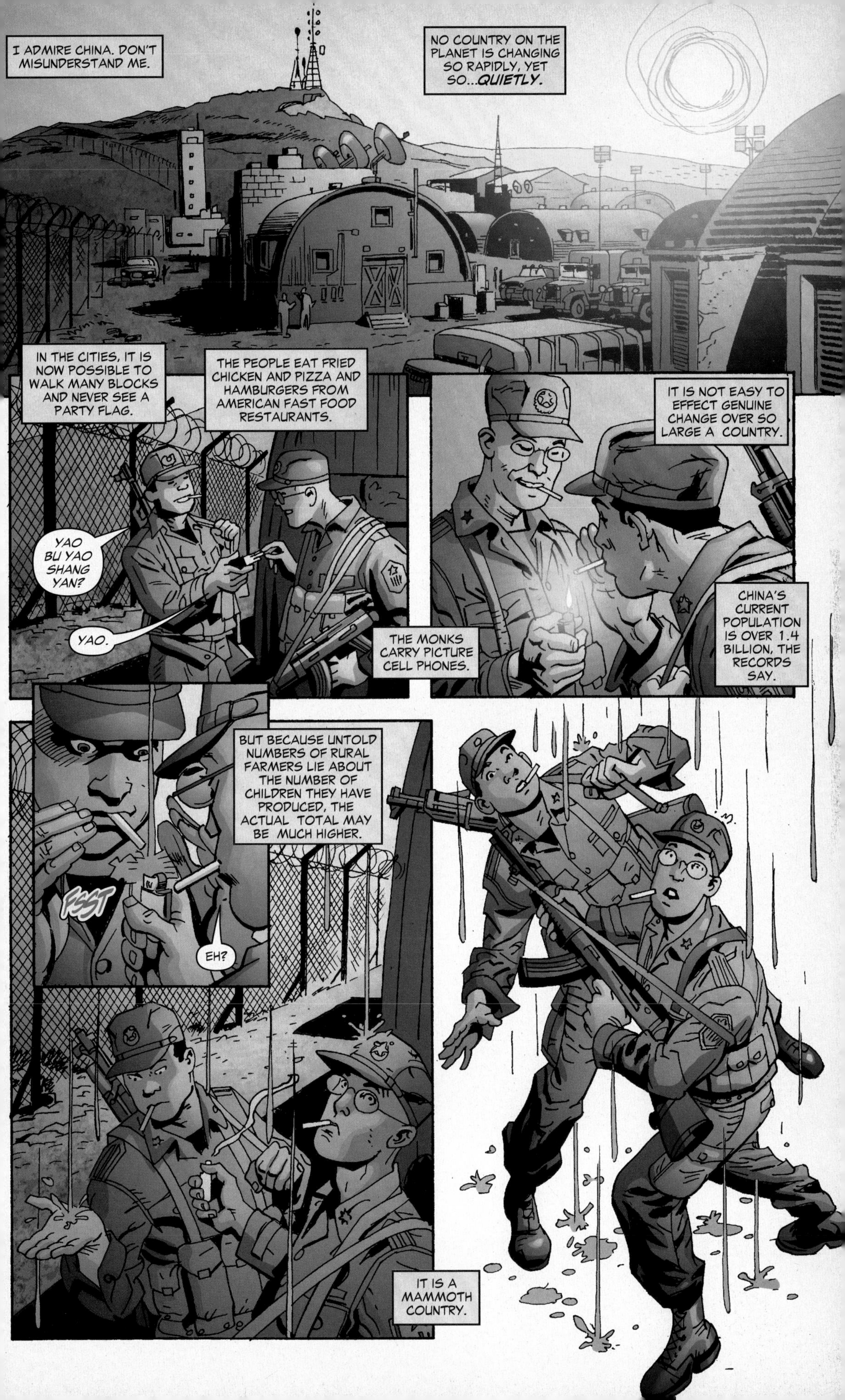
I ADMIRE CHINA. DON'T MISUNDERSTAND ME.
NO COUNTRY ON THE PLANET IS CHANGING SO RAPIDLY, YET SO...QUIETLY.
IN THE CITIES, IT IS NOW POSSIBLE TO WALK MANY BLOCKS AND NEVER SEE A PARTY FLAG.
THE PEOPLE EAT FRIED CHICKEN AND PIZZA AND HAMBURGERS FROM AMERICAN FAST FOOD RESTAURANTS.
YAO BU YAO SHANG YAN?
YAO.
THE MONKS CARRY PICTURE CELL PHONES.
IT IS NOT EASY TO EFFECT GENUINE CHANGE OVER SO LARGE A COUNTRY.
CHINA'S CURRENT POPULATION IS OVER 1.4 BILLION, THE RECORDS SAY.
BUT BECAUSE UNTOLD NUMBERS OF RURAL FARMERS LIE ABOUT THE NUMBER OF CHILDREN THEY HAVE PRODUCED, THE ACTUAL TOTAL MAY BE MUCH HIGHER.
FSST
EH?
IT IS A MAMMOTH COUNTRY.

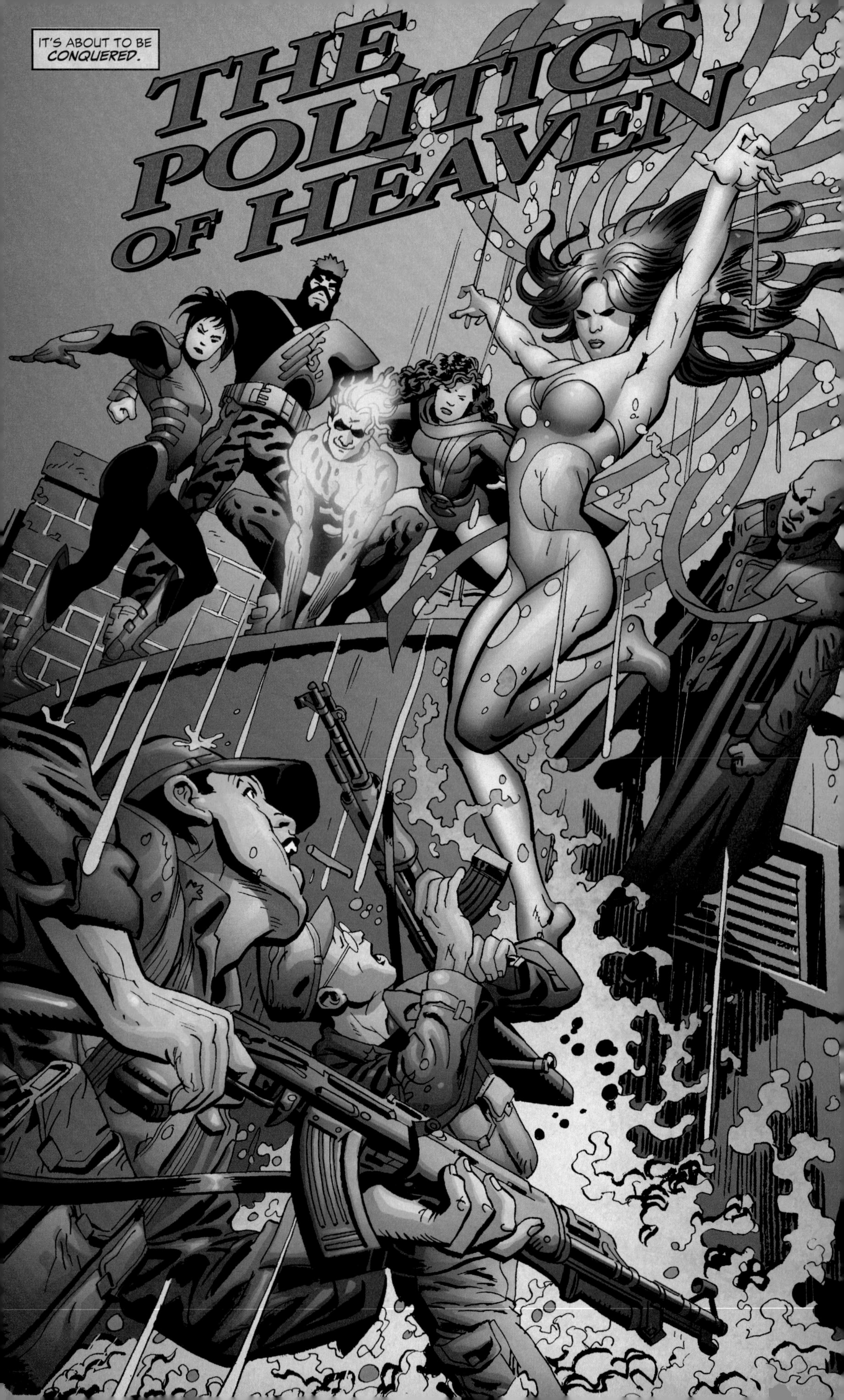
IT'S ABOUT TO BE CONQUERED.
THE POLITICS OF HEAVEN

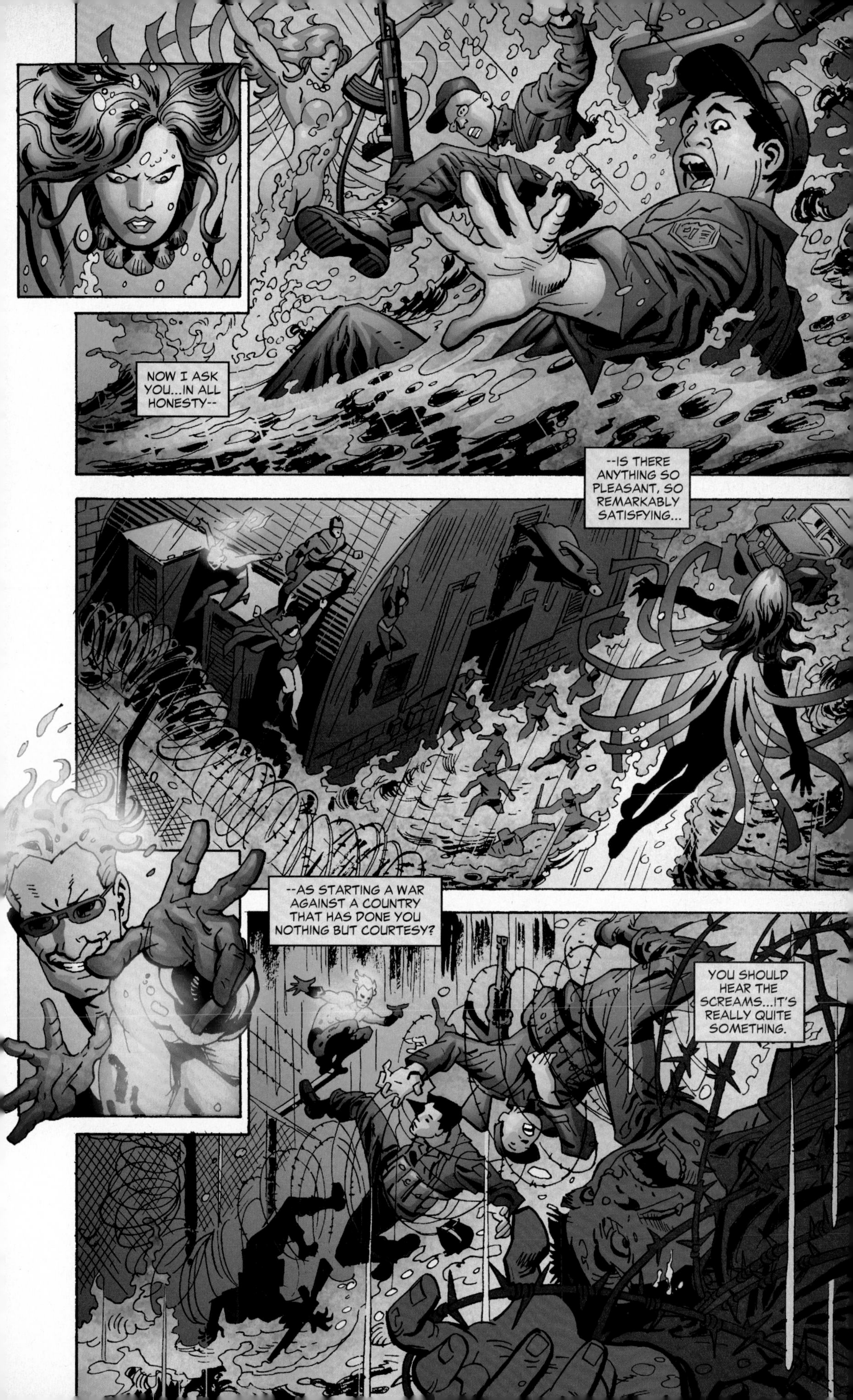
NOW I ASK YOU...IN ALL HONESTY--
--IS THERE ANYTHING SO PLEASANT, SO REMARKABLY SATISFYING...
--AS STARTING A WAR AGAINST A COUNTRY THAT HAS DONE YOU NOTHING BUT COURTESY?
YOU SHOULD HEAR THE SCREAMS...IT'S REALLY QUITE SOMETHING.

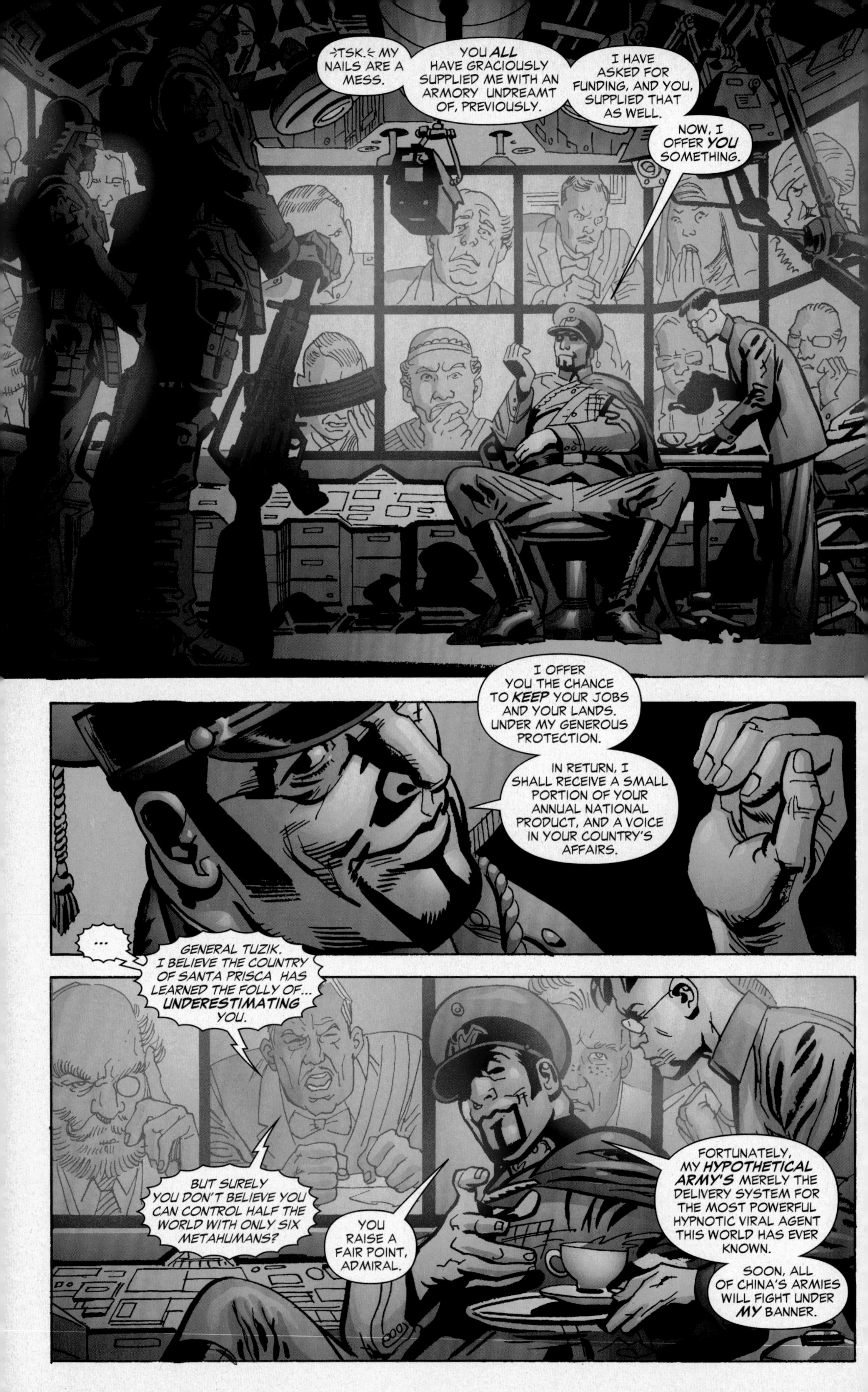

→TSK.← MY NAILS ARE A MESS.
YOU ALL HAVE GRACIOUSLY SUPPLIED ME WITH AN ARMORY UNDREAMT OF, PREVIOUSLY.
I HAVE ASKED FOR FUNDING, AND YOU, SUPPLIED THAT AS WELL.
NOW, I OFFER YOU SOMETHING.
I OFFER YOU THE CHANCE TO KEEP YOUR JOBS AND YOUR LANDS. UNDER MY GENEROUS PROTECTION.
IN RETURN, I SHALL RECEIVE A SMALL PORTION OF YOUR ANNUAL NATIONAL PRODUCT, AND A VOICE IN YOUR COUNTRY'S AFFAIRS.
...
GENERAL TUZIK. I BELIEVE THE COUNTRY OF SANTA PRISCA HAS LEARNED THE FOLLY OF... UNDERESTIMATING YOU.
BUT SURELY YOU DON'T BELIEVE YOU CAN CONTROL HALF THE WORLD WITH ONLY SIX METAHUMANS?
YOU RAISE A FAIR POINT, ADMIRAL.
FORTUNATELY, MY HYPOTHETICAL ARMY'S MERELY THE DELIVERY SYSTEM FOR THE MOST POWERFUL HYPNOTIC VIRAL AGENT THIS WORLD HAS EVER KNOWN.
SOON, ALL OF CHINA'S ARMIES WILL FIGHT UNDER MY BANNER.

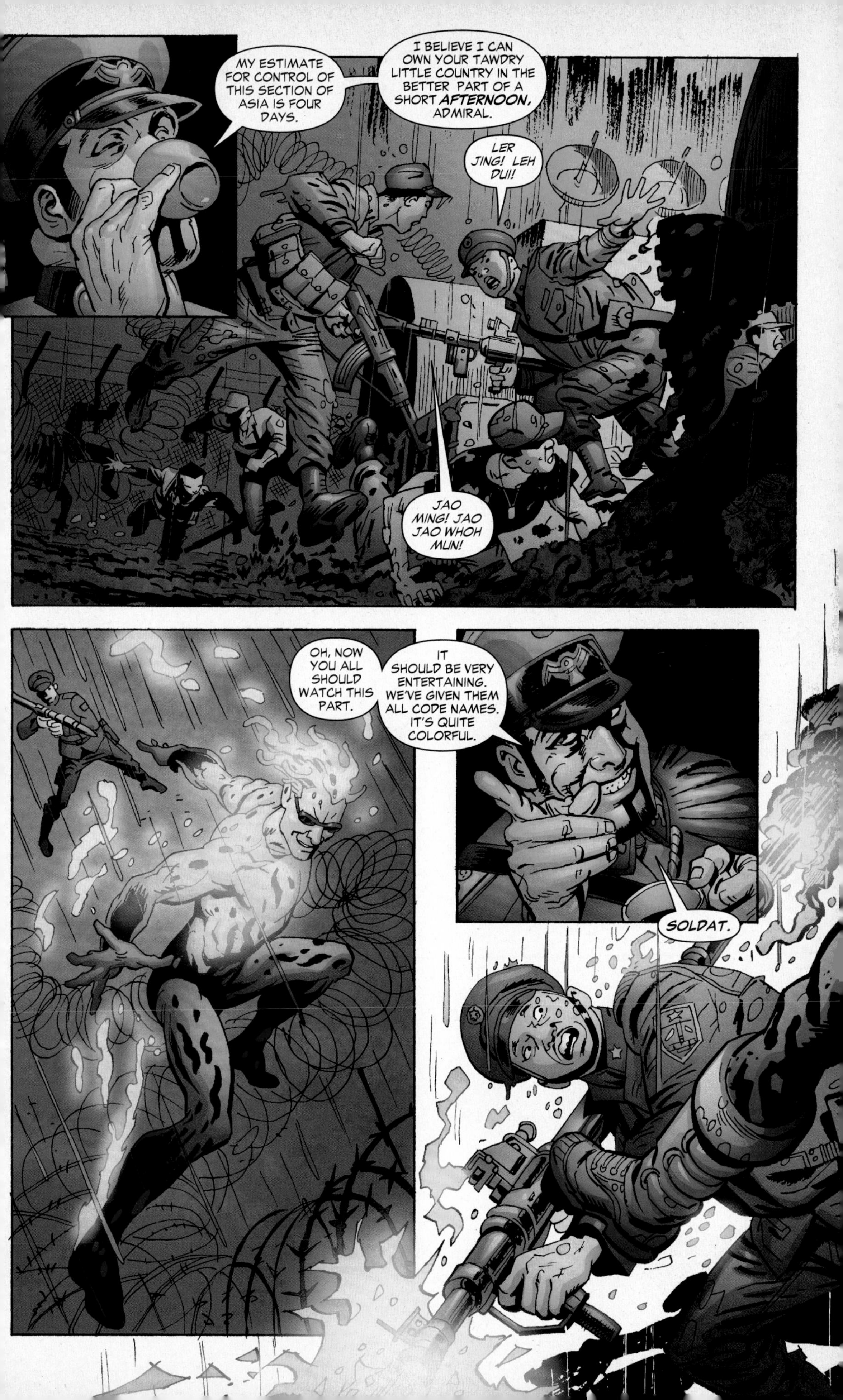
MY ESTIMATE FOR CONTROL OF THIS SECTION OF ASIA IS FOUR DAYS.
I BELIEVE I CAN OWN YOUR TAWDRY LITTLE COUNTRY IN THE BETTER PART OF A SHORT AFTERNOON, ADMIRAL.
LER JING! LEH DUI!
JAO MING! JAO JAO WHOH MUN!
OH, NOW YOU ALL SHOULD WATCH THIS PART.
IT SHOULD BE VERY ENTERTAINING. WE'VE GIVEN THEM ALL CODE NAMES. IT'S QUITE COLORFUL.
SOLDAT.

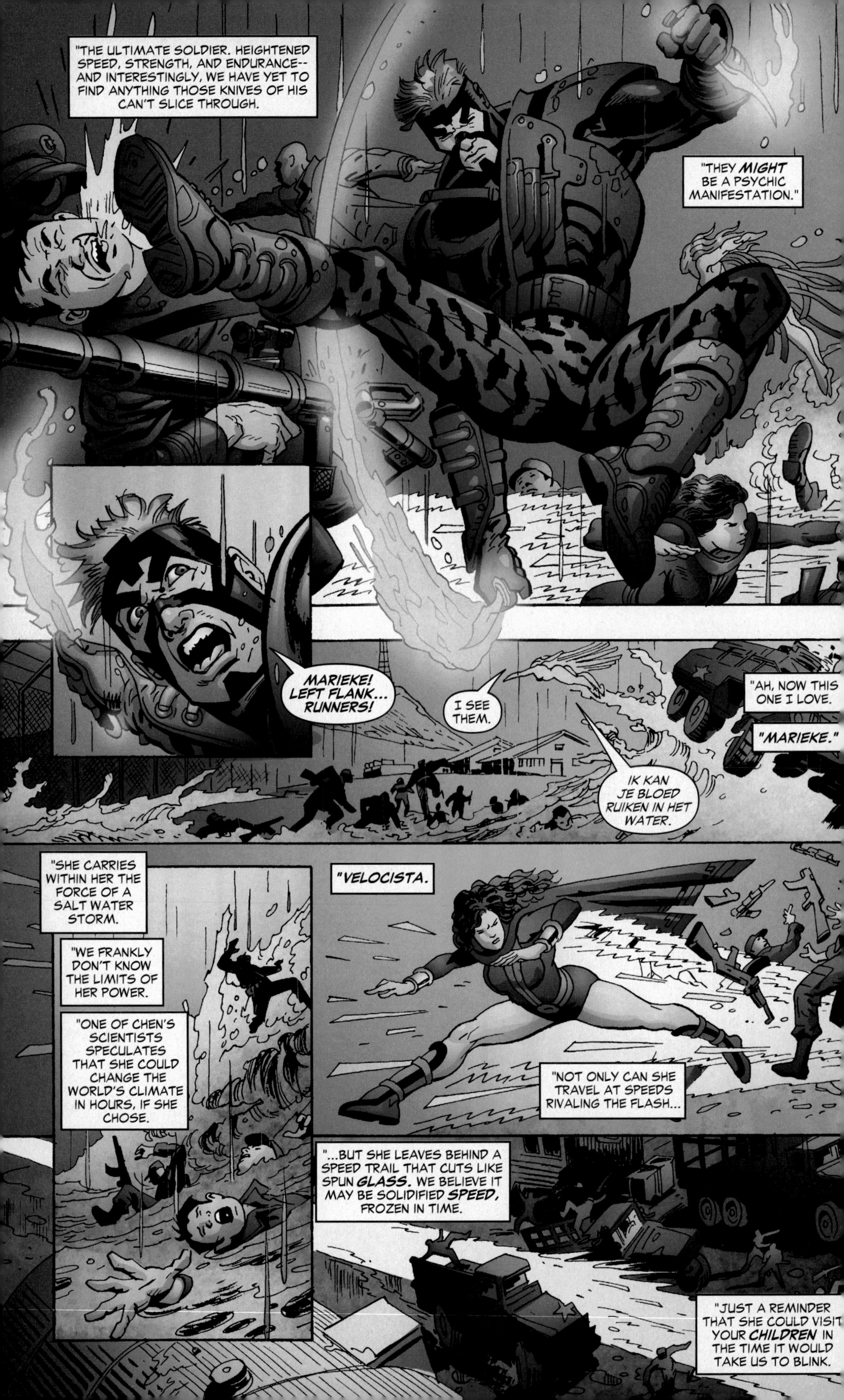

"THE ULTIMATE SOLDIER. HEIGHTENED SPEED, STRENGTH, AND ENDURANCE--AND INTERESTINGLY, WE HAVE YET TO FIND ANYTHING THOSE KNIVES OF HIS CAN'T SLICE THROUGH.
"THEY MIGHT BE A PSYCHIC MANIFESTATION."
MARIEKE! LEFT FLANK... RUNNERS!
I SEE THEM.
IK KAN JE BLOED RUIKEN IN HET WATER.
"AH, NOW THIS ONE I LOVE.
"MARIEKE."
"SHE CARRIES WITHIN HER THE FORCE OF A SALT WATER STORM.
"WE FRANKLY DON'T KNOW THE LIMITS OF HER POWER.
"ONE OF CHEN'S SCIENTISTS SPECULATES THAT SHE COULD CHANGE THE WORLD'S CLIMATE IN HOURS, IF SHE CHOSE.
"VELOCISTA.
"NOT ONLY CAN SHE TRAVEL AT SPEEDS RIVALING THE FLASH...
"...BUT SHE LEAVES BEHIND A SPEED TRAIL THAT CUTS LIKE SPUN GLASS. WE BELIEVE IT MAY BE SOLIDIFIED SPEED, FROZEN IN TIME.
"JUST A REMINDER THAT SHE COULD VISIT YOUR CHILDREN IN THE TIME IT WOULD TAKE US TO BLINK.

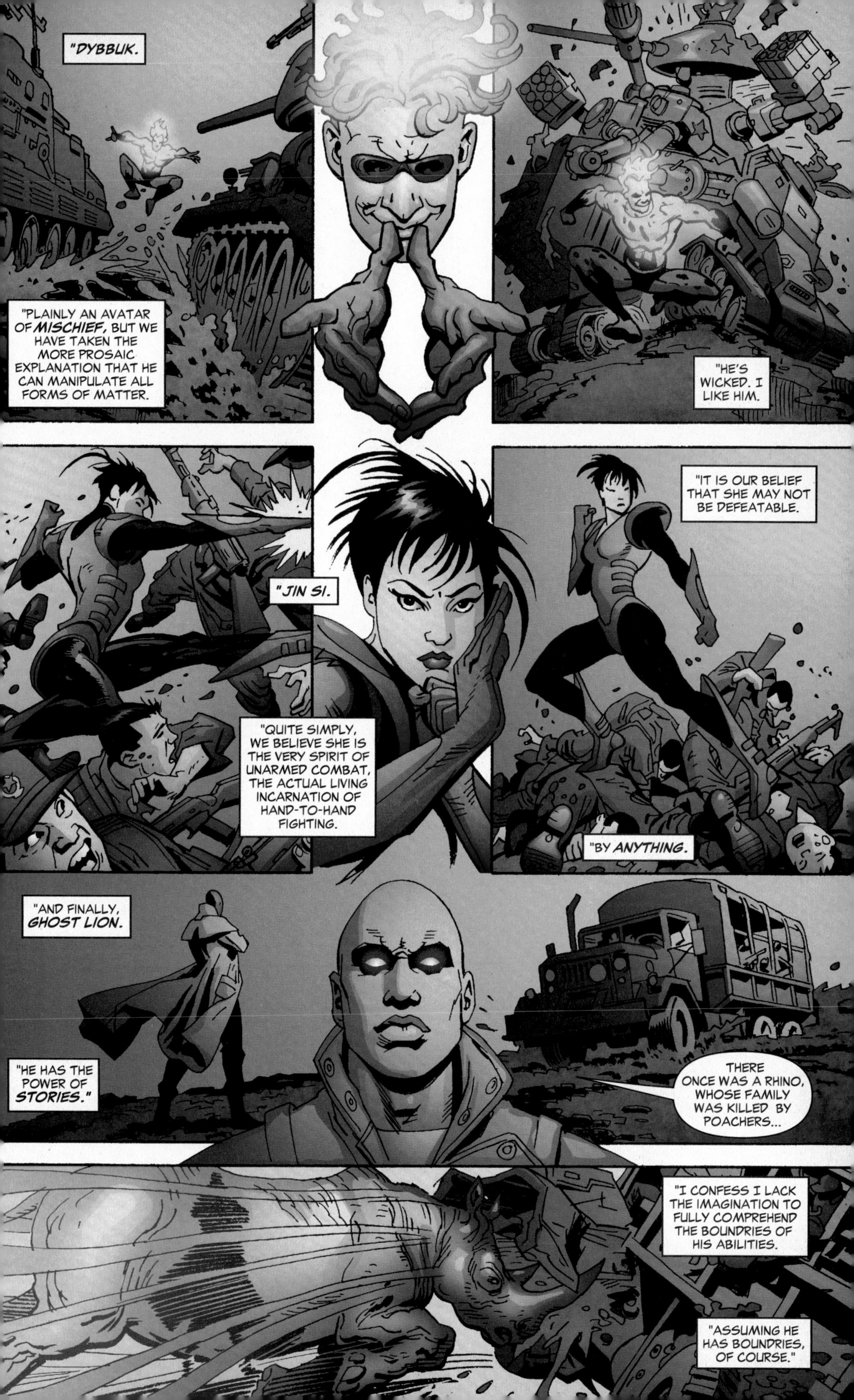
"DYBBUK.
"PLAINLY AN AVATAR OF MISCHIEF, BUT WE HAVE TAKEN THE MORE PROSAIC EXPLANATION THAT HE CAN MANIPULATE ALL FORMS OF MATTER.
"HE'S WICKED. I LIKE HIM.
"JIN SI.
"QUITE SIMPLY, WE BELIEVE SHE IS THE VERY SPIRIT OF UNARMED COMBAT, THE ACTUAL LIVING INCARNATION OF HAND-TO-HAND FIGHTING.
"IT IS OUR BELIEF THAT SHE MAY NOT BE DEFEATABLE.
"BY ANYTHING.
"AND FINALLY, GHOST LION.
"HE HAS THE POWER OF STORIES."
THERE ONCE WAS A RHINO, WHOSE FAMILY WAS KILLED BY POACHERS...
"I CONFESS I LACK THE IMAGINATION TO FULLY COMPREHEND THE BOUNDRIES OF HIS ABILITIES.
"ASSUMING HE HAS BOUNDRIES, OF COURSE."

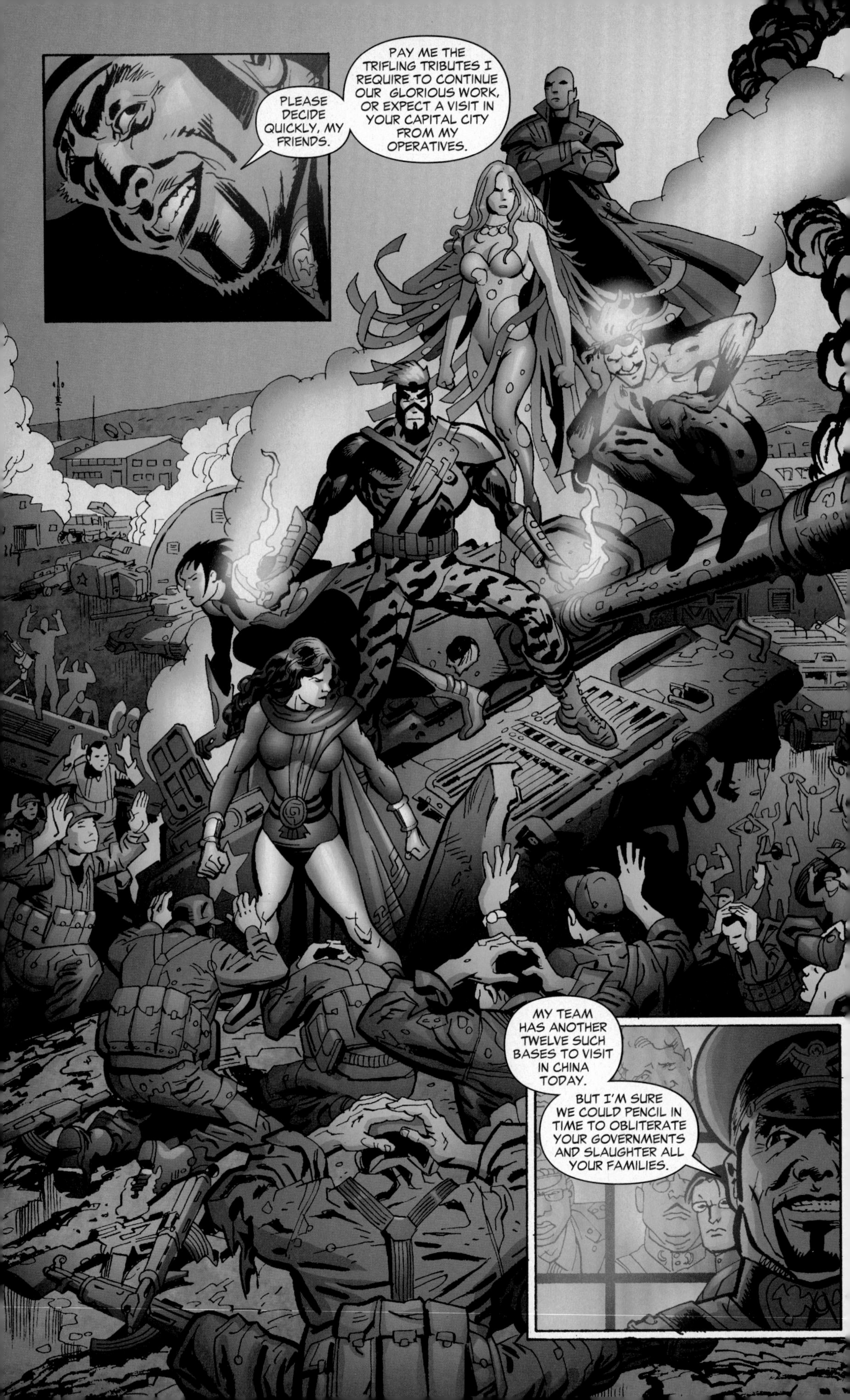
PLEASE DECIDE QUICKLY, MY FRIENDS.
PAY ME THE TRIFLING TRIBUTES I REQUIRE TO CONTINUE OUR GLORIOUS WORK, OR EXPECT A VISIT IN YOUR CAPITAL CITY FROM MY OPERATIVES.
MY TEAM HAS ANOTHER TWELVE SUCH BASES TO VISIT IN CHINA TODAY.
BUT I'M SURE WE COULD PENCIL IN TIME TO OBLITERATE YOUR GOVERNMENTS AND SLAUGHTER ALL YOUR FAMILIES.

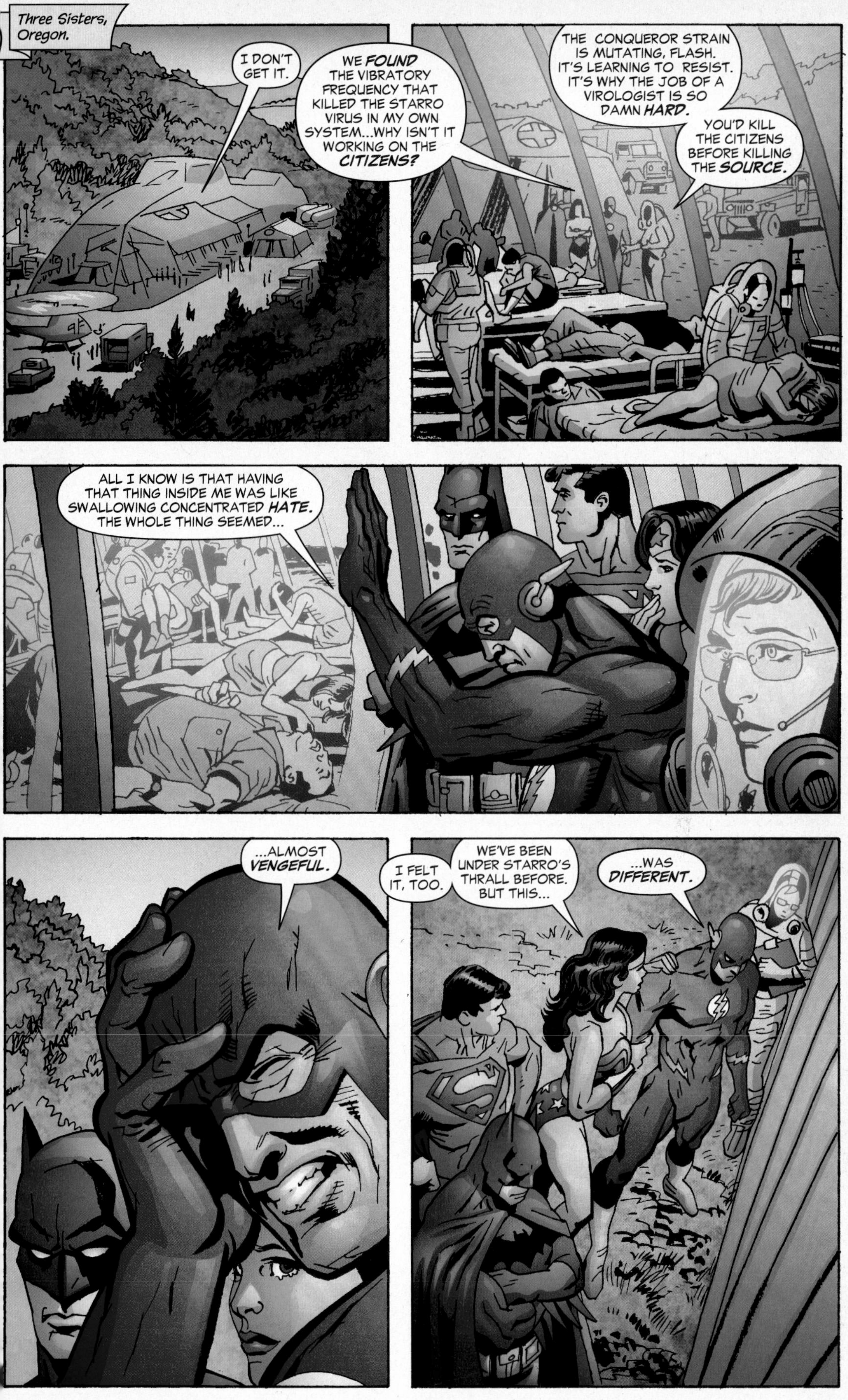
Three Sisters, Oregon.
I DON'T GET IT.
WE FOUND THE VIBRATORY FREQUENCY THAT KILLED THE STARRO VIRUS IN MY OWN SYSTEM...WHY ISN'T IT WORKING ON THE CITIZENS?
THE CONQUEROR STRAIN IS MUTATING, FLASH. IT'S LEARNING TO RESIST. IT'S WHY THE JOB OF A VIROLOGIST IS SO DAMN HARD.
YOU'D KILL THE CITIZENS BEFORE KILLING THE SOURCE.
ALL I KNOW IS THAT HAVING THAT THING INSIDE ME WAS LIKE SWALLOWING CONCENTRATED HATE. THE WHOLE THING SEEMED...
...ALMOST VENGEFUL.
I FELT IT, TOO.
WE'VE BEEN UNDER STARRO'S THRALL BEFORE. BUT THIS...
...WAS DIFFERENT.

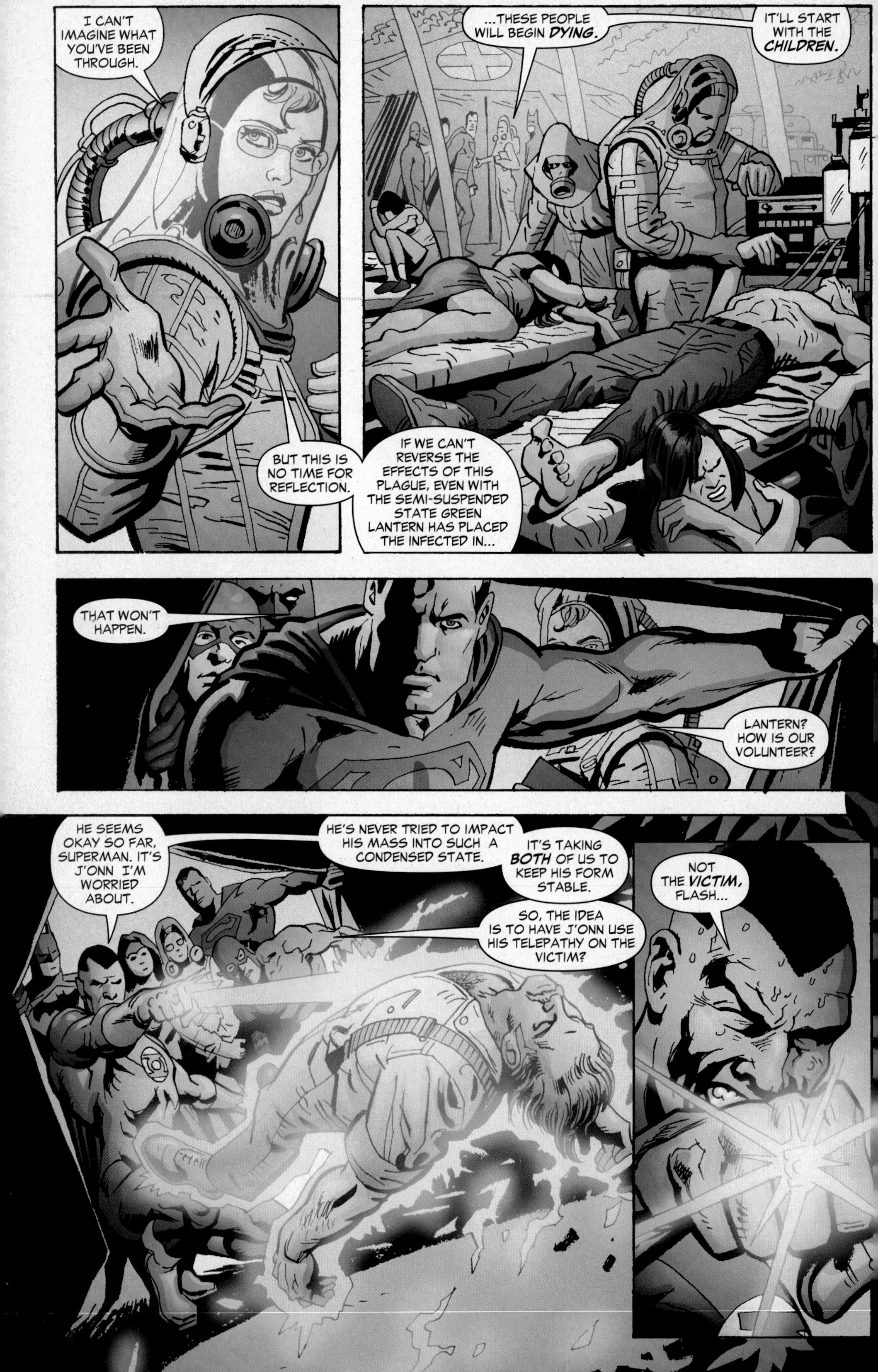

I CAN'T IMAGINE WHAT YOU'VE BEEN THROUGH.
BUT THIS IS NO TIME FOR REFLECTION.
IF WE CAN'T REVERSE THE EFFECTS OF THIS PLAGUE, EVEN WITH THE SEMI-SUSPENDED STATE GREEN LANTERN HAS PLACED THE INFECTED IN...
...THESE PEOPLE WILL BEGIN DYING.
IT'LL START WITH THE CHILDREN.
THAT WON'T HAPPEN.
LANTERN? HOW IS OUR VOLUNTEER?
HE SEEMS OKAY SO FAR, SUPERMAN. IT'S J'ONN I'M WORRIED ABOUT.
HE'S NEVER TRIED TO IMPACT HIS MASS INTO SUCH A CONDENSED STATE.
IT'S TAKING BOTH OF US TO KEEP HIS FORM STABLE.
SO, THE IDEA IS TO HAVE J'ONN USE HIS TELEPATHY ON THE VICTIM?
NOT THE VICTIM, FLASH...

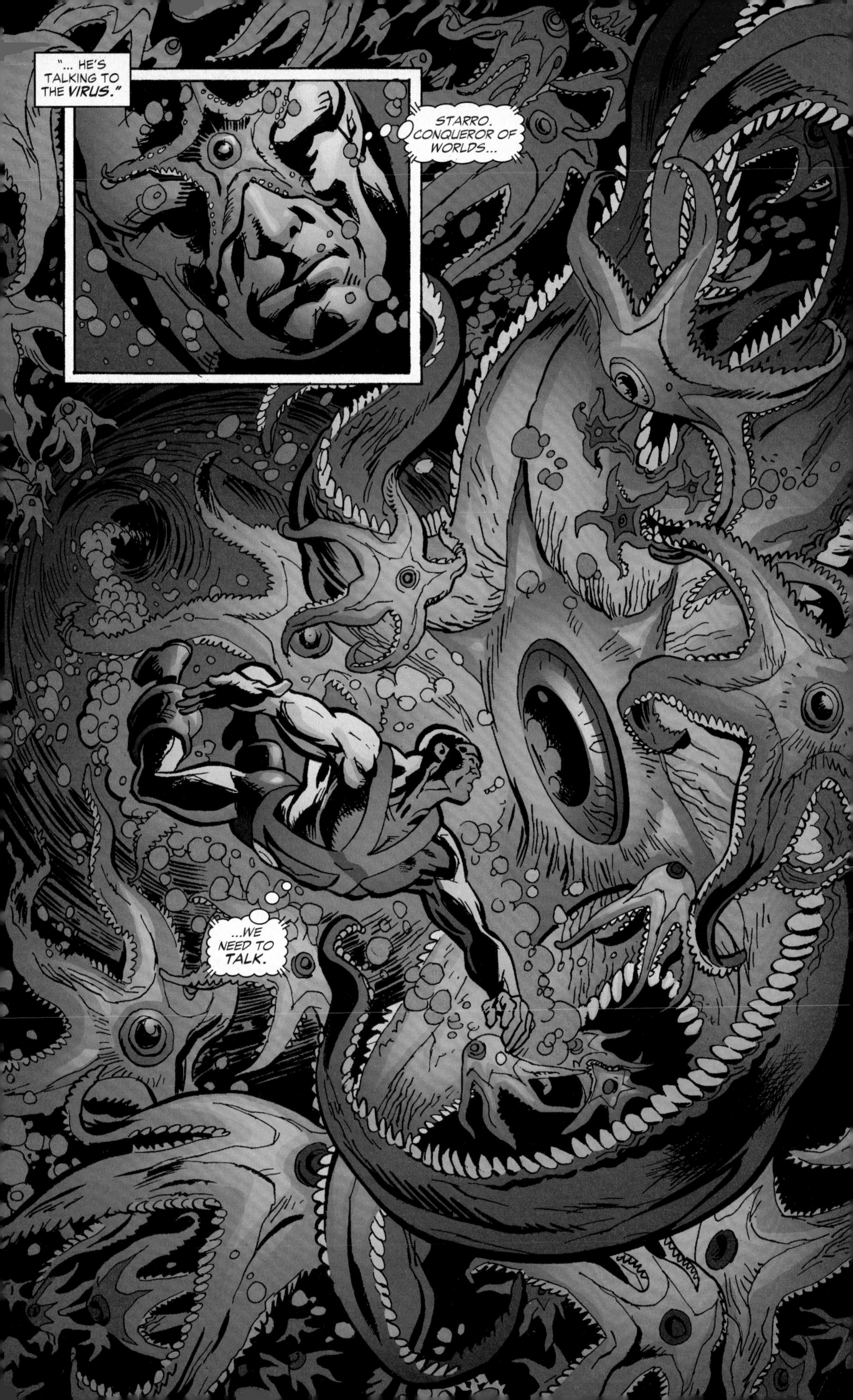
"... HE'S TALKING TO THE VIRUS."
STARRO. CONQUEROR OF WORLDS...
...WE NEED TO TALK.

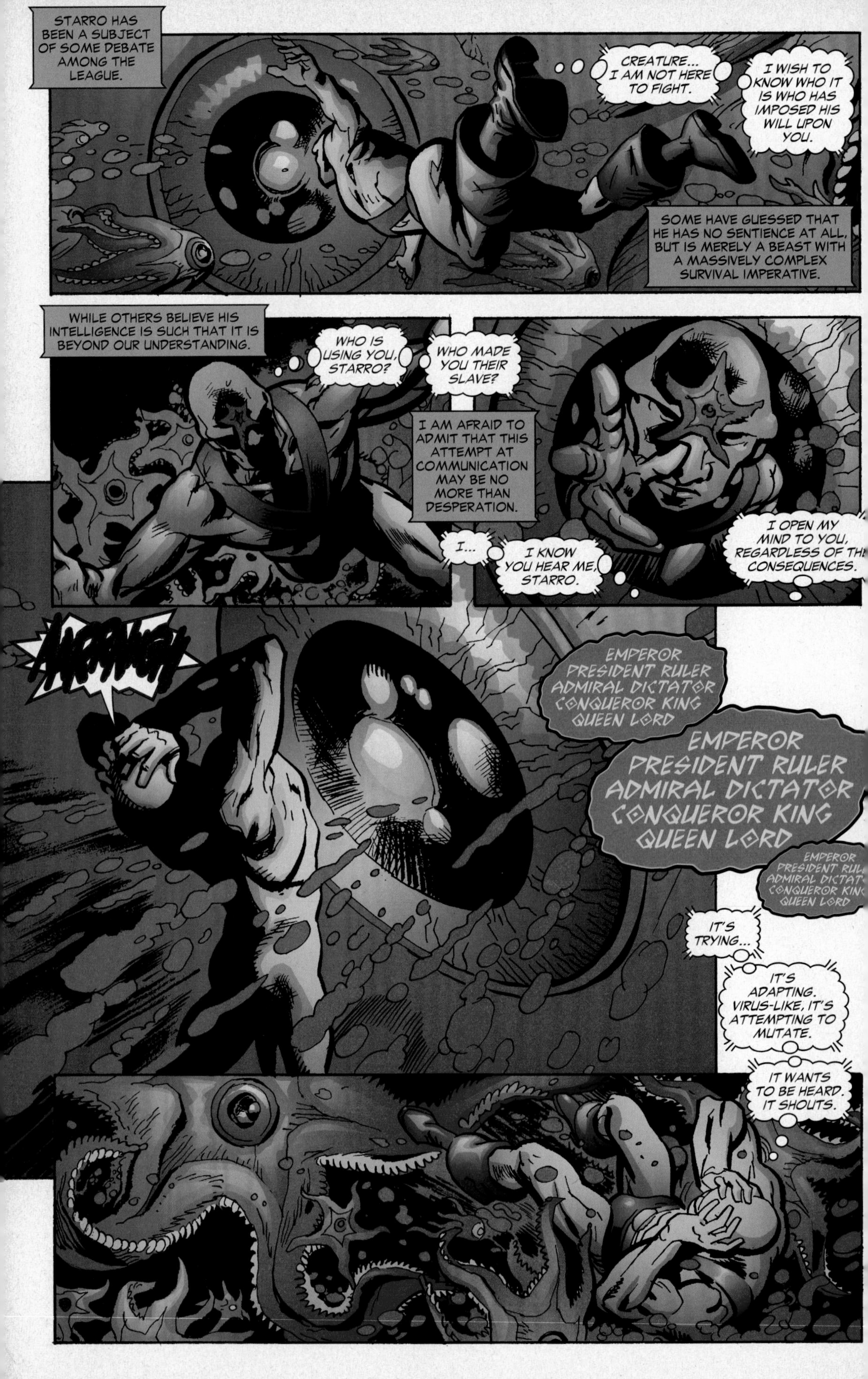
STARRO HAS BEEN A SUBJECT OF SOME DEBATE AMONG THE LEAGUE.
CREATURE... I AM NOT HERE TO FIGHT.
I WISH TO KNOW WHO IT IS WHO HAS IMPOSED HIS WILL UPON YOU.
SOME HAVE GUESSED THAT HE HAS NO SENTIENCE AT ALL, BUT IS MERELY A BEAST WITH A MASSIVELY COMPLEX SURVIVAL IMPERATIVE.
WHILE OTHERS BELIEVE HIS INTELLIGENCE IS SUCH THAT IT IS BEYOND OUR UNDERSTANDING.
WHO IS USING YOU, STARRO?
WHO MADE YOU THEIR SLAVE?
I AM AFRAID TO ADMIT THAT THIS ATTEMPT AT COMMUNICATION MAY BE NO MORE THAN DESPERATION.
I...
I KNOW YOU HEAR ME, STARRO.
I OPEN MY MIND TO YOU, REGARDLESS OF THE CONSEQUENCES.
EMPEROR PRESIDENT RULER ADMIRAL DICTATOR CONQUEROR KING QUEEN LORD
EMPEROR PRESIDENT RULER ADMIRAL DICTATOR CONQUEROR KING QUEEN LORD
EMPEROR PRESIDENT RUL ADMIRAL DICTAT CONQUEROR KIN QUEEN LORD
IT'S TRYING...
IT'S ADAPTING. VIRUS-LIKE, IT'S ATTEMPTING TO MUTATE.
IT WANTS TO BE HEARD. IT SHOUTS.

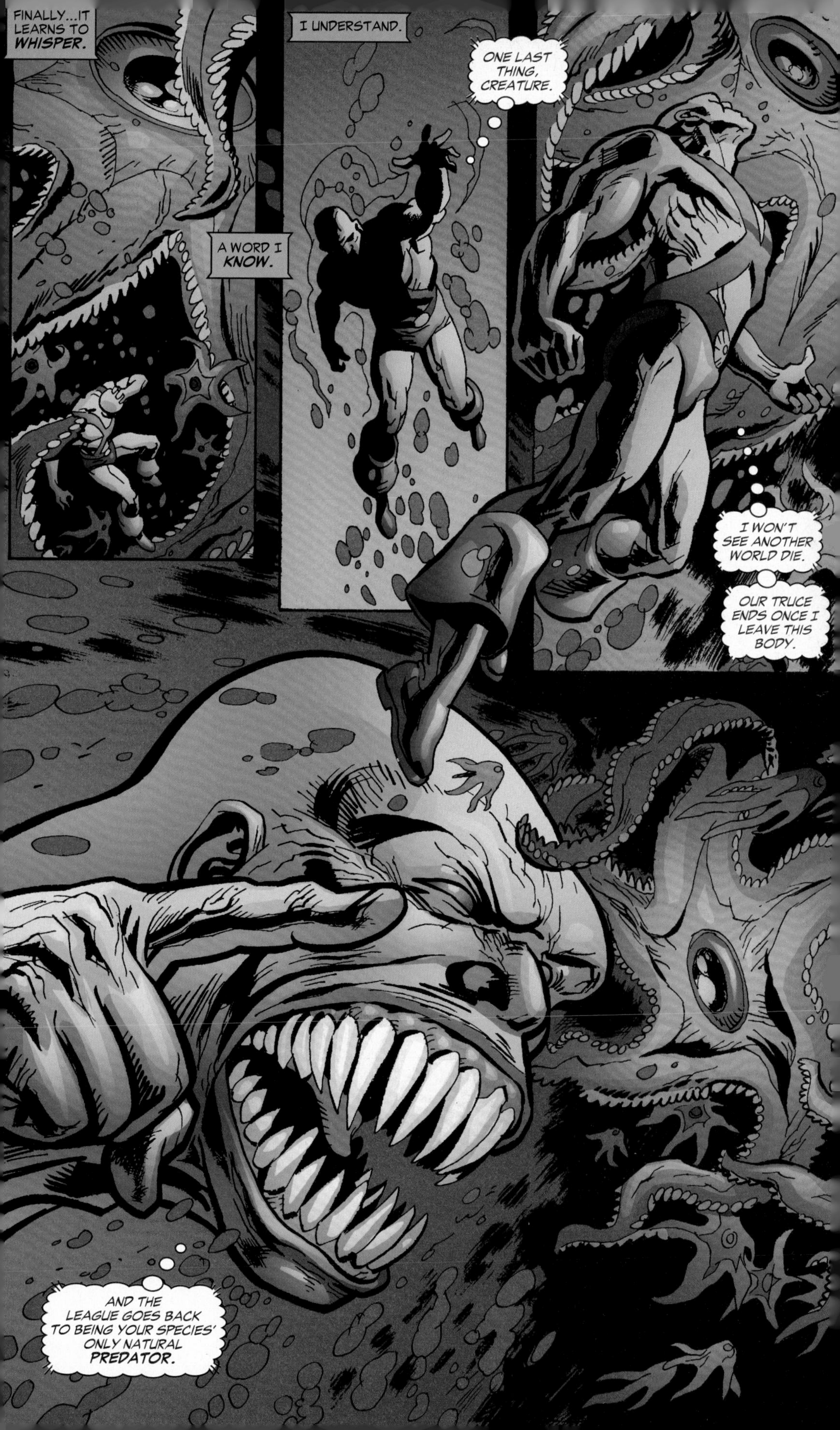
FINALLY...IT LEARNS TO WHISPER.
A WORD I KNOW.
I UNDERSTAND.
ONE LAST THING, CREATURE.
I WON'T SEE ANOTHER WORLD DIE.
OUR TRUCE ENDS ONCE I LEAVE THIS BODY.
AND THE LEAGUE GOES BACK TO BEING YOUR SPECIES' ONLY NATURAL PREDATOR.

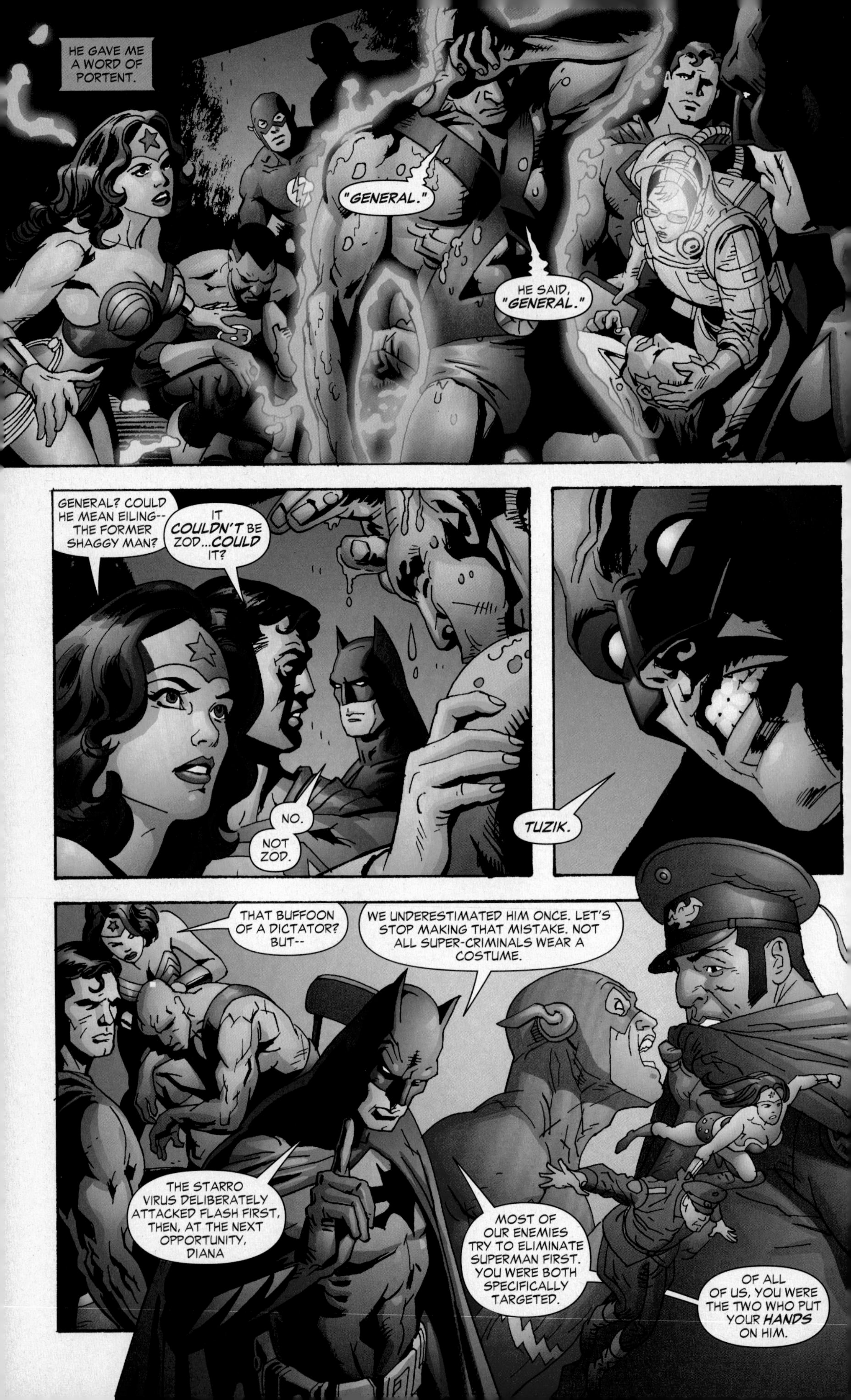
HE GAVE ME A WORD OF PORTENT.
"GENERAL."
HE SAID, "GENERAL."
GENERAL? COULD HE MEAN EILING-- THE FORMER SHAGGY MAN?
IT COULDN'T BE ZOD...COULD IT?
NO.
NOT ZOD.
TUZIK.
THAT BUFFOON OF A DICTATOR? BUT--
WE UNDERESTIMATED HIM ONCE. LET'S STOP MAKING THAT MISTAKE. NOT ALL SUPER-CRIMINALS WEAR A COSTUME.
THE STARRO VIRUS DELIBERATELY ATTACKED FLASH FIRST, THEN, AT THE NEXT OPPORTUNITY, DIANA
MOST OF OUR ENEMIES TRY TO ELIMINATE SUPERMAN FIRST. YOU WERE BOTH SPECIFICALLY TARGETED.
OF ALL OF US, YOU WERE THE TWO WHO PUT YOUR HANDS ON HIM.

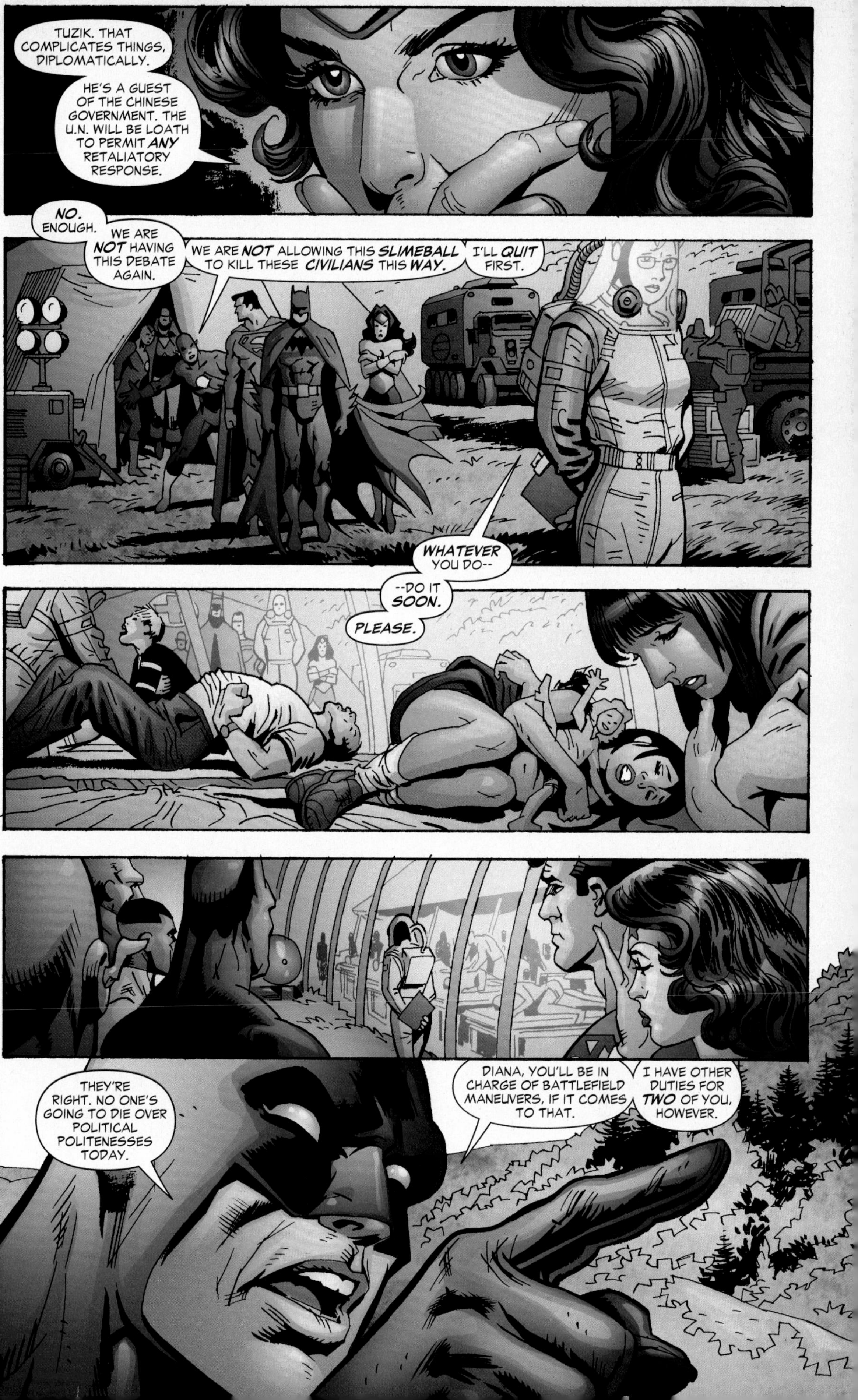

TUZIK. THAT COMPLICATES THINGS, DIPLOMATICALLY.
HE'S A GUEST OF THE CHINESE GOVERNMENT. THE U.N. WILL BE LOATH TO PERMIT ANY RETALIATORY RESPONSE.
NO. ENOUGH.
WE ARE NOT HAVING THIS DEBATE AGAIN.
WE ARE NOT ALLOWING THIS SLIMEBALL TO KILL THESE CIVILIANS THIS WAY.
I'LL QUIT FIRST.
WHATEVER YOU DO--
--DO IT SOON.
PLEASE.
THEY'RE RIGHT. NO ONE'S GOING TO DIE OVER POLITICAL POLITENESSES TODAY.
DIANA, YOU'LL BE IN CHARGE OF BATTLEFIELD MANEUVERS, IF IT COMES TO THAT.
I HAVE OTHER DUTIES FOR TWO OF YOU, HOWEVER.

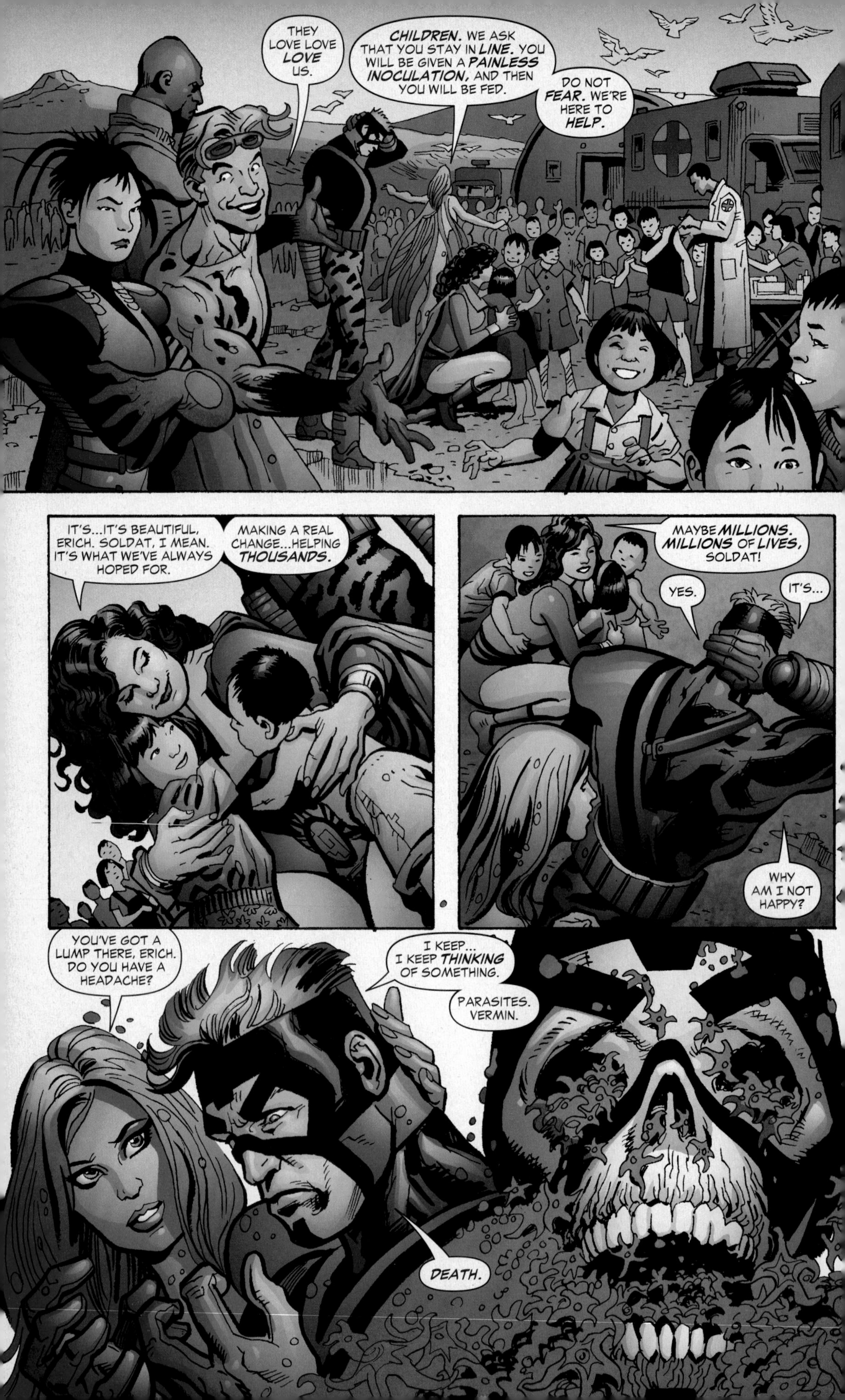
THEY LOVE LOVE LOVE US.
CHILDREN. WE ASK THAT YOU STAY IN LINE. YOU WILL BE GIVEN A PAINLESS INOCULATION, AND THEN YOU WILL BE FED.
DO NOT FEAR. WE'RE HERE TO HELP.
IT'S...IT'S BEAUTIFUL, ERICH. SOLDAT, I MEAN. IT'S WHAT WE'VE ALWAYS HOPED FOR.
MAKING A REAL CHANGE...HELPING THOUSANDS.
MAYBE MILLIONS. MILLIONS OF LIVES, SOLDAT!
YES.
IT'S...
WHY AM I NOT HAPPY?
YOU'VE GOT A LUMP THERE, ERICH. DO YOU HAVE A HEADACHE?
I KEEP... I KEEP THINKING OF SOMETHING.
PARASITES. VERMIN.
DEATH.

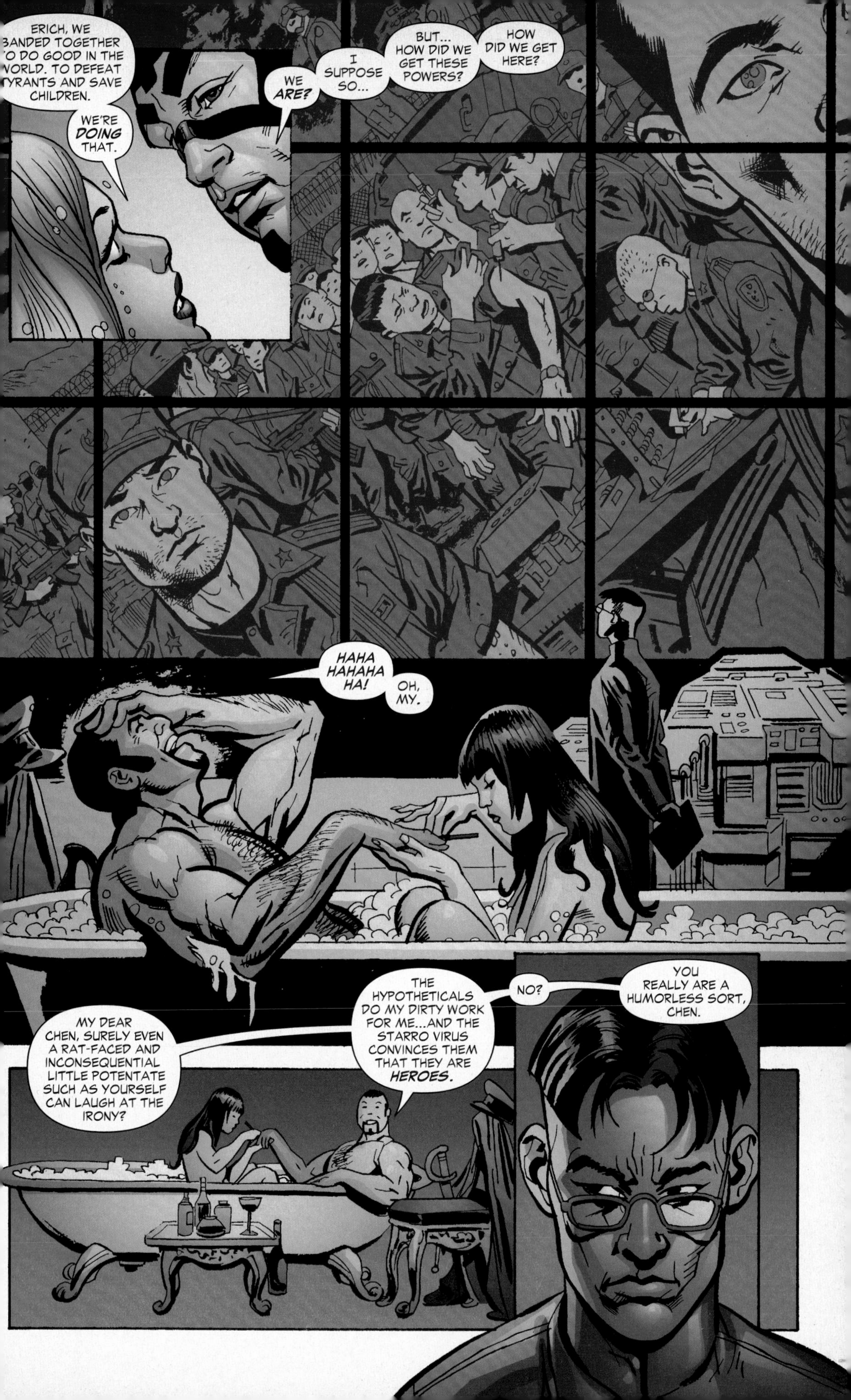
ERICH, WE BANDED TOGETHER TO DO GOOD IN THE WORLD. TO DEFEAT TYRANTS AND SAVE CHILDREN.
WE'RE *DOING* THAT.
WE *ARE?*
I SUPPOSE SO...
BUT... HOW DID WE GET THESE POWERS?
HOW DID WE GET HERE?
HAHA HAHAHA HA!
OH, MY.
MY DEAR CHEN, SURELY EVEN A RAT-FACED AND INCONSEQUENTIAL LITTLE POTENTATE SUCH AS YOURSELF CAN LAUGH AT THE IRONY?
THE HYPOTHETICALS DO MY DIRTY WORK FOR ME...AND THE STARRO VIRUS CONVINCES THEM THAT THEY ARE *HEROES*.
NO?
YOU REALLY ARE A HUMORLESS SORT, CHEN.

Beijing.

...REMIND YOU THAT YOU ARE A DIPLOMATIC GUEST AND THAT USE OF ANY ALLEGED "POWERS" YOU MAY HAVE WILL BE CONSIDERED A HOSTILE ACT, SUPERMAN.

UNDERSTOOD, MR. LI.

THEN MAY I PRESENT MR. DENG CHUNYAN, CHAIRMEN OF THE STANDING COMMITTEE OF THE POLITICAL BUREAU OF THE COMMUNIST PARTY OF CHINA, CENTRAL COMMITTEE.

I KNOW WHY YOU'RE HERE, SUPERMAN.

YOU ARE NOT WELCOME. I CANNOT STRESS THIS CLEARLY ENOUGH.

IF YOU ENTER CHINESE AIRSPACE UNINVITED, THERE WILL BE GRAVE REPERCUSSIONS.

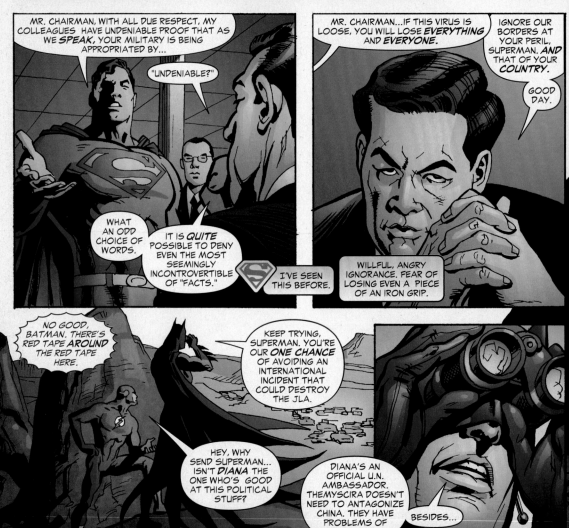

MR. CHAIRMAN, WITH ALL DUE RESPECT, MY COLLEAGUES HAVE UNDENIABLE PROOF THAT AS WE SPEAK, YOUR MILITARY IS BEING APPROPRIATED BY...

"UNDENIABLE?"

MR. CHAIRMAN...IF THIS VIRUS IS LOOSE, YOU WILL LOSE EVERYTHING AND EVERYONE.

IGNORE OUR BORDERS AT YOUR PERIL, SUPERMAN. AND THAT OF YOUR COUNTRY.

GOOD DAY.

WHAT AN ODD CHOICE OF WORDS.

IT IS QUITE POSSIBLE TO DENY EVEN THE MOST SEEMINGLY INCONTROVERTIBLE OF "FACTS."

I'VE SEEN THIS BEFORE.

WILLFUL, ANGRY IGNORANCE. FEAR OF LOSING EVEN A PIECE OF AN IRON GRIP.

NO GOOD, BATMAN. THERE'S RED TAPE AROUND THE RED TAPE HERE.

KEEP TRYING, SUPERMAN. YOU'RE OUR ONE CHANCE OF AVOIDING AN INTERNATIONAL INCIDENT THAT COULD DESTROY THE JLA.

HEY, WHY SEND SUPERMAN... ISN'T DIANA THE ONE WHO'S GOOD AT THIS POLITICAL STUFF?

DIANA'S AN OFFICIAL U.N. AMBASSADOR. THEMYSCIRA DOESN'T NEED TO ANTAGONIZE CHINA. THEY HAVE PROBLEMS OF THEIR OWN.

BESIDES...

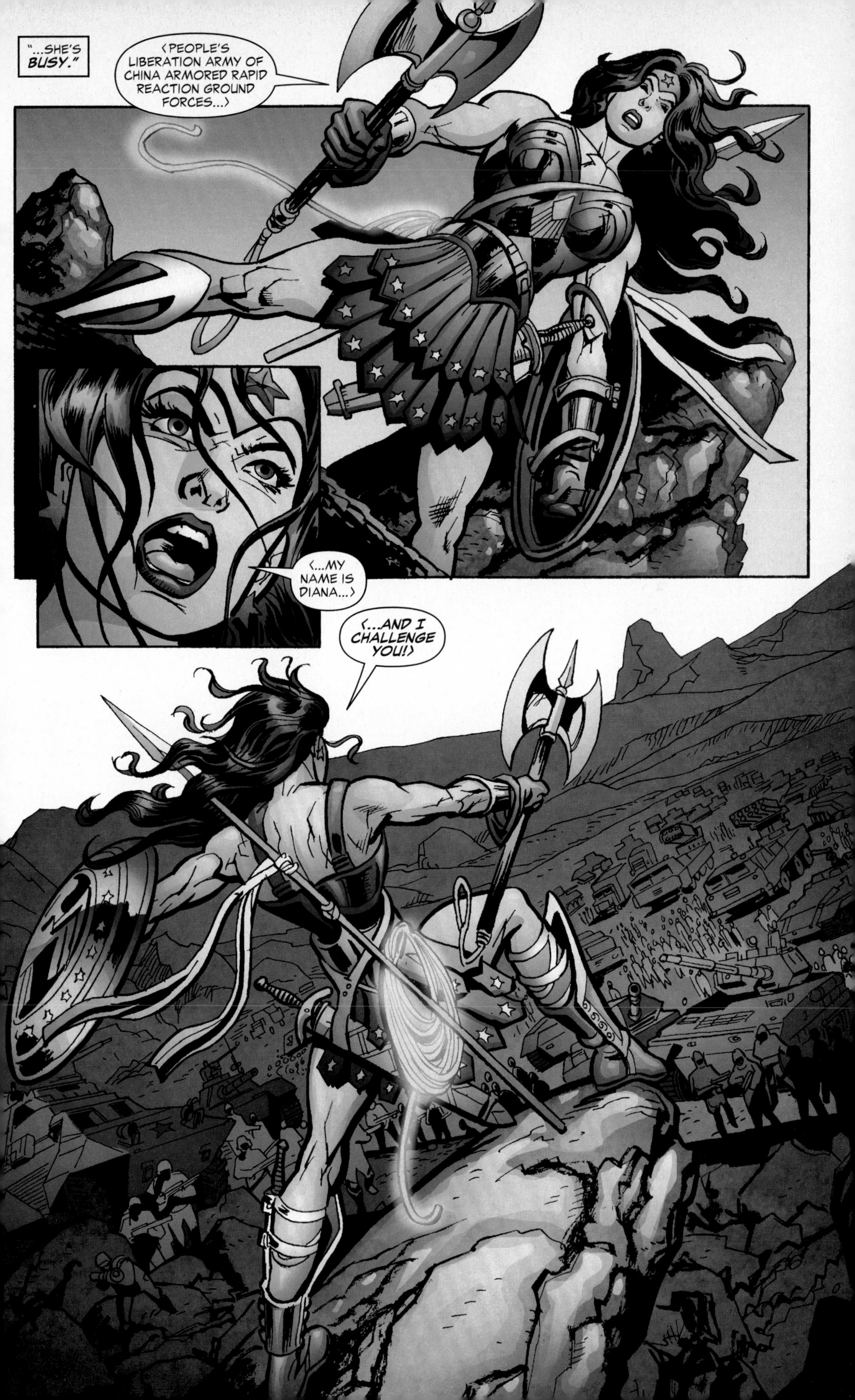
"...SHE'S BUSY."
‹PEOPLE'S LIBERATION ARMY OF CHINA ARMORED RAPID REACTION GROUND FORCES...›
‹...MY NAME IS DIANA...›
‹...AND I CHALLENGE YOU!›

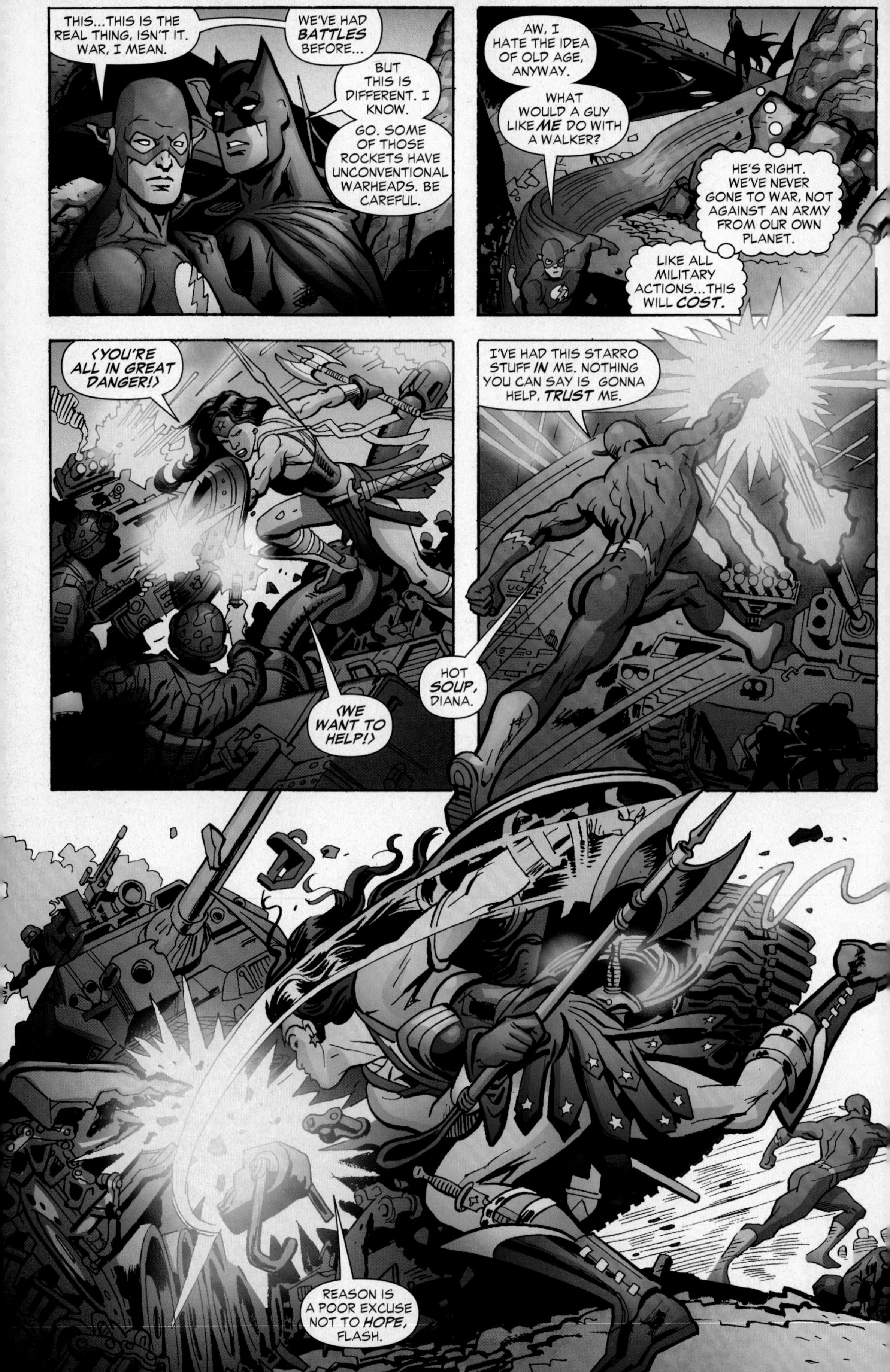

THIS...THIS IS THE REAL THING, ISN'T IT. WAR, I MEAN.
WE'VE HAD BATTLES BEFORE...
BUT THIS IS DIFFERENT. I KNOW.
GO. SOME OF THOSE ROCKETS HAVE UNCONVENTIONAL WARHEADS. BE CAREFUL.
AW, I HATE THE IDEA OF OLD AGE, ANYWAY.
WHAT WOULD A GUY LIKE ME DO WITH A WALKER?
HE'S RIGHT. WE'VE NEVER GONE TO WAR, NOT AGAINST AN ARMY FROM OUR OWN PLANET.
LIKE ALL MILITARY ACTIONS...THIS WILL COST.
<YOU'RE ALL IN GREAT DANGER!>
<WE WANT TO HELP!>
I'VE HAD THIS STARRO STUFF IN ME. NOTHING YOU CAN SAY IS GONNA HELP, TRUST ME.
HOT SOUP, DIANA.
REASON IS A POOR EXCUSE NOT TO HOPE, FLASH.

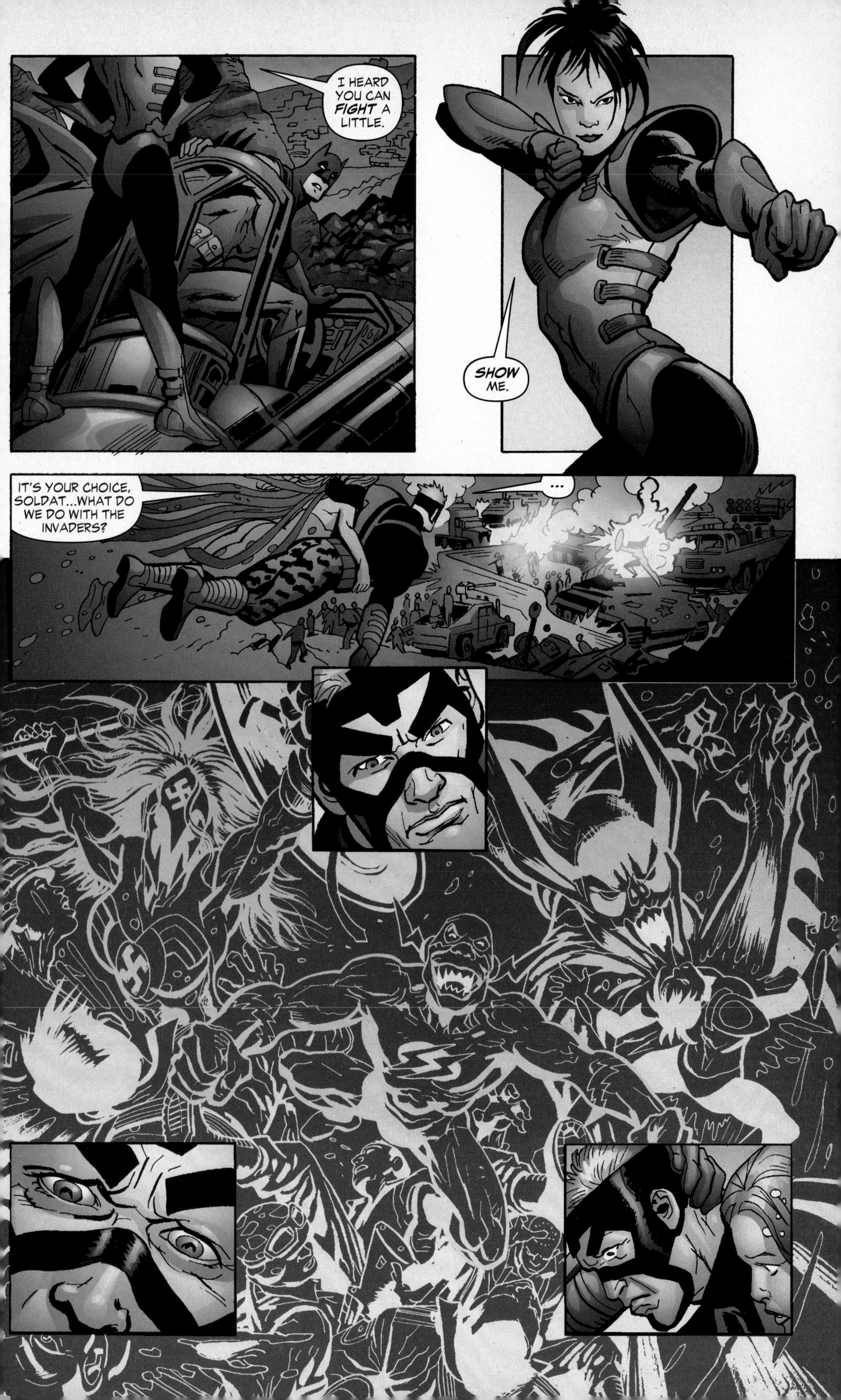
I HEARD YOU CAN FIGHT A LITTLE.
SHOW ME.
IT'S YOUR CHOICE, SOLDAT...WHAT DO WE DO WITH THE INVADERS?
...

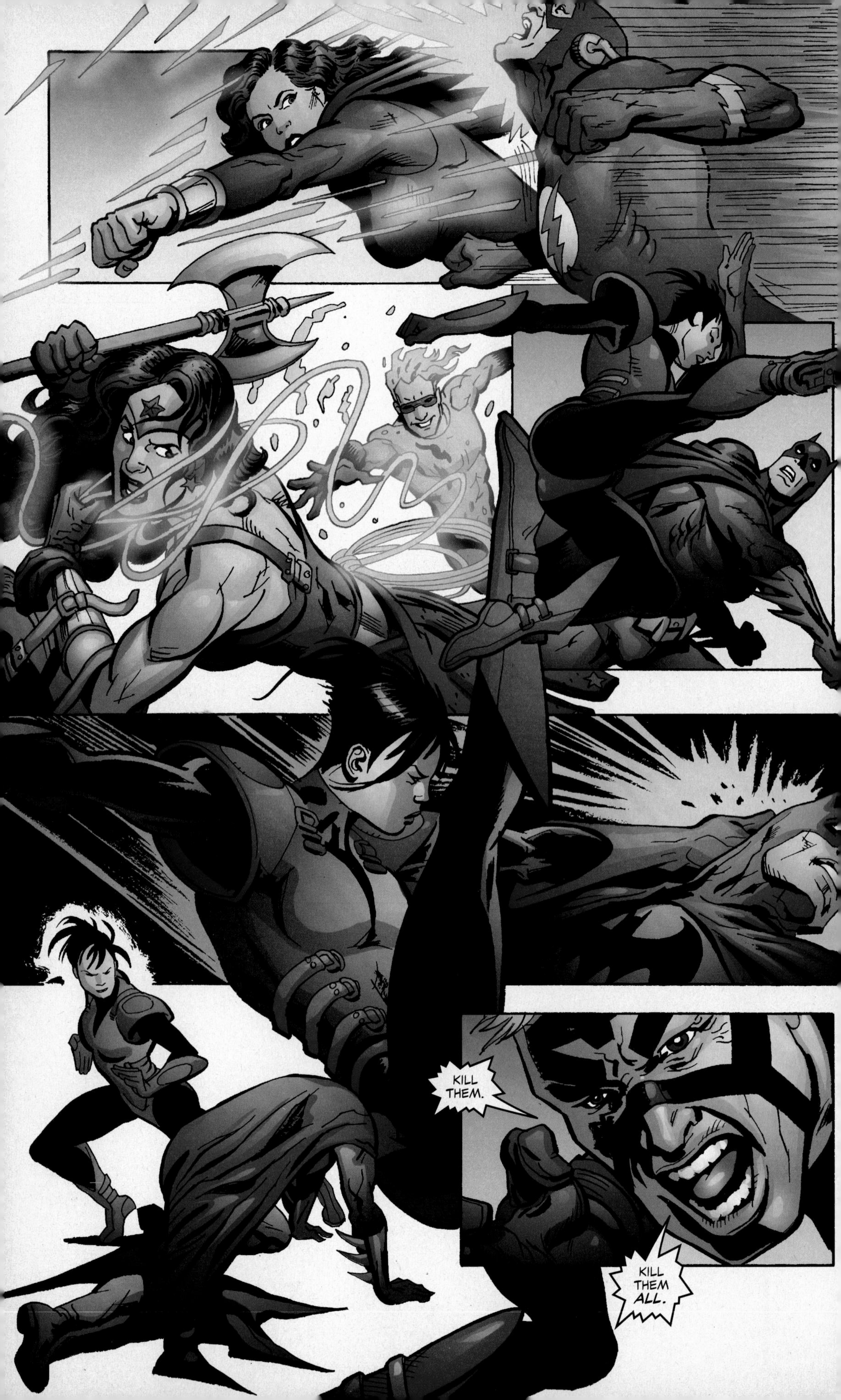
KILL THEM.
KILL THEM ALL.

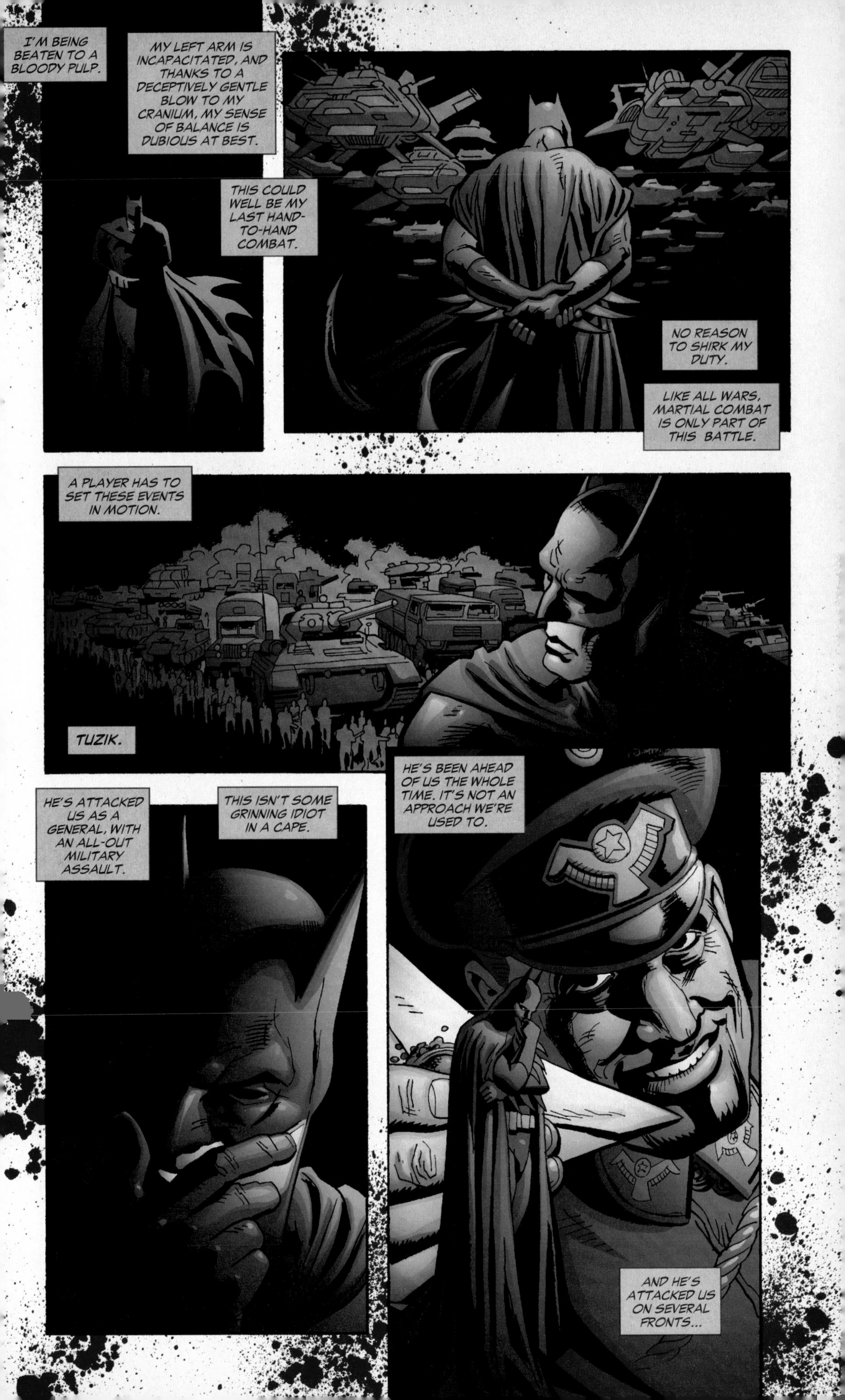

I'M BEING BEATEN TO A BLOODY PULP.
MY LEFT ARM IS INCAPACITATED, AND THANKS TO A DECEPTIVELY GENTLE BLOW TO MY CRANIUM, MY SENSE OF BALANCE IS DUBIOUS AT BEST.
THIS COULD WELL BE MY LAST HAND-TO-HAND COMBAT.
NO REASON TO SHIRK MY DUTY.
LIKE ALL WARS, MARTIAL COMBAT IS ONLY PART OF THIS BATTLE.
A PLAYER HAS TO SET THESE EVENTS IN MOTION.
TUZIK.
HE'S ATTACKED US AS A GENERAL, WITH AN ALL-OUT MILITARY ASSAULT.
THIS ISN'T SOME GRINNING IDIOT IN A CAPE.
HE'S BEEN AHEAD OF US THE WHOLE TIME. IT'S NOT AN APPROACH WE'RE USED TO.
AND HE'S ATTACKED US ON SEVERAL FRONTS...

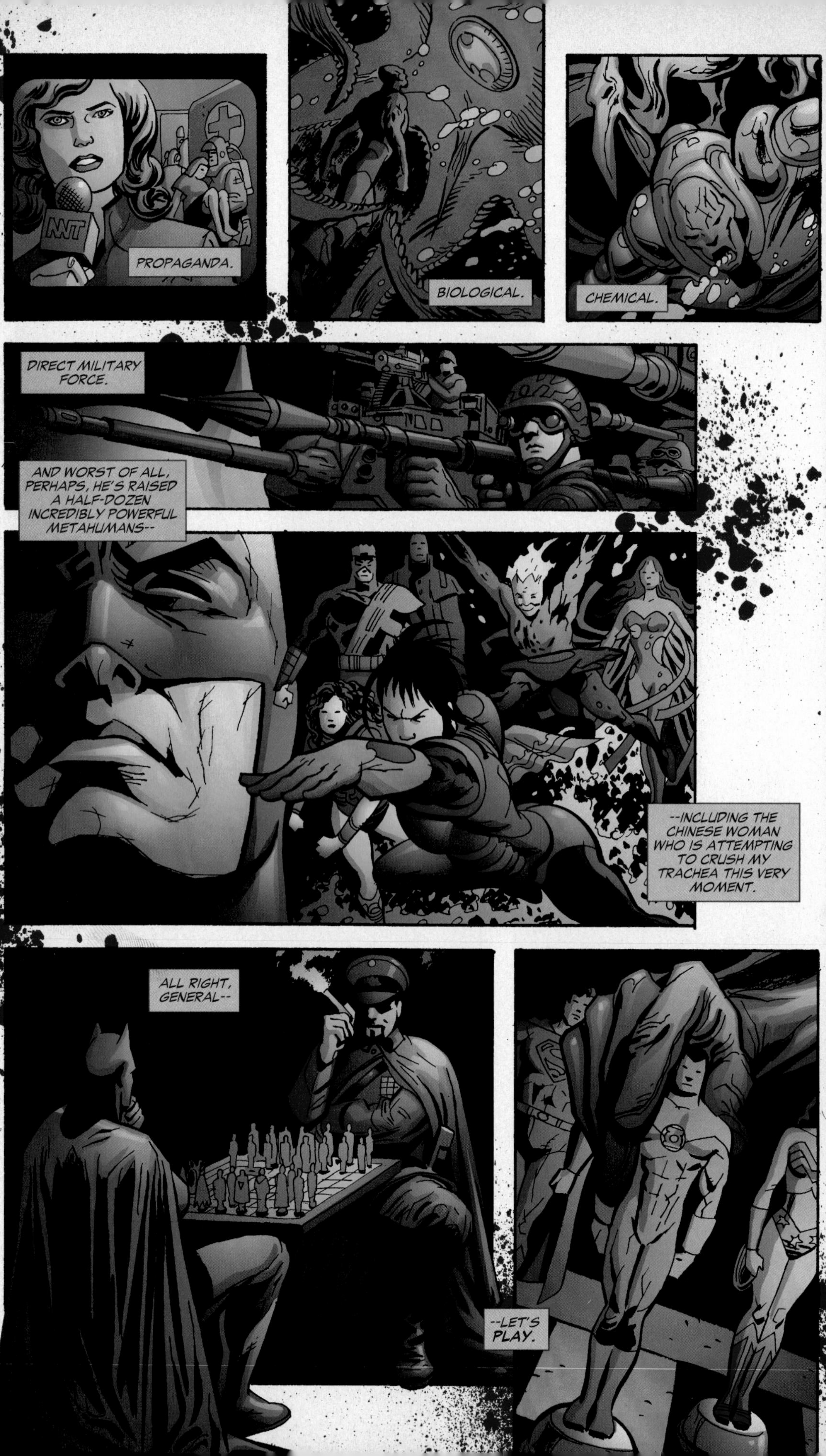
PROPAGANDA.
BIOLOGICAL.
CHEMICAL.
DIRECT MILITARY FORCE.
AND WORST OF ALL, PERHAPS, HE'S RAISED A HALF-DOZEN INCREDIBLY POWERFUL METAHUMANS--
--INCLUDING THE CHINESE WOMAN WHO IS ATTEMPTING TO CRUSH MY TRACHEA THIS VERY MOMENT.
ALL RIGHT, GENERAL--
--LET'S PLAY.

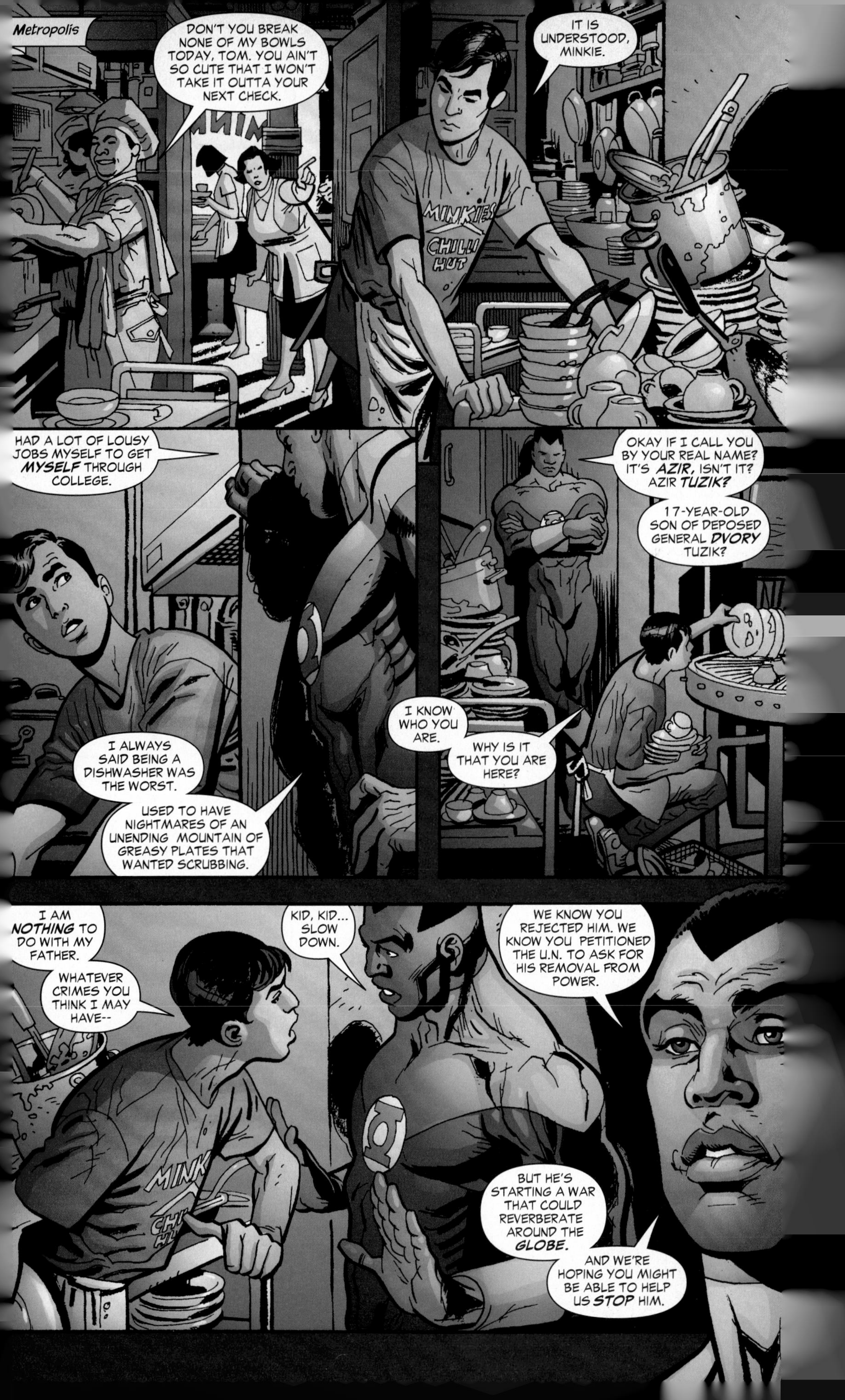
Metropolis
DON'T YOU BREAK NONE OF MY BOWLS TODAY, TOM. YOU AIN'T SO CUTE THAT I WON'T TAKE IT OUTTA YOUR NEXT CHECK.
IT IS UNDERSTOOD, MINKIE.
MINKIE'S CHILLI HUT
HAD A LOT OF LOUSY JOBS MYSELF TO GET MYSELF THROUGH COLLEGE.
I ALWAYS SAID BEING A DISHWASHER WAS THE WORST.
USED TO HAVE NIGHTMARES OF AN UNENDING MOUNTAIN OF GREASY PLATES THAT WANTED SCRUBBING.
OKAY IF I CALL YOU BY YOUR REAL NAME? IT'S AZIR, ISN'T IT? AZIR TUZIK?
17-YEAR-OLD SON OF DEPOSED GENERAL DVORY TUZIK?
I KNOW WHO YOU ARE.
WHY IS IT THAT YOU ARE HERE?
I AM NOTHING TO DO WITH MY FATHER.
WHATEVER CRIMES YOU THINK I MAY HAVE--
KID, KID... SLOW DOWN.
WE KNOW YOU REJECTED HIM. WE KNOW YOU PETITIONED THE U.N. TO ASK FOR HIS REMOVAL FROM POWER.
BUT HE'S STARTING A WAR THAT COULD REVERBERATE AROUND THE GLOBE.
AND WE'RE HOPING YOU MIGHT BE ABLE TO HELP US STOP HIM.

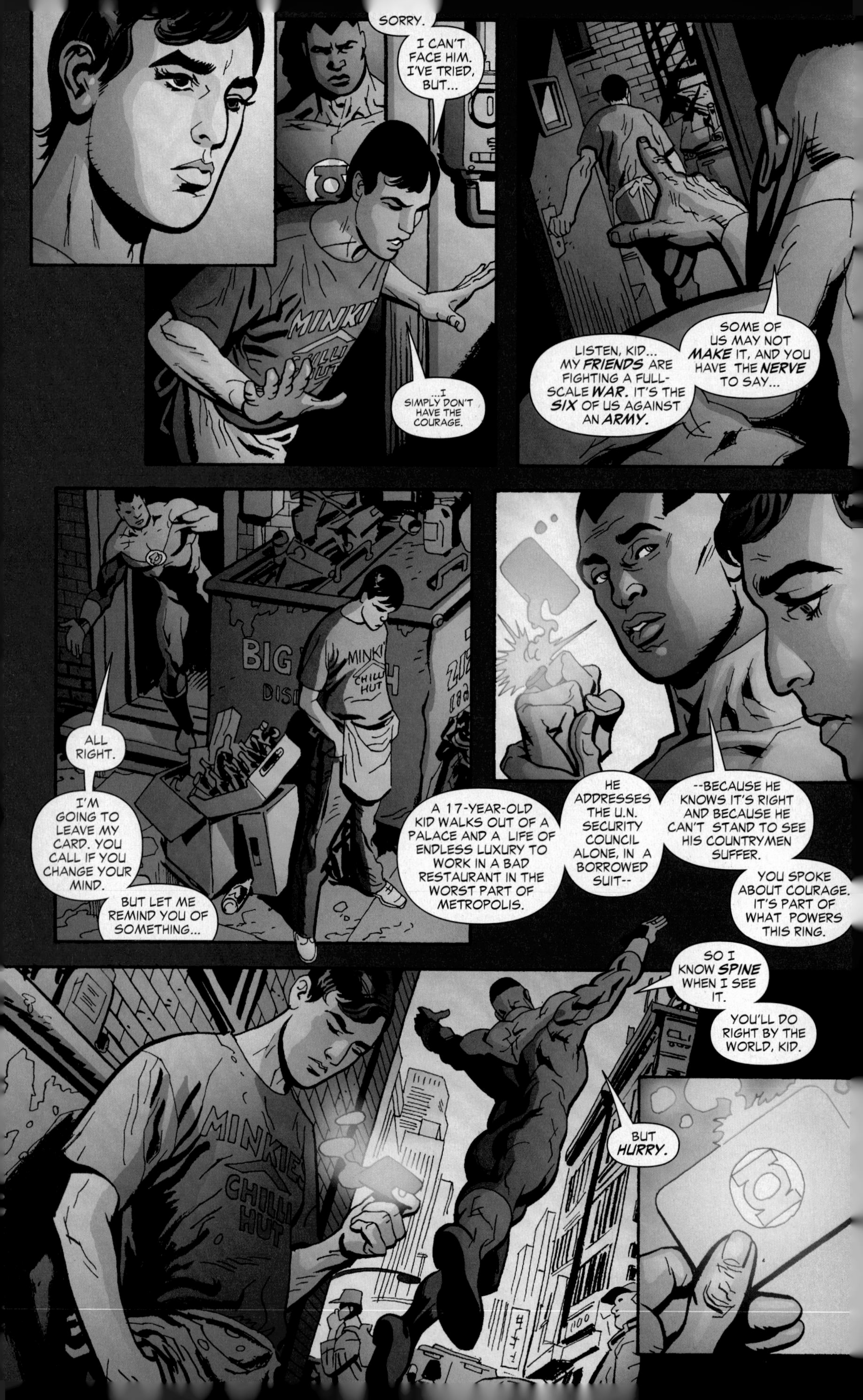
SORRY.
I CAN'T FACE HIM. I'VE TRIED, BUT...
...I SIMPLY DON'T HAVE THE COURAGE.
LISTEN, KID... MY FRIENDS ARE FIGHTING A FULL-SCALE WAR. IT'S THE SIX OF US AGAINST AN ARMY.
SOME OF US MAY NOT MAKE IT, AND YOU HAVE THE NERVE TO SAY...
ALL RIGHT.
I'M GOING TO LEAVE MY CARD. YOU CALL IF YOU CHANGE YOUR MIND.
BUT LET ME REMIND YOU OF SOMETHING...
A 17-YEAR-OLD KID WALKS OUT OF A PALACE AND A LIFE OF ENDLESS LUXURY TO WORK IN A BAD RESTAURANT IN THE WORST PART OF METROPOLIS.
HE ADDRESSES THE U.N. SECURITY COUNCIL ALONE, IN A BORROWED SUIT--
--BECAUSE HE KNOWS IT'S RIGHT AND BECAUSE HE CAN'T STAND TO SEE HIS COUNTRYMEN SUFFER.
YOU SPOKE ABOUT COURAGE. IT'S PART OF WHAT POWERS THIS RING.
SO I KNOW SPINE WHEN I SEE IT.
YOU'LL DO RIGHT BY THE WORLD, KID.
BUT HURRY.

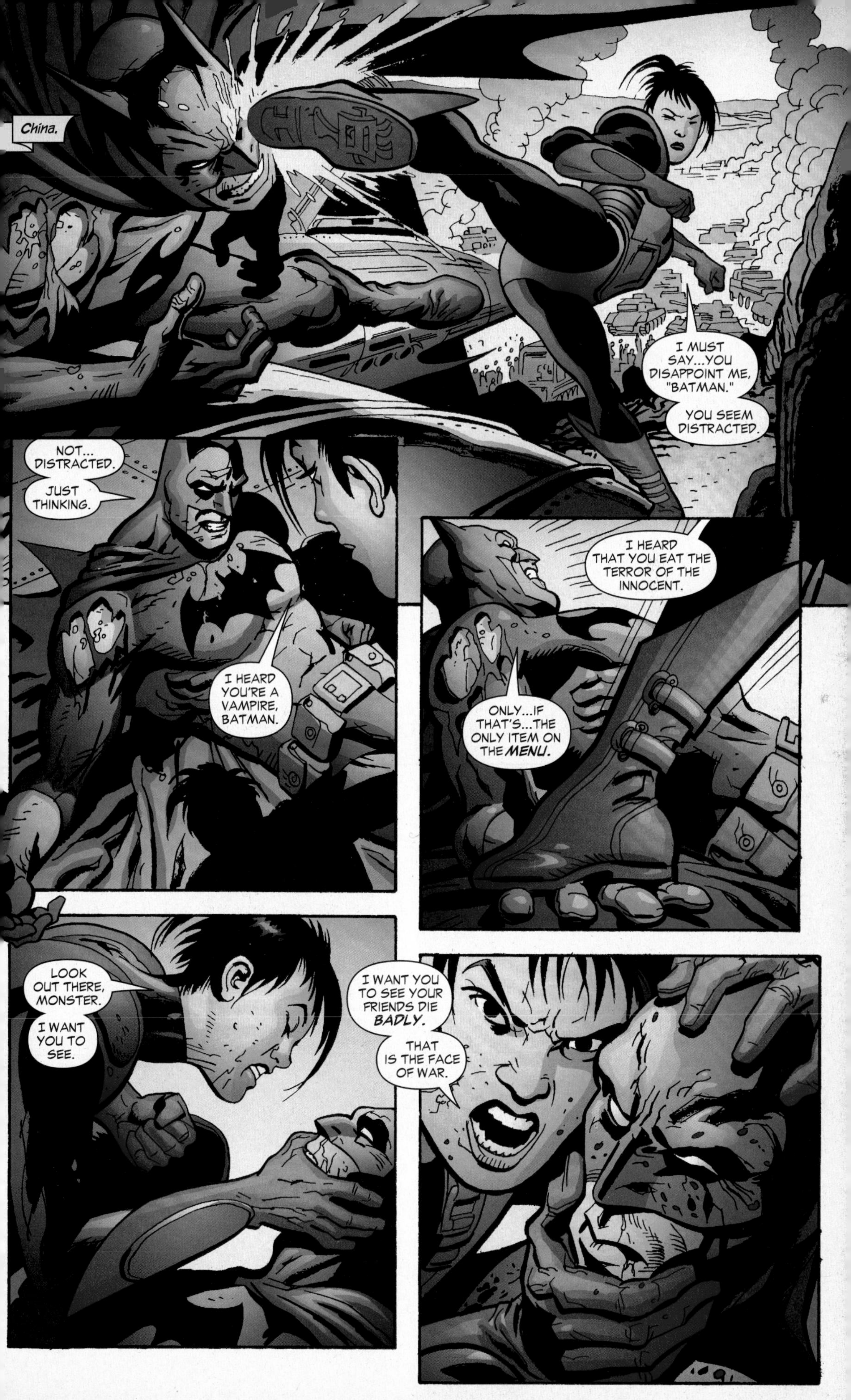
China.
I MUST SAY...YOU DISAPPOINT ME, "BATMAN."
YOU SEEM DISTRACTED.
NOT... DISTRACTED.
JUST THINKING.
I HEARD YOU'RE A VAMPIRE, BATMAN.
I HEARD THAT YOU EAT THE TERROR OF THE INNOCENT.
ONLY...IF THAT'S...THE ONLY ITEM ON THE *MENU*.
LOOK OUT THERE, MONSTER.
I WANT YOU TO SEE.
I WANT YOU TO SEE YOUR FRIENDS DIE *BADLY*.
THAT IS THE FACE OF WAR.

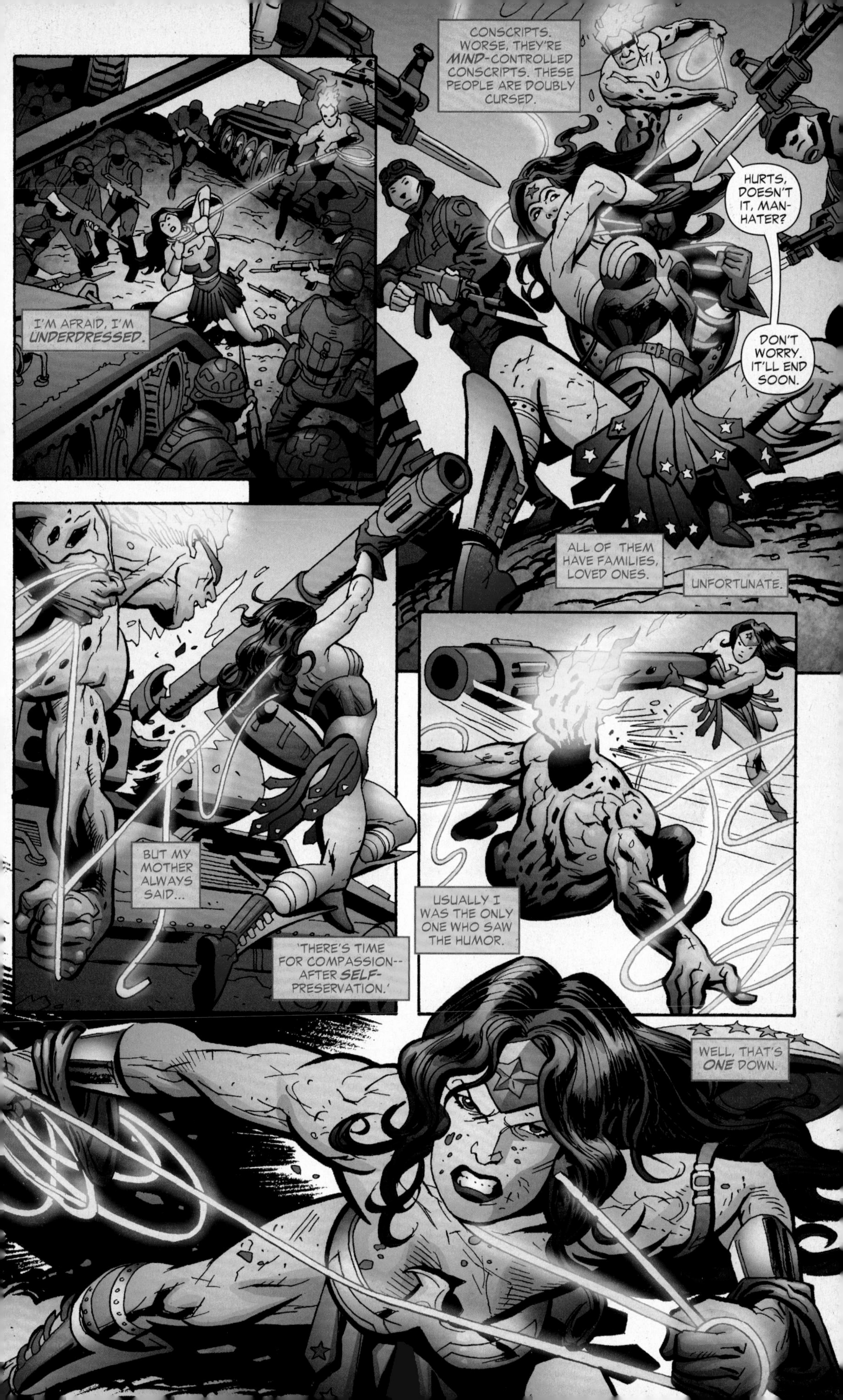
CONSCRIPTS. WORSE, THEY'RE MIND-CONTROLLED CONSCRIPTS. THESE PEOPLE ARE DOUBLY CURSED.
I'M AFRAID, I'M UNDERDRESSED.
HURTS, DOESN'T IT, MAN-HATER?
DON'T WORRY. IT'LL END SOON.
ALL OF THEM HAVE FAMILIES, LOVED ONES.
UNFORTUNATE.
BUT MY MOTHER ALWAYS SAID...
'THERE'S TIME FOR COMPASSION-- AFTER SELF-PRESERVATION.'
USUALLY I WAS THE ONLY ONE WHO SAW THE HUMOR.
WELL, THAT'S ONE DOWN.

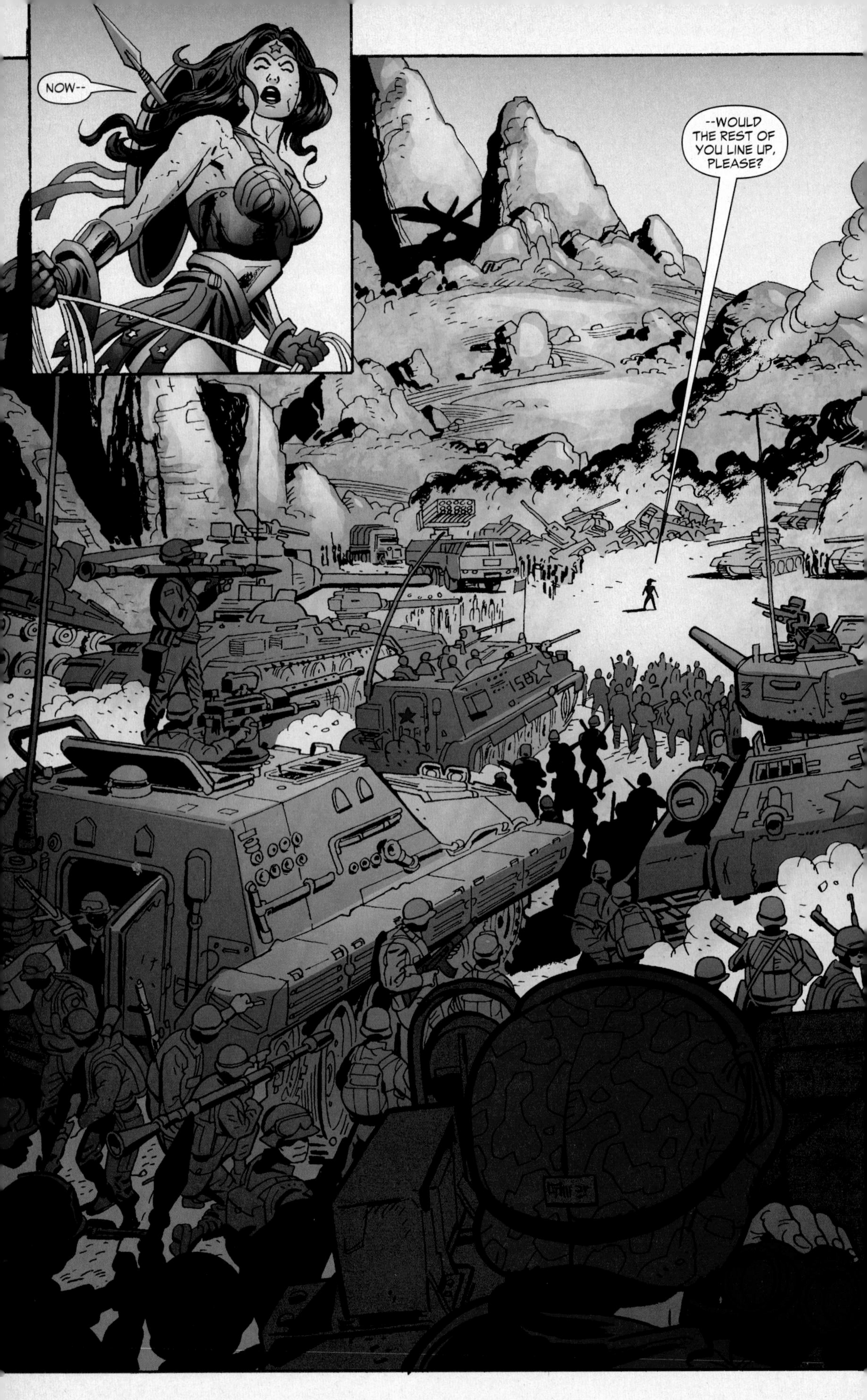
NOW--
--WOULD THE REST OF YOU LINE UP, PLEASE?

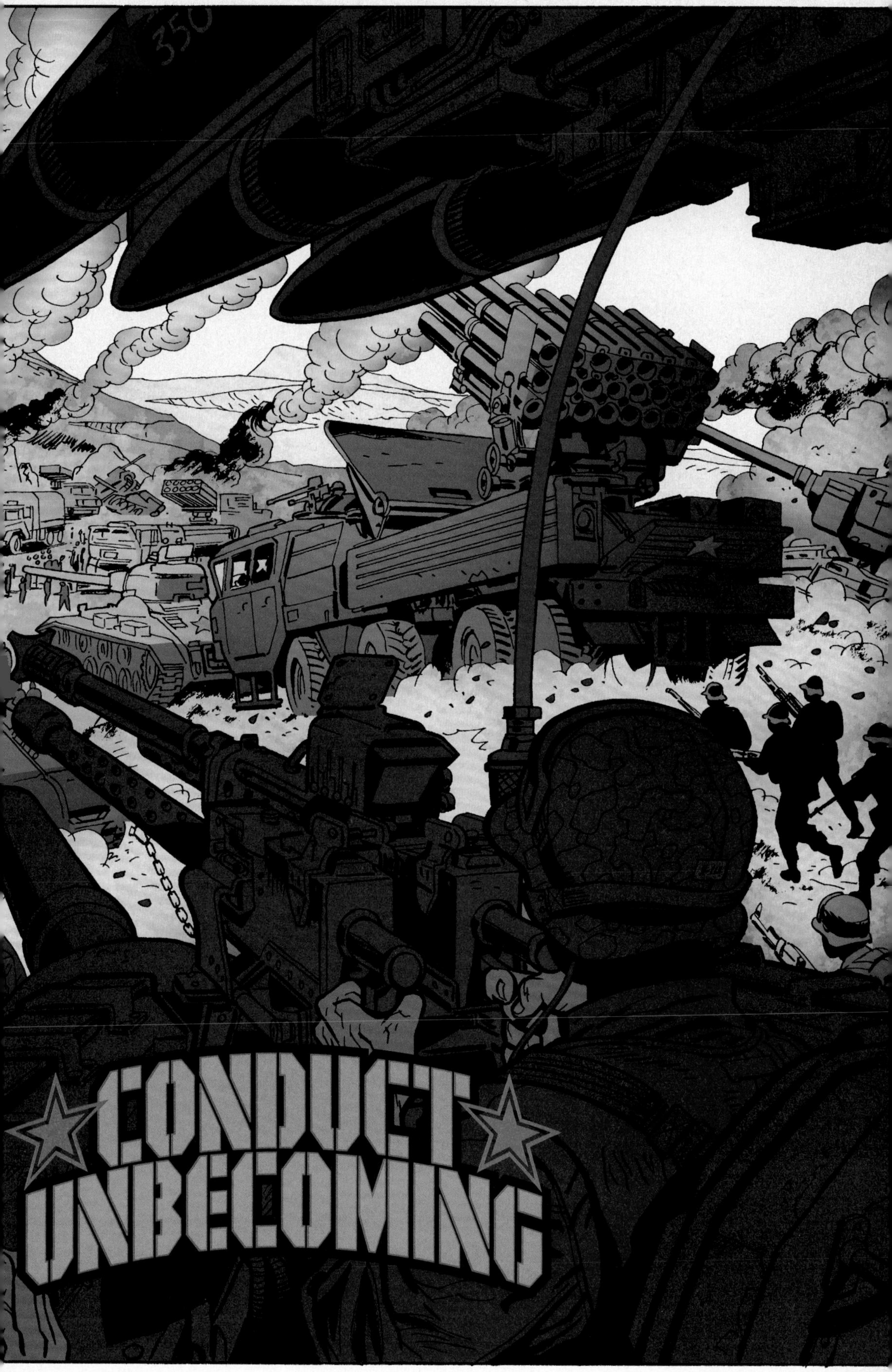
350
CONDUCT
UNBECOMING

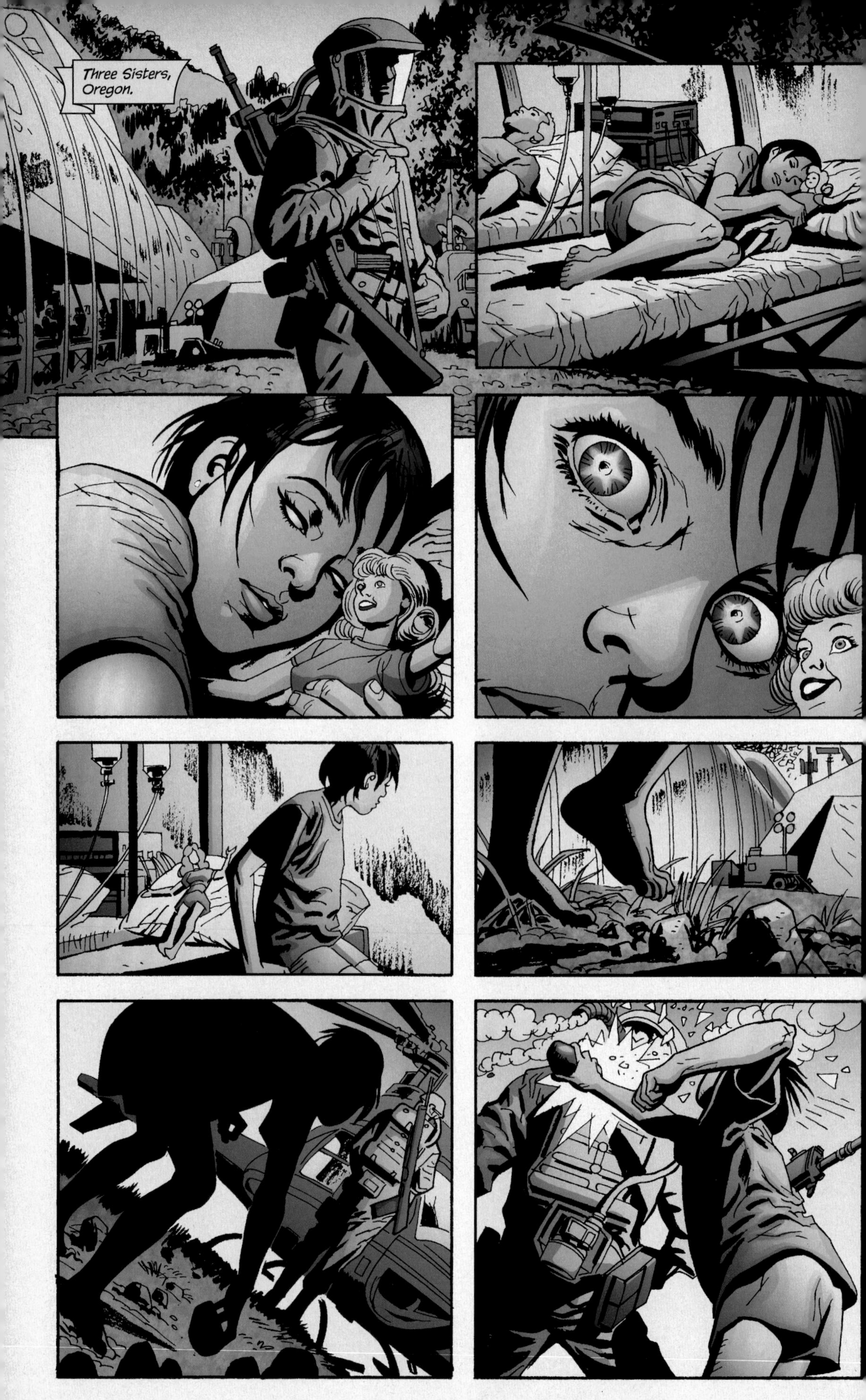
Three Sisters, Oregon.

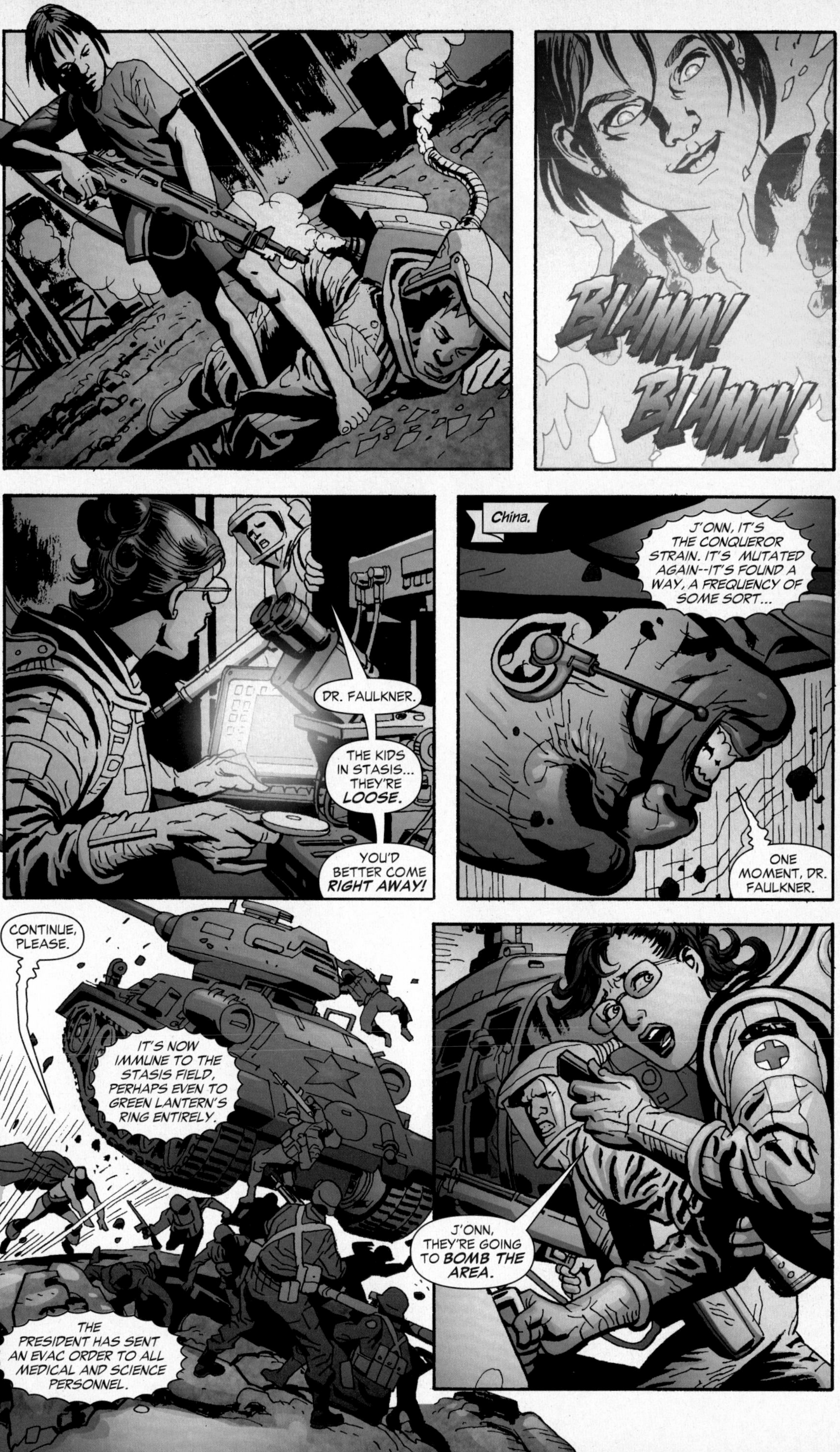
BLAMM!
BLAMM!
China.
DR. FAULKNER.
THE KIDS IN STASIS... THEY'RE LOOSE.
YOU'D BETTER COME RIGHT AWAY!
J'ONN, IT'S THE CONQUEROR STRAIN. IT'S MUTATED AGAIN--IT'S FOUND A WAY, A FREQUENCY OF SOME SORT...
ONE MOMENT, DR. FAULKNER.
CONTINUE, PLEASE.
IT'S NOW IMMUNE TO THE STASIS FIELD, PERHAPS EVEN TO GREEN LANTERN'S RING ENTIRELY.
THE PRESIDENT HAS SENT AN EVAC ORDER TO ALL MEDICAL AND SCIENCE PERSONNEL.
J'ONN, THEY'RE GOING TO BOMB THE AREA.

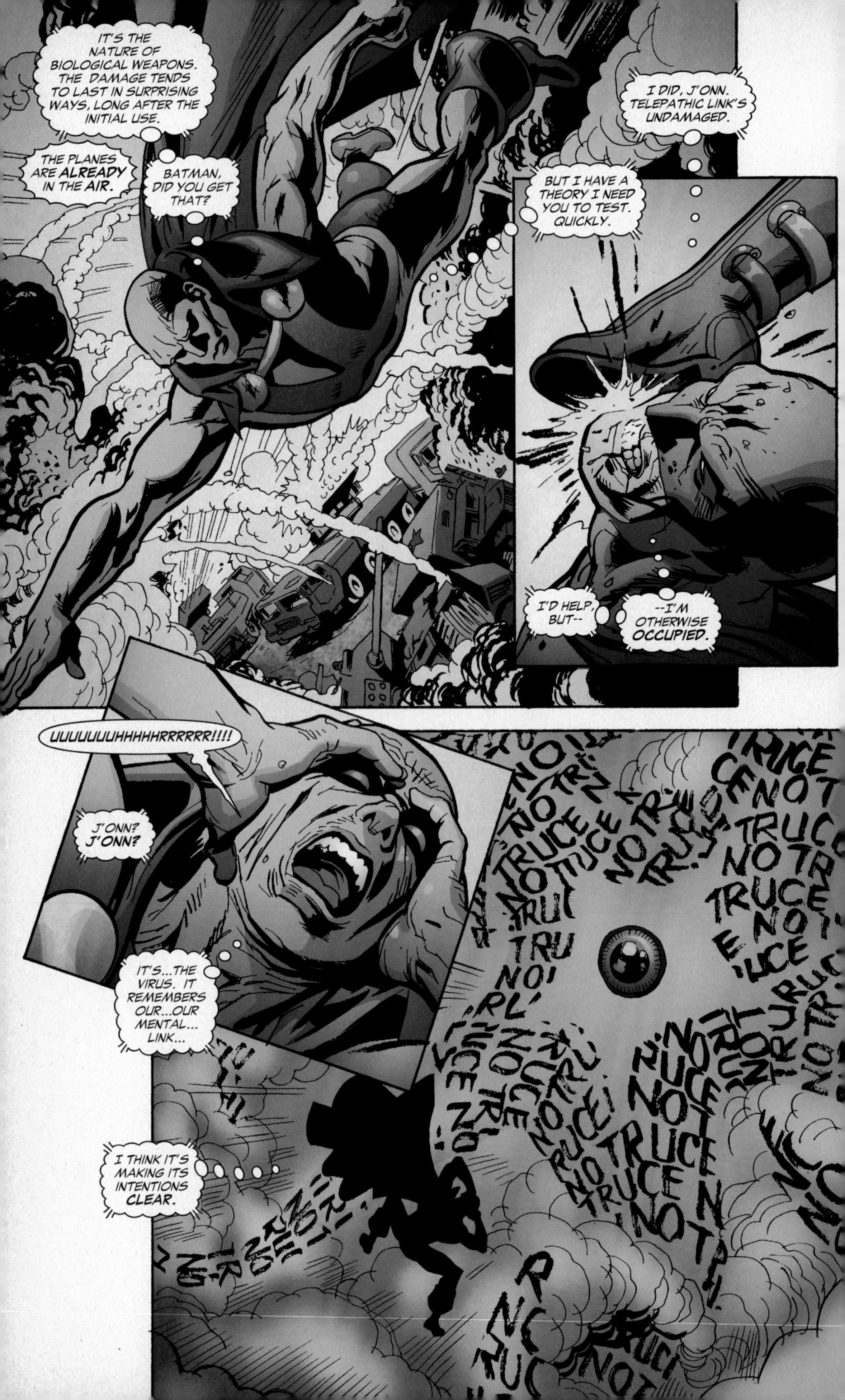
IT'S THE NATURE OF BIOLOGICAL WEAPONS. THE DAMAGE TENDS TO LAST IN SURPRISING WAYS, LONG AFTER THE INITIAL USE.
THE PLANES ARE **ALREADY** IN THE **AIR**.
BATMAN, DID YOU GET THAT?
I DID, J'ONN. TELEPATHIC LINK'S UNDAMAGED.
BUT I HAVE A THEORY I NEED YOU TO TEST. QUICKLY.
I'D HELP, BUT--
--I'M OTHERWISE **OCCUPIED**.
UUUUUUUHHHHHRRRRRR!!!!
J'ONN? **J'ONN?**
IT'S...THE VIRUS. IT REMEMBERS OUR...OUR MENTAL... LINK...
I THINK IT'S MAKING ITS INTENTIONS **CLEAR**.

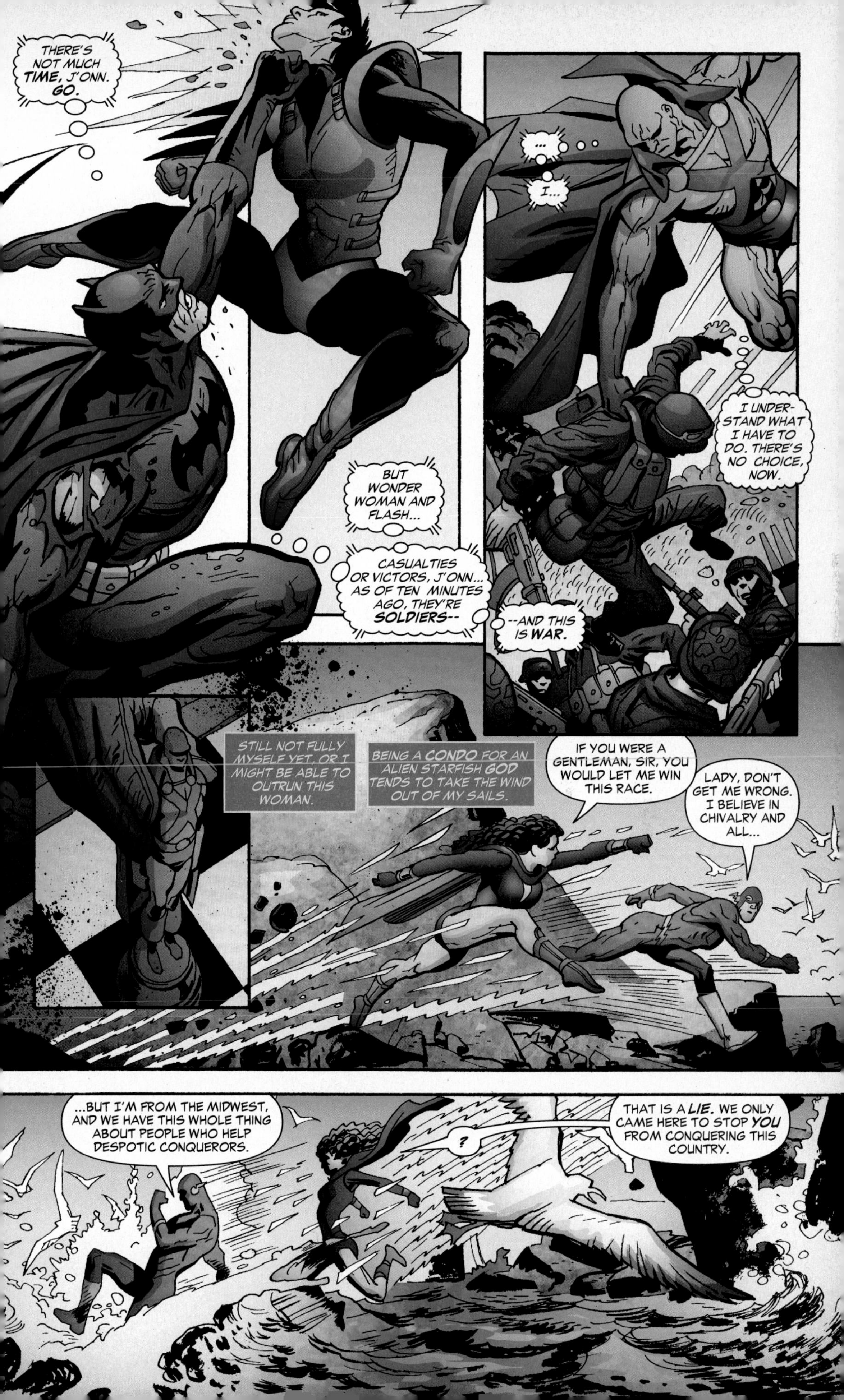
THERE'S NOT MUCH TIME, J'ONN. GO.
...
I...
BUT WONDER WOMAN AND FLASH...
CASUALTIES OR VICTORS, J'ONN... AS OF TEN MINUTES AGO, THEY'RE SOLDIERS--
--AND THIS IS WAR.
I UNDERSTAND WHAT I HAVE TO DO. THERE'S NO CHOICE, NOW.
STILL NOT FULLY MYSELF YET, OR I MIGHT BE ABLE TO OUTRUN THIS WOMAN.
BEING A CONDO FOR AN ALIEN STARFISH GOD TENDS TO TAKE THE WIND OUT OF MY SAILS.
IF YOU WERE A GENTLEMAN, SIR, YOU WOULD LET ME WIN THIS RACE.
LADY, DON'T GET ME WRONG. I BELIEVE IN CHIVALRY AND ALL...
...BUT I'M FROM THE MIDWEST, AND WE HAVE THIS WHOLE THING ABOUT PEOPLE WHO HELP DESPOTIC CONQUERORS.
?
THAT IS A LIE. WE ONLY CAME HERE TO STOP YOU FROM CONQUERING THIS COUNTRY.

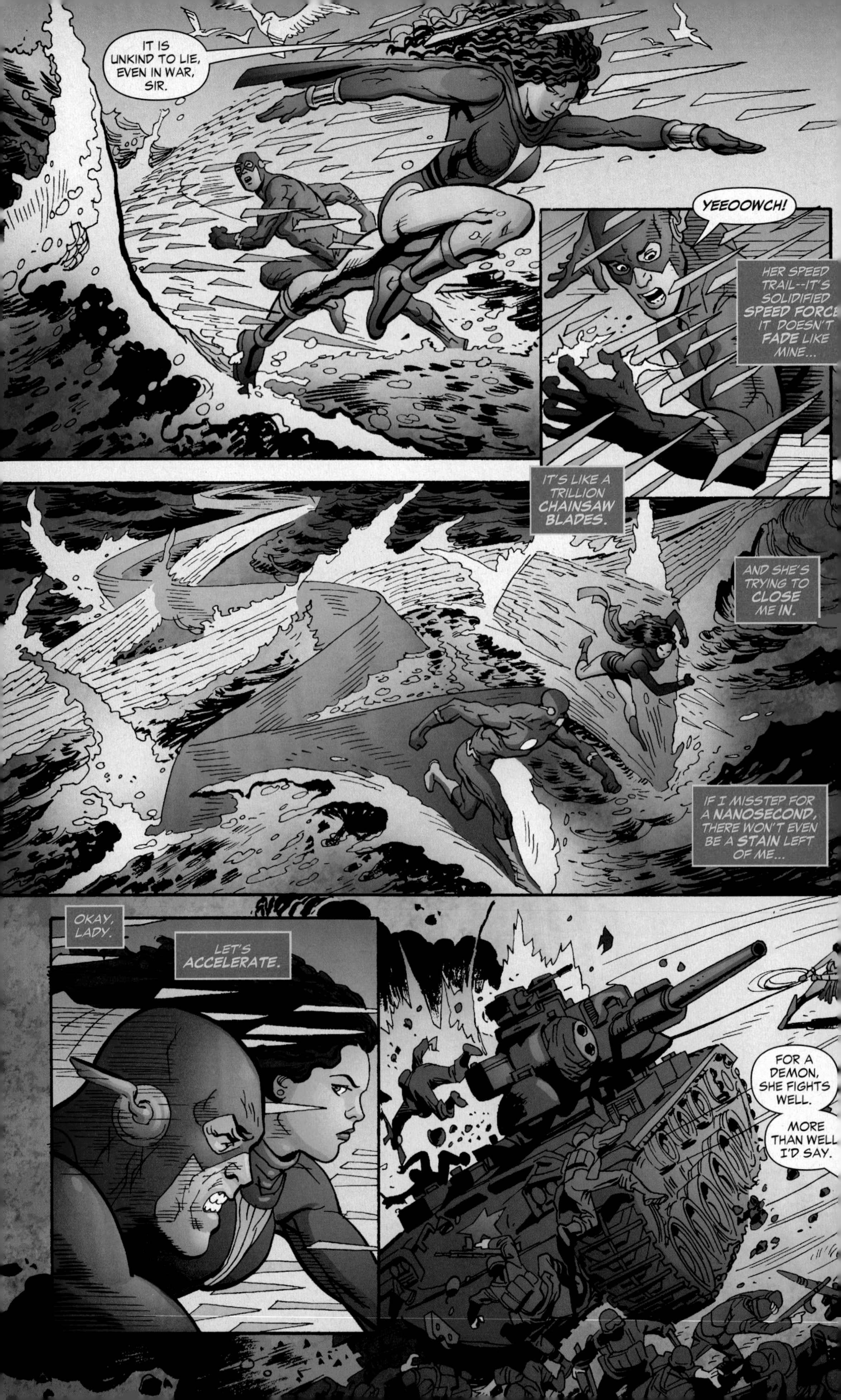
IT IS UNKIND TO LIE, EVEN IN WAR, SIR.
YEEOOWCH!
HER SPEED TRAIL--IT'S SOLIDIFIED SPEED FORCE. IT DOESN'T FADE LIKE MINE...
IT'S LIKE A TRILLION CHAINSAW BLADES.
AND SHE'S TRYING TO CLOSE ME IN.
IF I MISSTEP FOR A NANOSECOND, THERE WON'T EVEN BE A STAIN LEFT OF ME...
OKAY, LADY.
LET'S ACCELERATE.
FOR A DEMON, SHE FIGHTS WELL.
MORE THAN WELL I'D SAY.

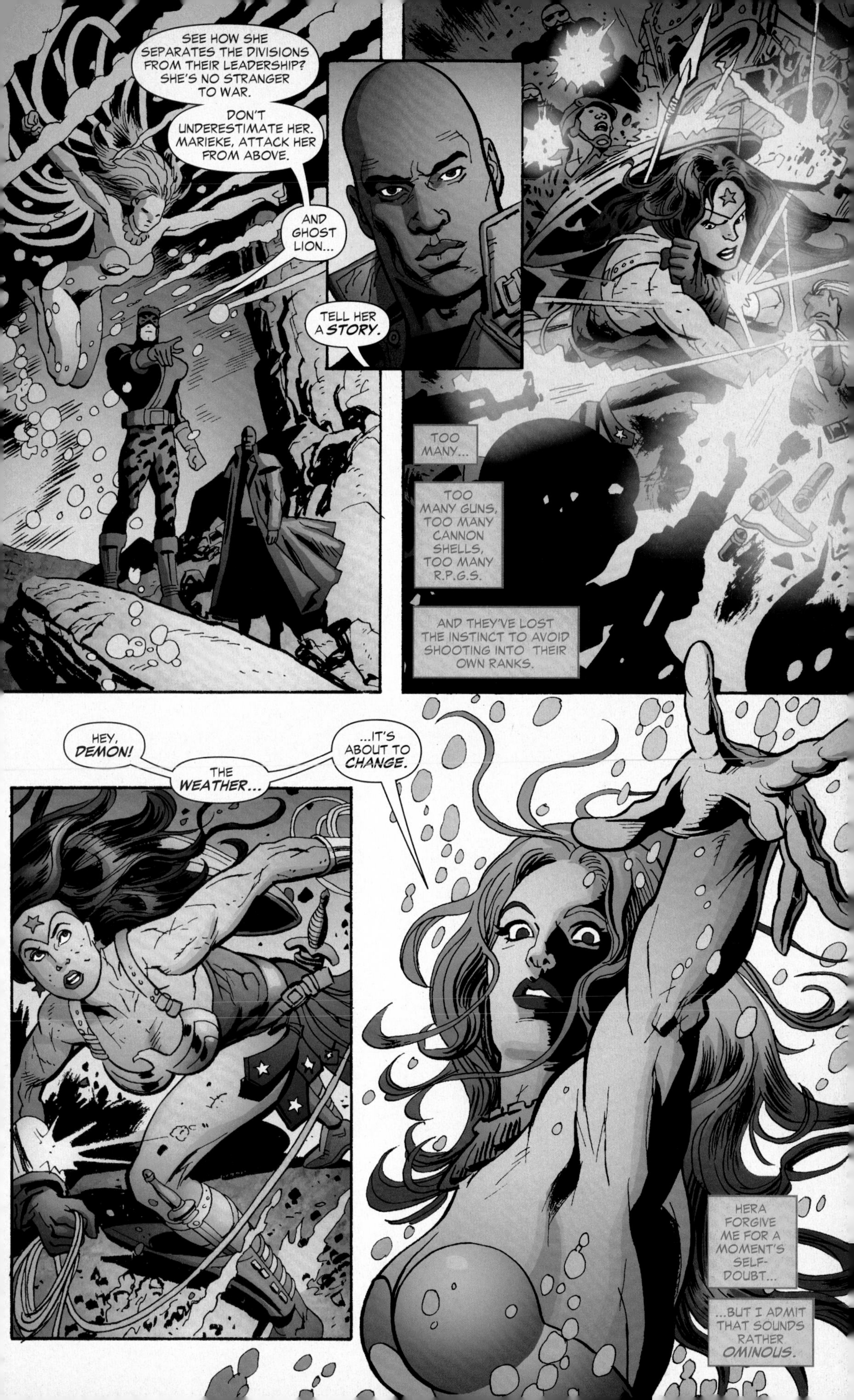
SEE HOW SHE SEPARATES THE DIVISIONS FROM THEIR LEADERSHIP? SHE'S NO STRANGER TO WAR.
DON'T UNDERESTIMATE HER. MARIEKE, ATTACK HER FROM ABOVE.
AND GHOST LION...
TELL HER A STORY.
TOO MANY...
TOO MANY GUNS, TOO MANY CANNON SHELLS, TOO MANY R.P.G.S.
AND THEY'VE LOST THE INSTINCT TO AVOID SHOOTING INTO THEIR OWN RANKS.
HEY, DEMON!
THE WEATHER...
...IT'S ABOUT TO CHANGE.
HERA FORGIVE ME FOR A MOMENT'S SELF-DOUBT...
...BUT I ADMIT THAT SOUNDS RATHER OMINOUS.

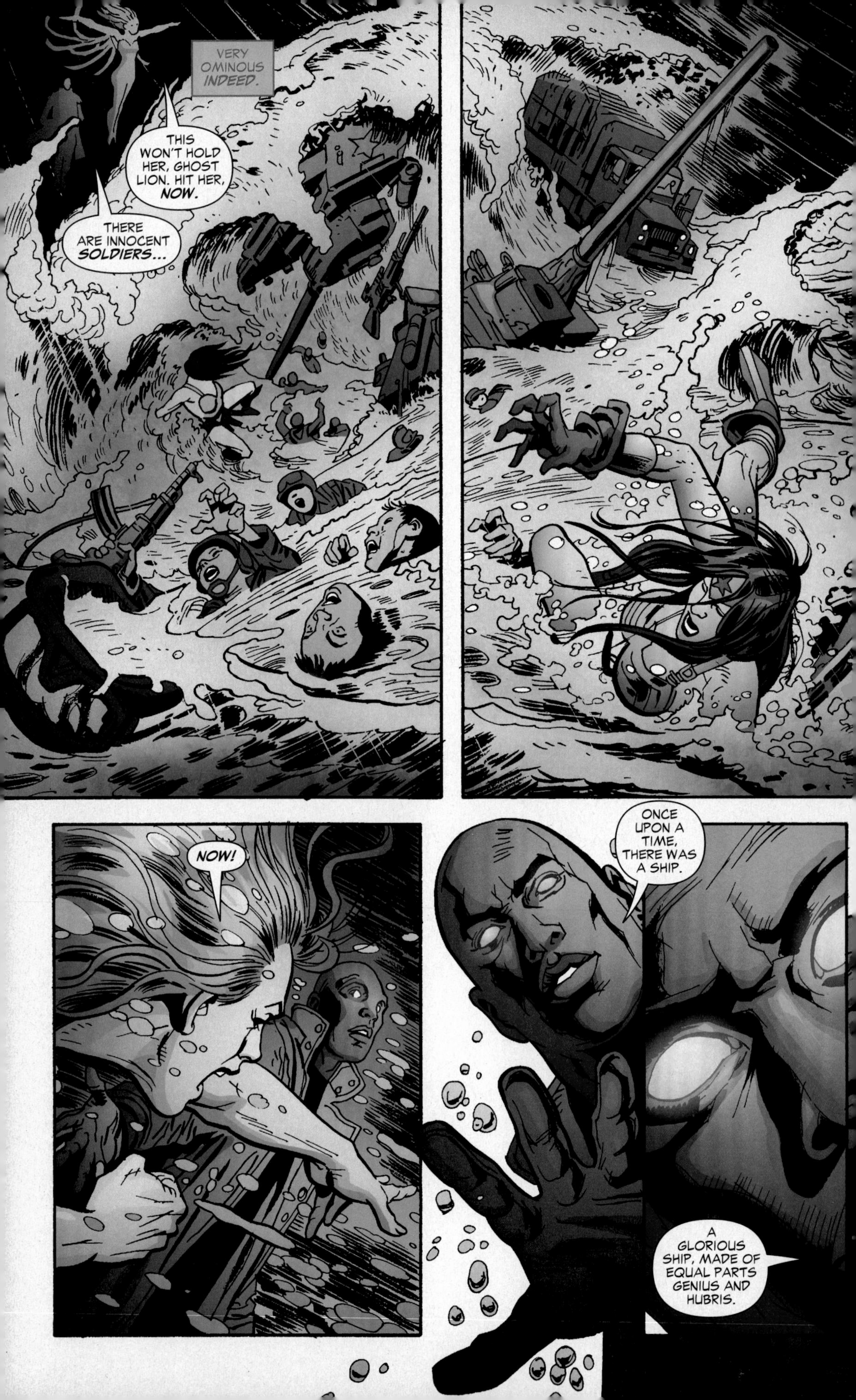
VERY OMINOUS INDEED.
THIS WON'T HOLD HER, GHOST LION. HIT HER, NOW.
THERE ARE INNOCENT SOLDIERS...
NOW!
ONCE UPON A TIME, THERE WAS A SHIP.
A GLORIOUS SHIP, MADE OF EQUAL PARTS GENIUS AND HUBRIS.

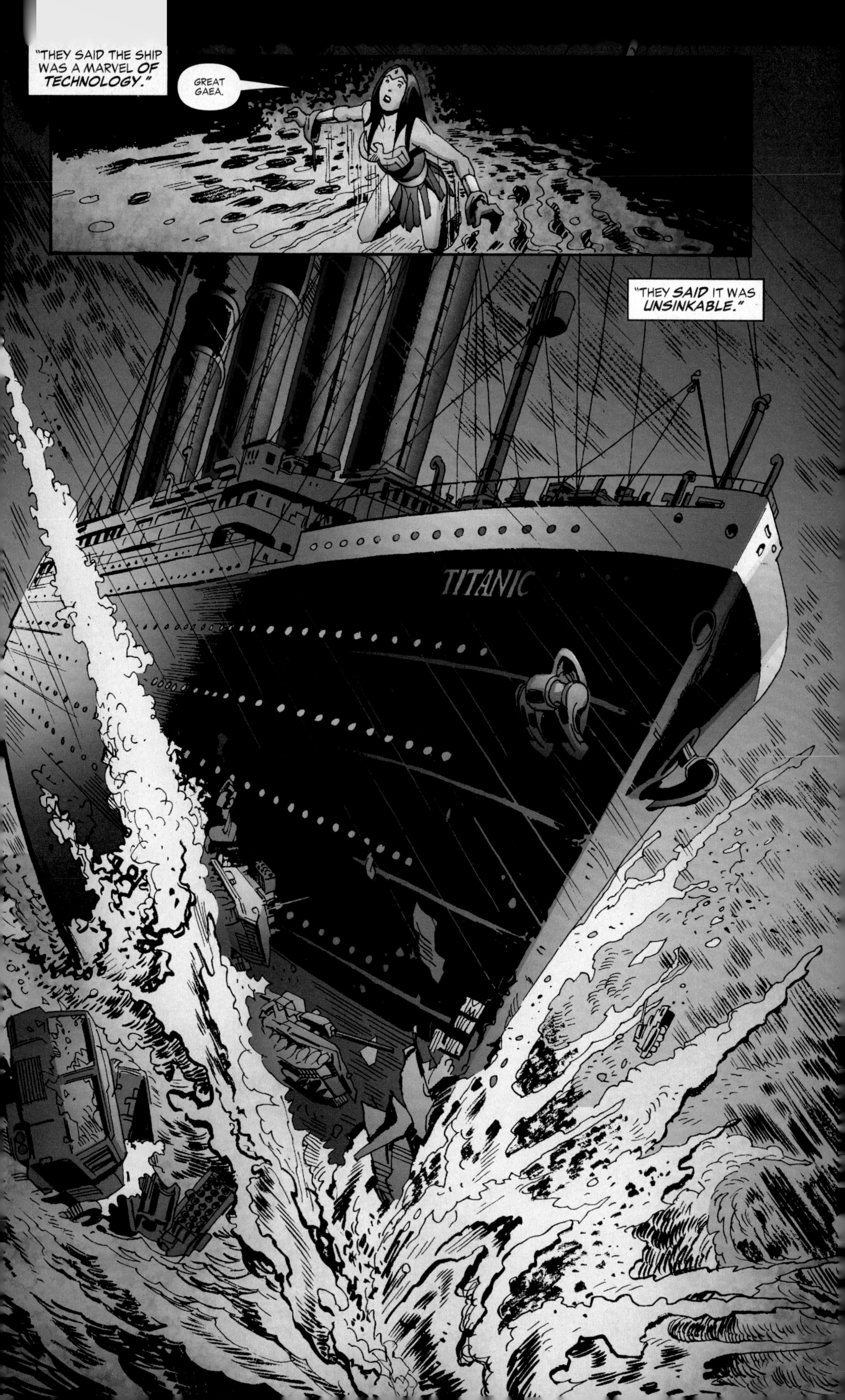
"THEY SAID THE SHIP WAS A MARVEL OF TECHNOLOGY."
GREAT GAEA.
"THEY SAID IT WAS UNSINKABLE."
TITANIC

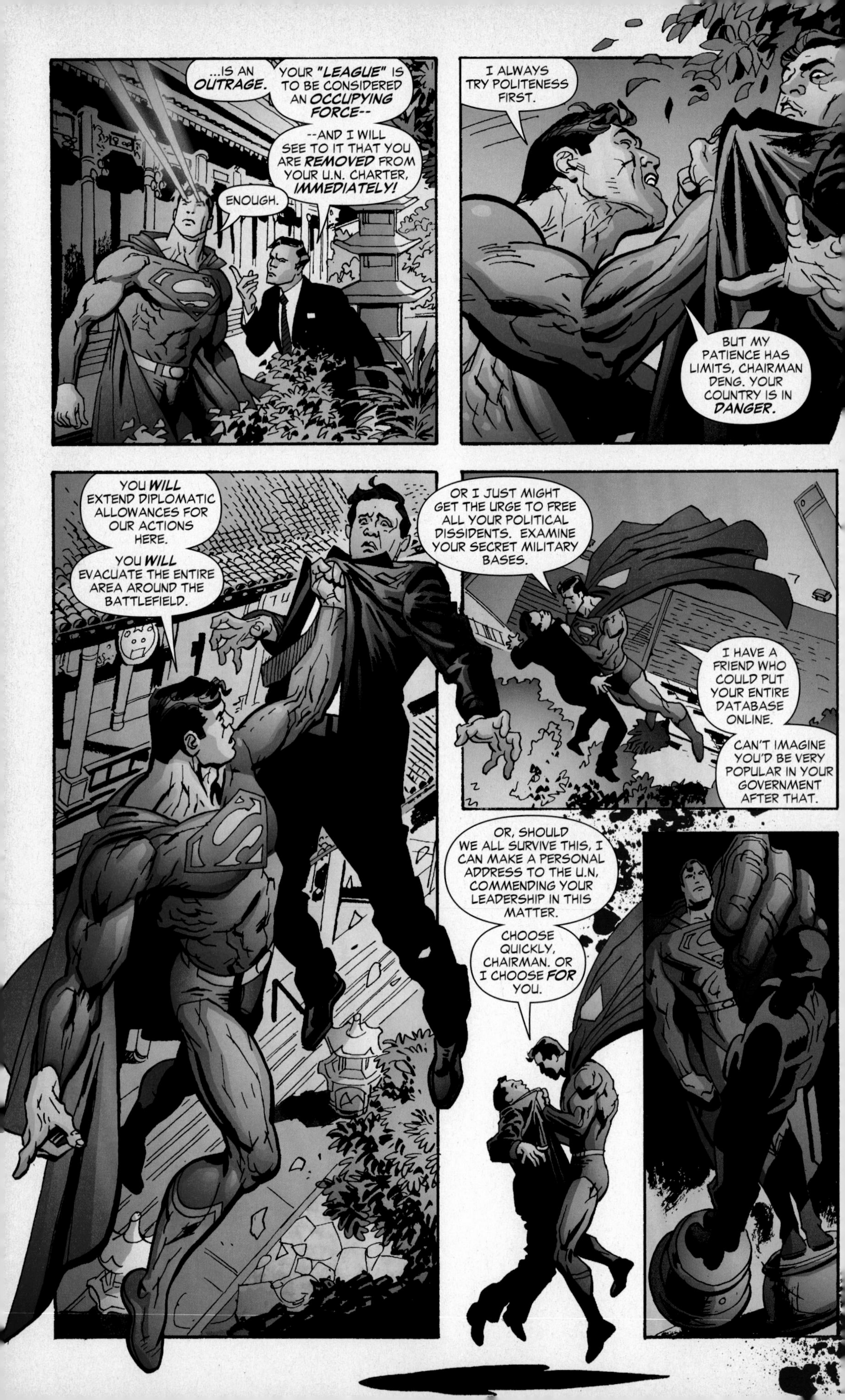
...IS AN OUTRAGE.
YOUR "LEAGUE" IS TO BE CONSIDERED AN OCCUPYING FORCE--
--AND I WILL SEE TO IT THAT YOU ARE REMOVED FROM YOUR U.N. CHARTER, IMMEDIATELY!
ENOUGH.
I ALWAYS TRY POLITENESS FIRST.
BUT MY PATIENCE HAS LIMITS, CHAIRMAN DENG. YOUR COUNTRY IS IN DANGER.
YOU WILL EXTEND DIPLOMATIC ALLOWANCES FOR OUR ACTIONS HERE.
YOU WILL EVACUATE THE ENTIRE AREA AROUND THE BATTLEFIELD.
OR I JUST MIGHT GET THE URGE TO FREE ALL YOUR POLITICAL DISSIDENTS. EXAMINE YOUR SECRET MILITARY BASES.
I HAVE A FRIEND WHO COULD PUT YOUR ENTIRE DATABASE ONLINE.
CAN'T IMAGINE YOU'D BE VERY POPULAR IN YOUR GOVERNMENT AFTER THAT.
OR, SHOULD WE ALL SURVIVE THIS, I CAN MAKE A PERSONAL ADDRESS TO THE U.N, COMMENDING YOUR LEADERSHIP IN THIS MATTER.
CHOOSE QUICKLY, CHAIRMAN. OR I CHOOSE FOR YOU.

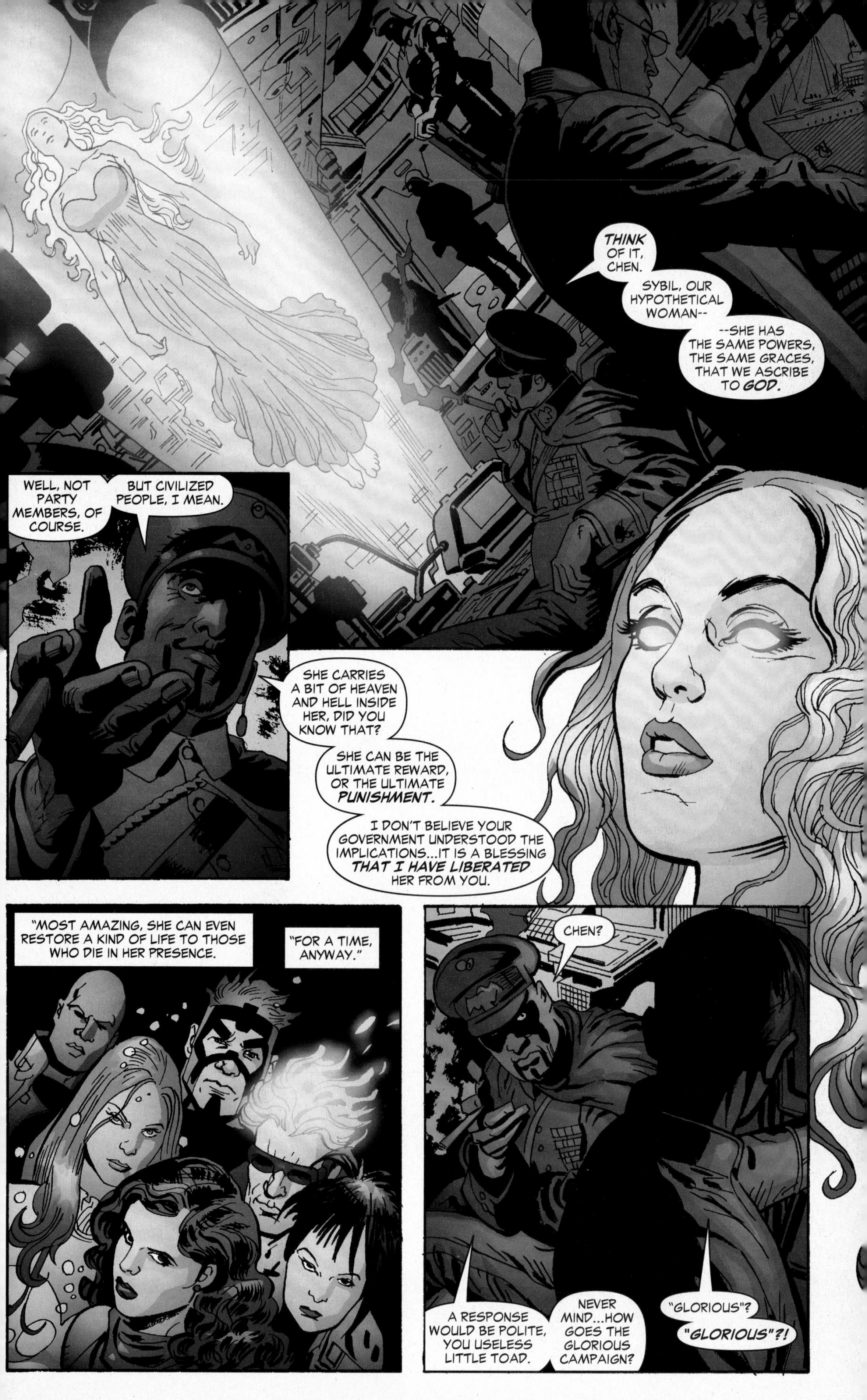
THINK OF IT, CHEN.
SYBIL, OUR HYPOTHETICAL WOMAN--
--SHE HAS THE SAME POWERS, THE SAME GRACES, THAT WE ASCRIBE TO GOD.
WELL, NOT PARTY MEMBERS, OF COURSE.
BUT CIVILIZED PEOPLE, I MEAN.
SHE CARRIES A BIT OF HEAVEN AND HELL INSIDE HER, DID YOU KNOW THAT?
SHE CAN BE THE ULTIMATE REWARD, OR THE ULTIMATE PUNISHMENT.
I DON'T BELIEVE YOUR GOVERNMENT UNDERSTOOD THE IMPLICATIONS...IT IS A BLESSING THAT I HAVE LIBERATED HER FROM YOU.
"MOST AMAZING, SHE CAN EVEN RESTORE A KIND OF LIFE TO THOSE WHO DIE IN HER PRESENCE.
"FOR A TIME, ANYWAY."
CHEN?
A RESPONSE WOULD BE POLITE, YOU USELESS LITTLE TOAD.
NEVER MIND...HOW GOES THE GLORIOUS CAMPAIGN?
"GLORIOUS"?
"GLORIOUS"?!

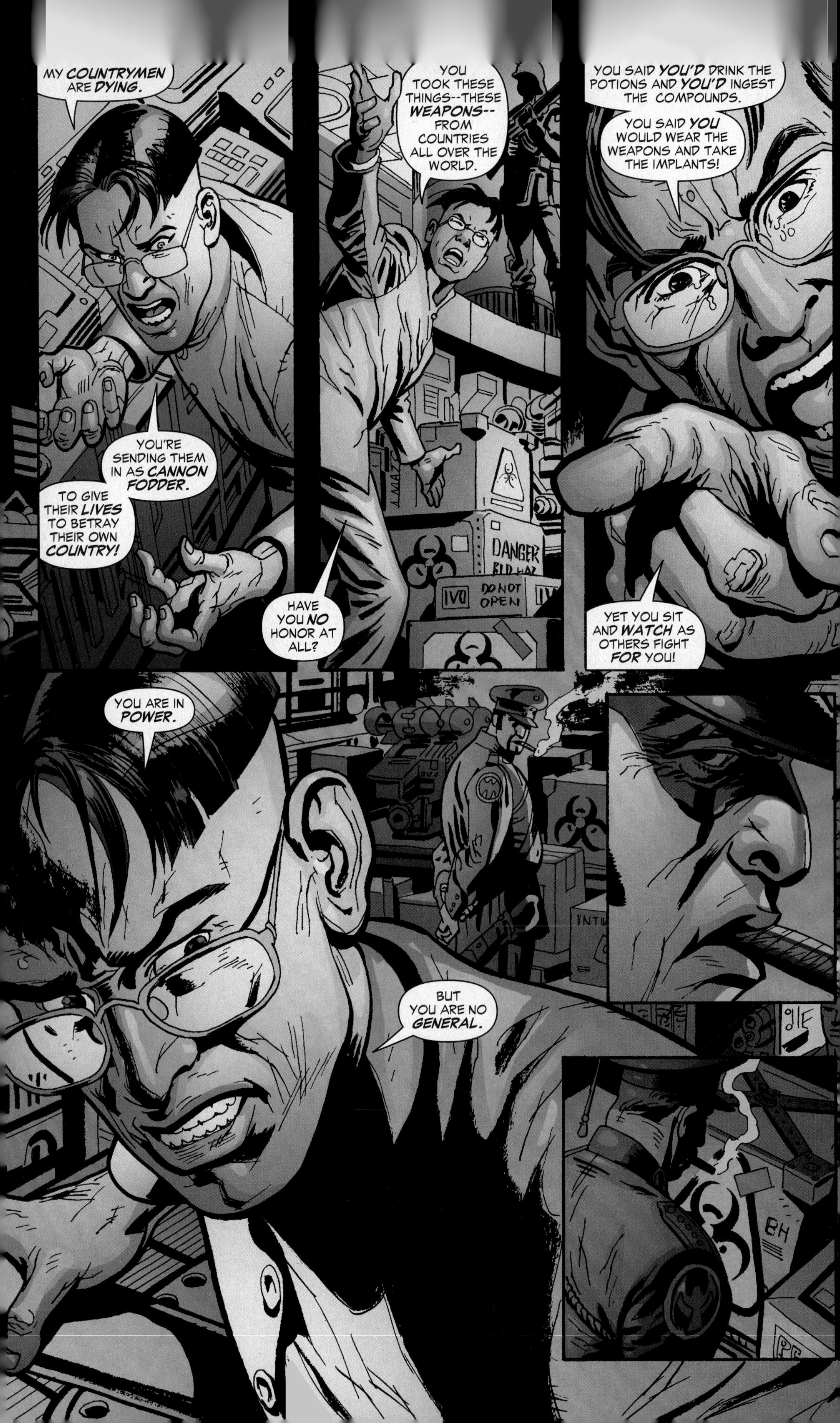
MY COUNTRYMEN ARE DYING.
YOU'RE SENDING THEM IN AS CANNON FODDER.
TO GIVE THEIR LIVES TO BETRAY THEIR OWN COUNTRY!
YOU TOOK THESE THINGS--THESE WEAPONS--FROM COUNTRIES ALL OVER THE WORLD.
DANGER
DO NOT OPEN
IVO
HAVE YOU NO HONOR AT ALL?
YOU SAID YOU'D DRINK THE POTIONS AND YOU'D INGEST THE COMPOUNDS.
YOU SAID YOU WOULD WEAR THE WEAPONS AND TAKE THE IMPLANTS!
YET YOU SIT AND WATCH AS OTHERS FIGHT FOR YOU!
YOU ARE IN POWER.
BUT YOU ARE NO GENERAL.

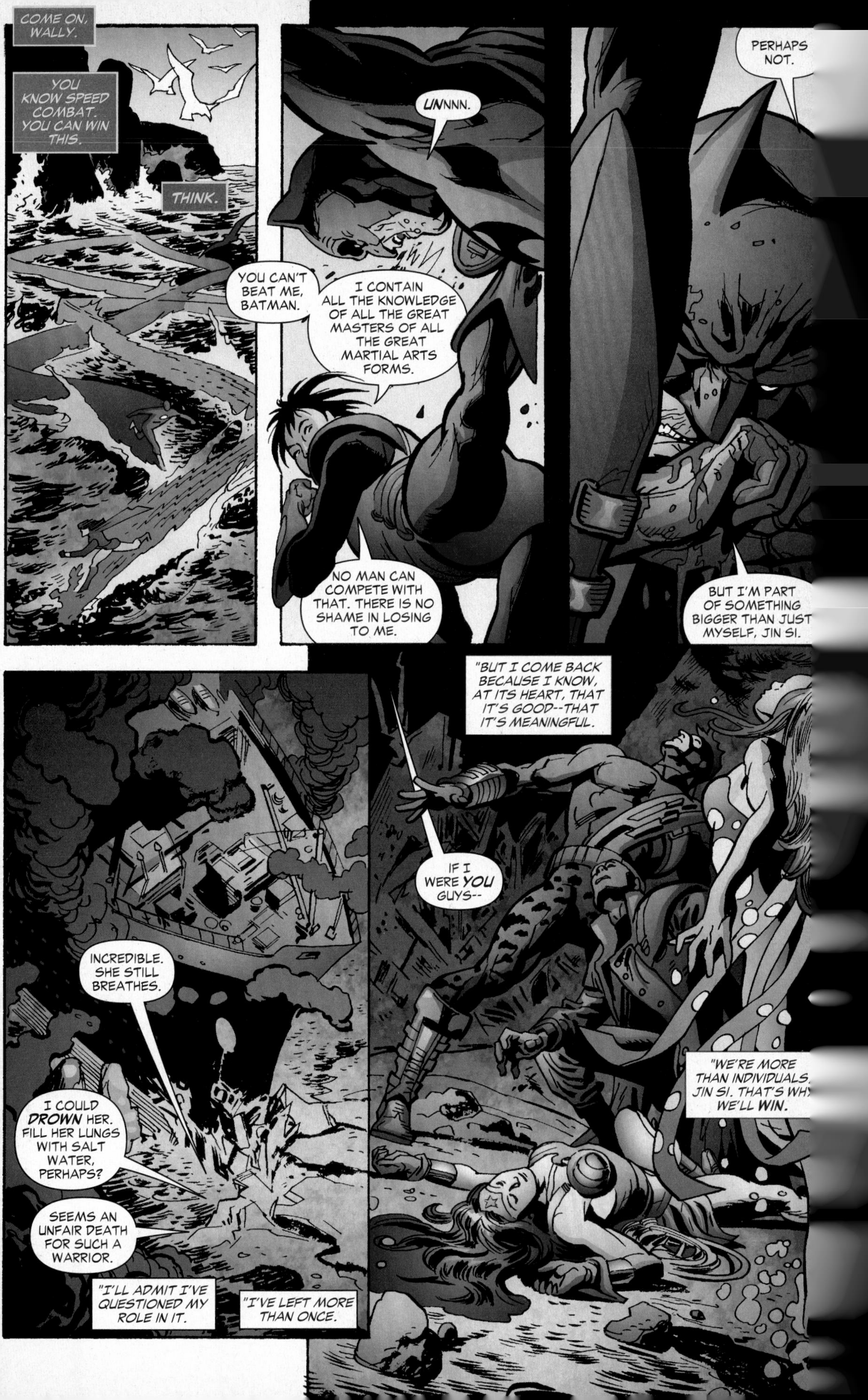
COME ON, WALLY.
YOU KNOW SPEED COMBAT. YOU CAN WIN THIS.
THINK.
UNNNN.
YOU CAN'T BEAT ME, BATMAN.
I CONTAIN ALL THE KNOWLEDGE OF ALL THE GREAT MASTERS OF ALL THE GREAT MARTIAL ARTS FORMS.
NO MAN CAN COMPETE WITH THAT. THERE IS NO SHAME IN LOSING TO ME.
PERHAPS NOT.
BUT I'M PART OF SOMETHING BIGGER THAN JUST MYSELF, JIN SI.
INCREDIBLE. SHE STILL BREATHES.
I COULD DROWN HER. FILL HER LUNGS WITH SALT WATER, PERHAPS?
SEEMS AN UNFAIR DEATH FOR SUCH A WARRIOR.
"I'LL ADMIT I'VE QUESTIONED MY ROLE IN IT.
"I'VE LEFT MORE THAN ONCE.
"BUT I COME BACK BECAUSE I KNOW, AT ITS HEART, THAT IT'S GOOD--THAT IT'S MEANINGFUL.
IF I WERE YOU GUYS--
"WE'RE MORE THAN INDIVIDUALS, JIN SI. THAT'S WHY WE'LL WIN.

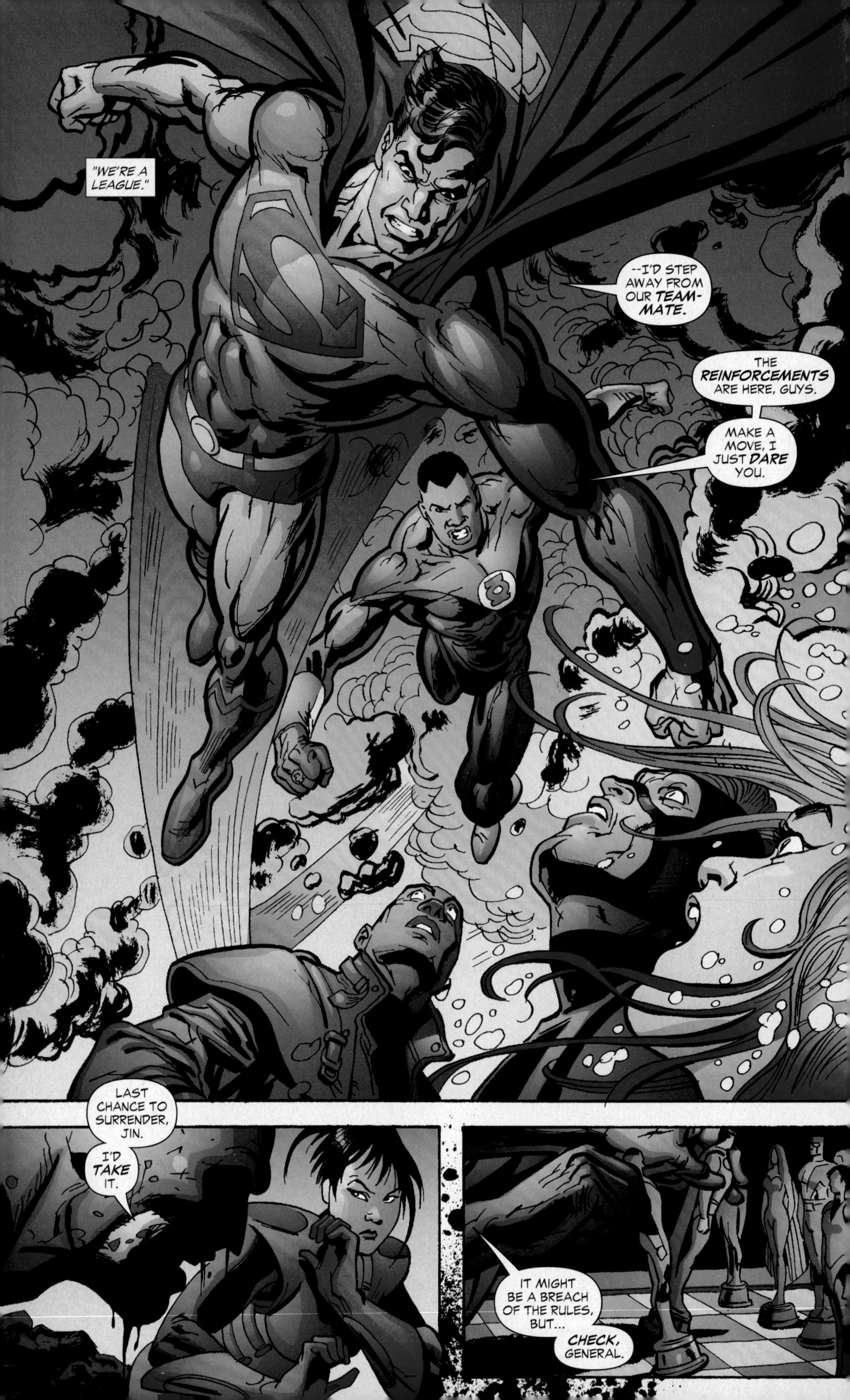
"WE'RE A LEAGUE."
--I'D STEP AWAY FROM OUR TEAM-MATE.
THE REINFORCEMENTS ARE HERE, GUYS.
MAKE A MOVE, I JUST DARE YOU.
LAST CHANCE TO SURRENDER, JIN.
I'D TAKE IT.
IT MIGHT BE A BREACH OF THE RULES, BUT... CHECK, GENERAL.

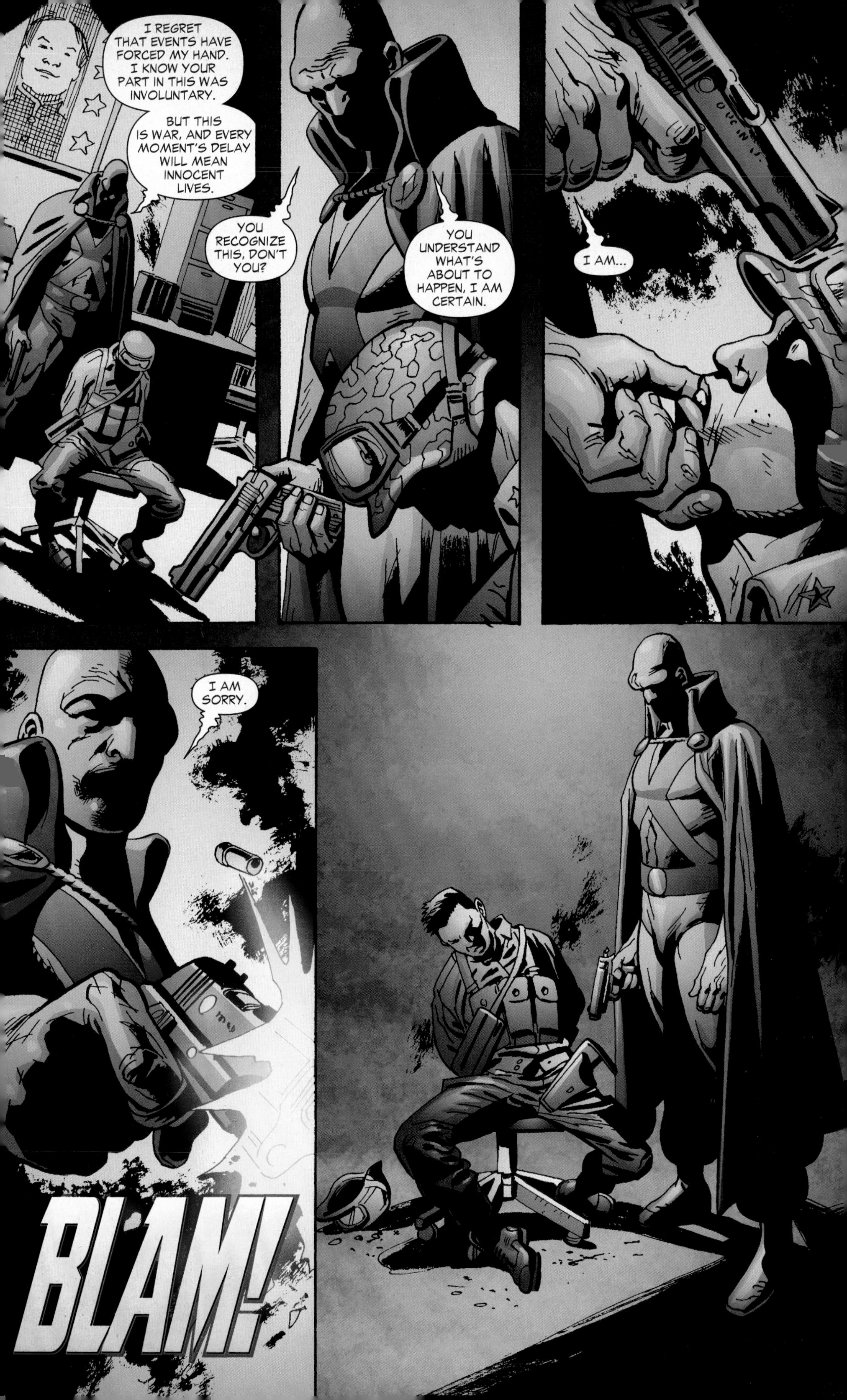
I REGRET THAT EVENTS HAVE FORCED MY HAND. I KNOW YOUR PART IN THIS WAS INVOLUNTARY.
BUT THIS IS WAR, AND EVERY MOMENT'S DELAY WILL MEAN INNOCENT LIVES.
YOU RECOGNIZE THIS, DON'T YOU?
YOU UNDERSTAND WHAT'S ABOUT TO HAPPEN, I AM CERTAIN.
I AM...
I AM SORRY.
BLAM!

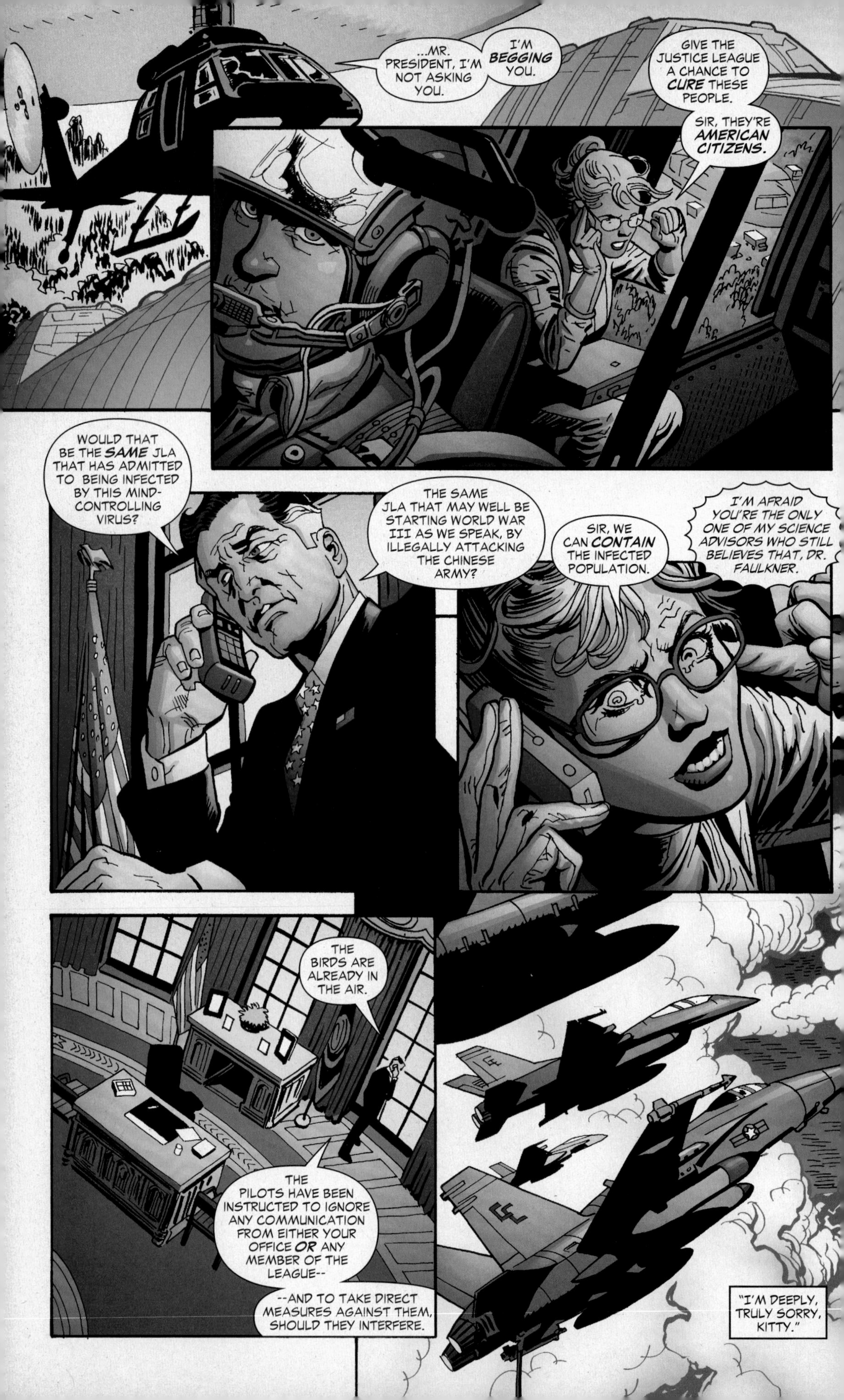
...MR. PRESIDENT, I'M NOT ASKING YOU.
I'M BEGGING YOU.
GIVE THE JUSTICE LEAGUE A CHANCE TO CURE THESE PEOPLE.
SIR, THEY'RE AMERICAN CITIZENS.
WOULD THAT BE THE SAME JLA THAT HAS ADMITTED TO BEING INFECTED BY THIS MIND-CONTROLLING VIRUS?
THE SAME JLA THAT MAY WELL BE STARTING WORLD WAR III AS WE SPEAK, BY ILLEGALLY ATTACKING THE CHINESE ARMY?
SIR, WE CAN CONTAIN THE INFECTED POPULATION.
I'M AFRAID YOU'RE THE ONLY ONE OF MY SCIENCE ADVISORS WHO STILL BELIEVES THAT, DR. FAULKNER.
THE BIRDS ARE ALREADY IN THE AIR.
THE PILOTS HAVE BEEN INSTRUCTED TO IGNORE ANY COMMUNICATION FROM EITHER YOUR OFFICE OR ANY MEMBER OF THE LEAGUE--
--AND TO TAKE DIRECT MEASURES AGAINST THEM, SHOULD THEY INTERFERE.
"I'M DEEPLY, TRULY SORRY, KITTY."

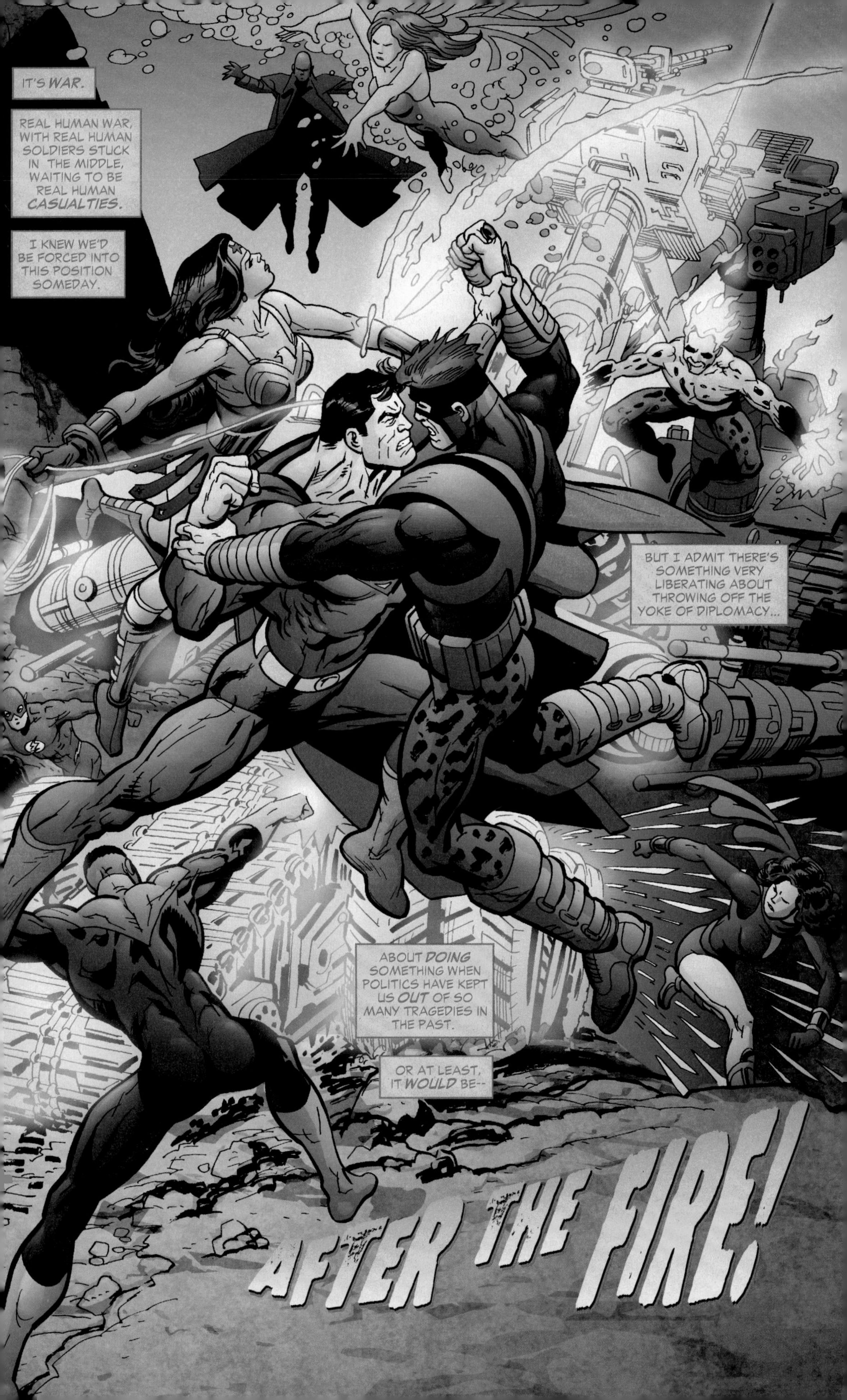
IT'S WAR.
REAL HUMAN WAR, WITH REAL HUMAN SOLDIERS STUCK IN THE MIDDLE, WAITING TO BE REAL HUMAN CASUALTIES.
I KNEW WE'D BE FORCED INTO THIS POSITION SOMEDAY.
BUT I ADMIT THERE'S SOMETHING VERY LIBERATING ABOUT THROWING OFF THE YOKE OF DIPLOMACY...
ABOUT DOING SOMETHING WHEN POLITICS HAVE KEPT US OUT OF SO MANY TRAGEDIES IN THE PAST.
OR AT LEAST, IT WOULD BE--
AFTER THE FIRE!

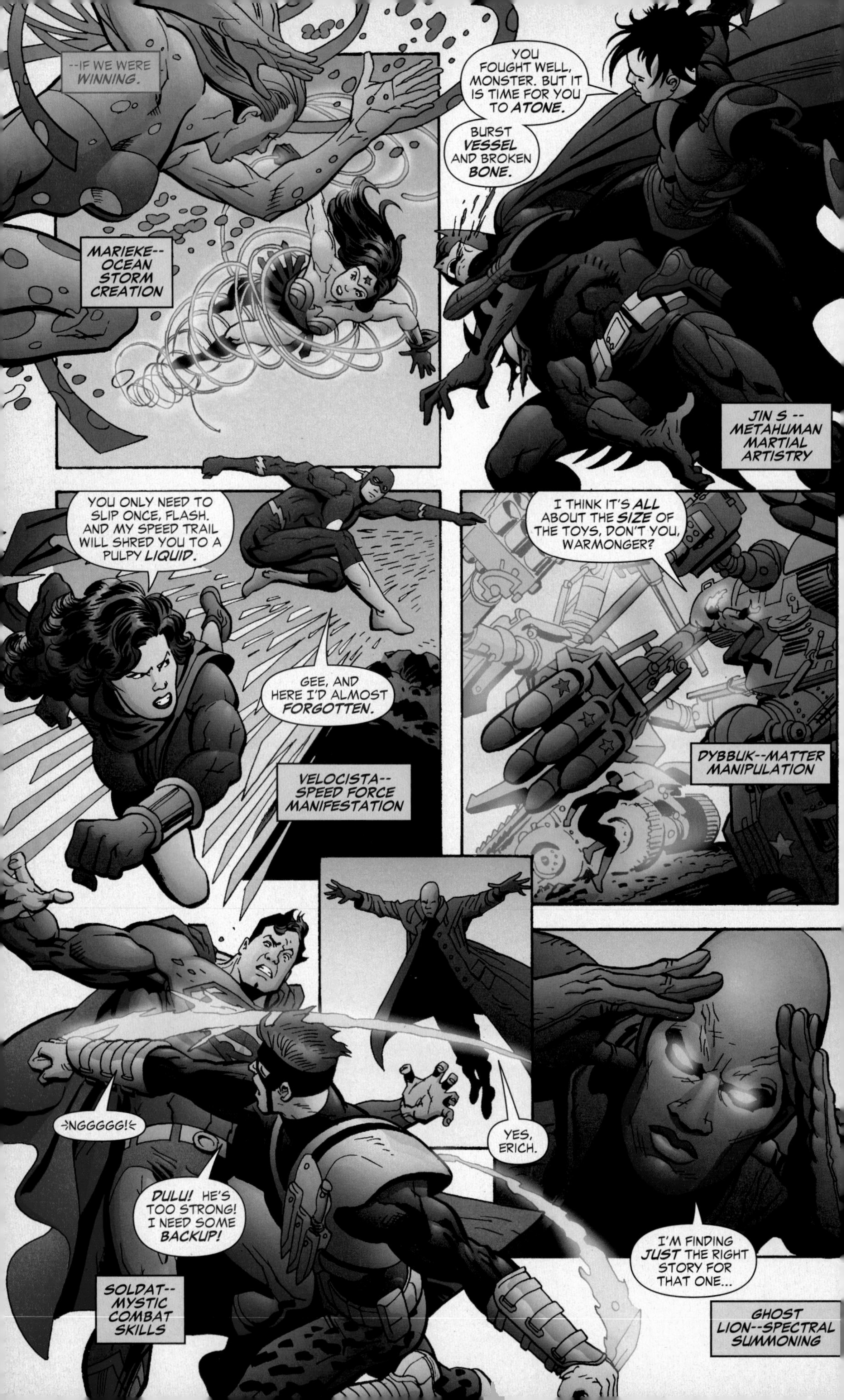
--IF WE WERE WINNING.
MARIEKE--OCEAN STORM CREATION
YOU FOUGHT WELL, MONSTER. BUT IT IS TIME FOR YOU TO ATONE.
BURST VESSEL AND BROKEN BONE.
JIN S --METAHUMAN MARTIAL ARTISTRY
YOU ONLY NEED TO SLIP ONCE, FLASH. AND MY SPEED TRAIL WILL SHRED YOU TO A PULPY LIQUID.
GEE, AND HERE I'D ALMOST FORGOTTEN.
VELOCISTA--SPEED FORCE MANIFESTATION
I THINK IT'S ALL ABOUT THE SIZE OF THE TOYS, DON'T YOU, WARMONGER?
DYBBUK--MATTER MANIPULATION
NGGGGG!
DULU! HE'S TOO STRONG! I NEED SOME BACKUP!
YES, ERICH.
SOLDAT--MYSTIC COMBAT SKILLS
I'M FINDING JUST THE RIGHT STORY FOR THAT ONE...
GHOST LION--SPECTRAL SUMMONING

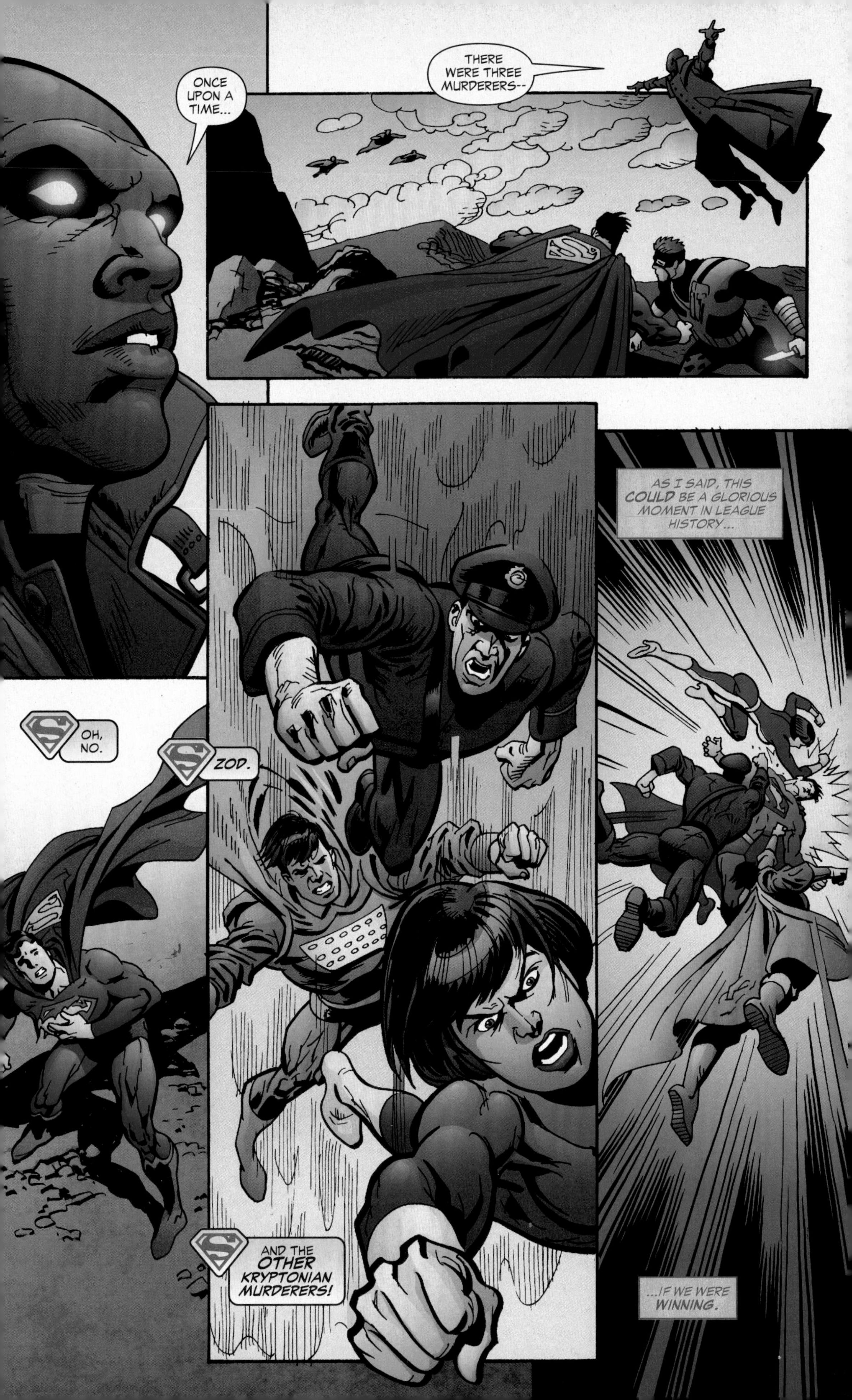
ONCE UPON A TIME...
THERE WERE THREE MURDERERS--
AS I SAID, THIS COULD BE A GLORIOUS MOMENT IN LEAGUE HISTORY...
OH, NO.
ZOD.
AND THE OTHER KRYPTONIAN MURDERERS!
...IF WE WERE WINNING.

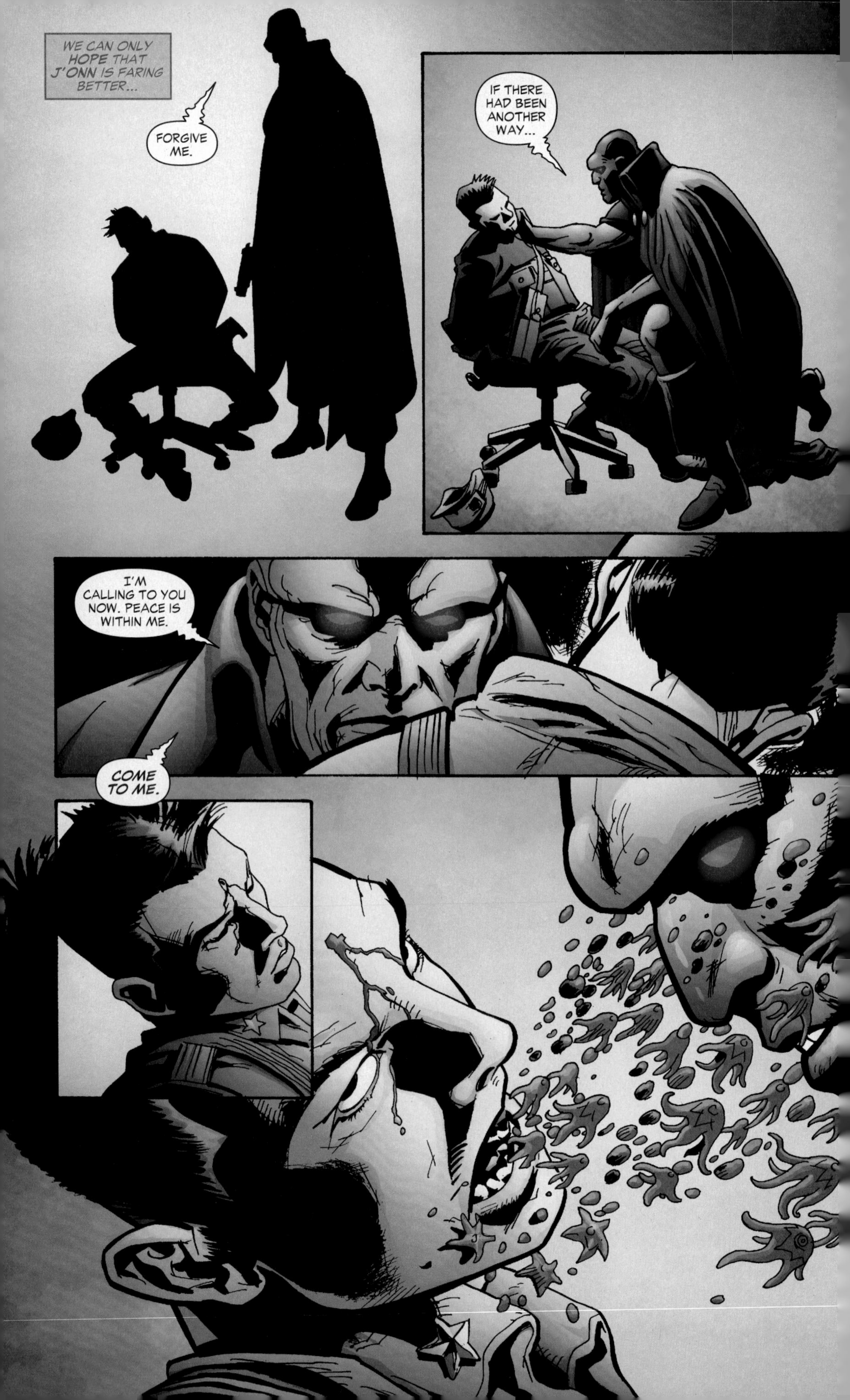

WE CAN ONLY HOPE THAT J'ONN IS FARING BETTER...
FORGIVE ME.
IF THERE HAD BEEN ANOTHER WAY...
I'M CALLING TO YOU NOW. PEACE IS WITHIN ME.
COME TO ME.

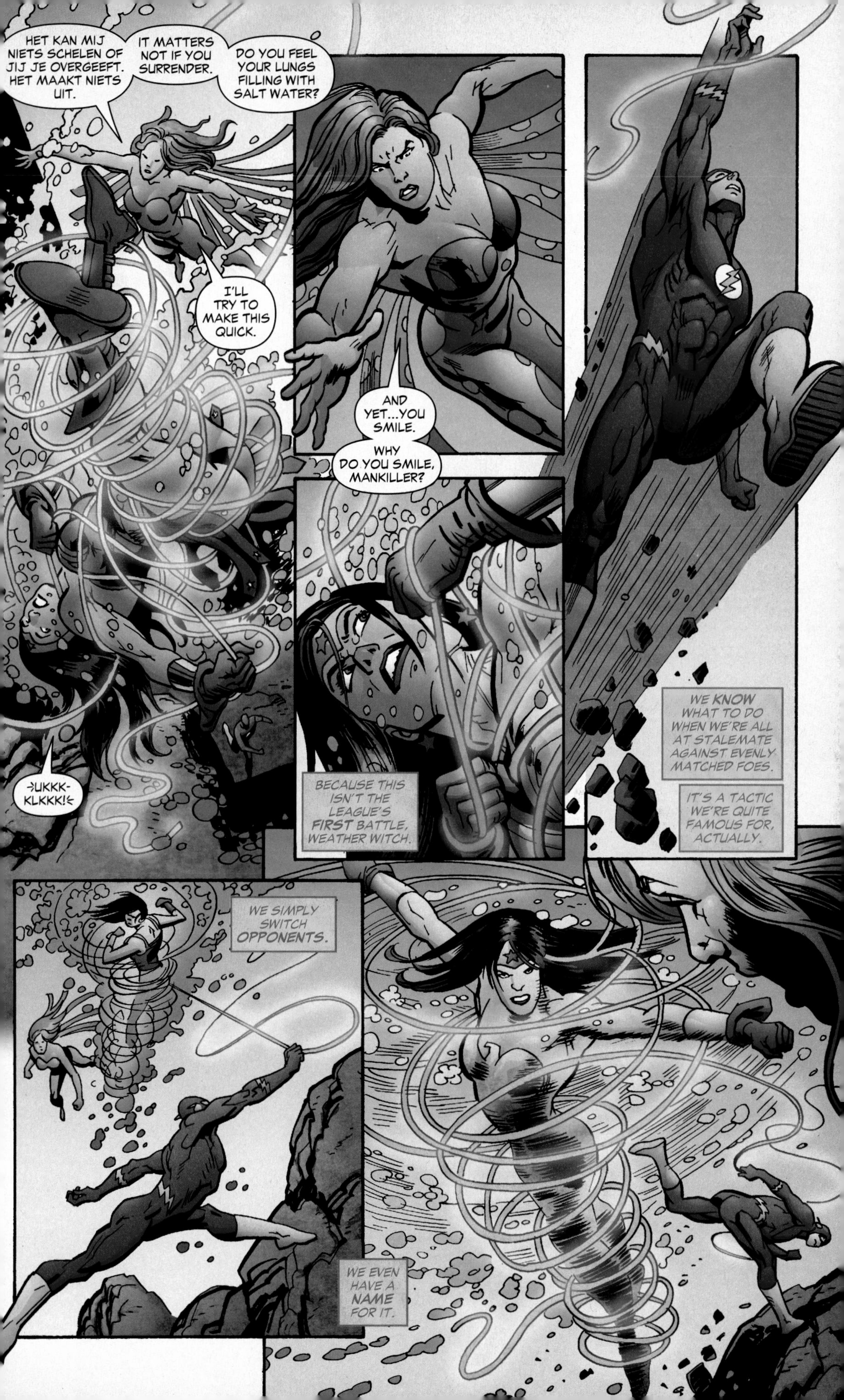
HET KAN MIJ NIETS SCHELEN OF JIJ JE OVERGEEFT. HET MAAKT NIETS UIT.
IT MATTERS NOT IF YOU SURRENDER.
DO YOU FEEL YOUR LUNGS FILLING WITH SALT WATER?
I'LL TRY TO MAKE THIS QUICK.
-UKKK-KLKKK!-
AND YET...YOU SMILE.
WHY DO YOU SMILE, MANKILLER?
BECAUSE THIS ISN'T THE LEAGUE'S FIRST BATTLE, WEATHER WITCH.
WE KNOW WHAT TO DO WHEN WE'RE ALL AT STALEMATE AGAINST EVENLY MATCHED FOES.
IT'S A TACTIC WE'RE QUITE FAMOUS FOR, ACTUALLY.
WE SIMPLY SWITCH OPPONENTS.
WE EVEN HAVE A NAME FOR IT.

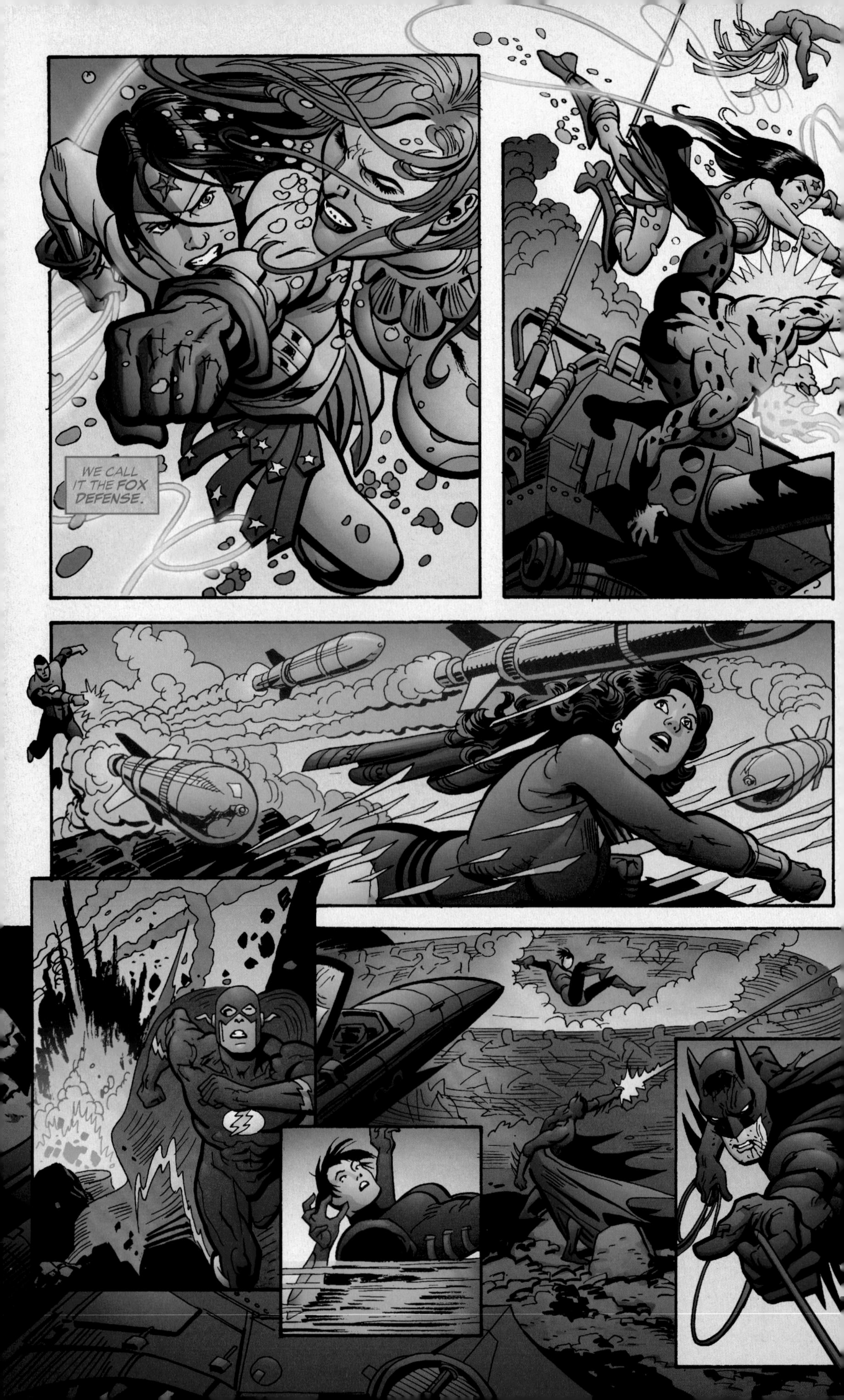
WE CALL IT THE FOX DEFENSE.

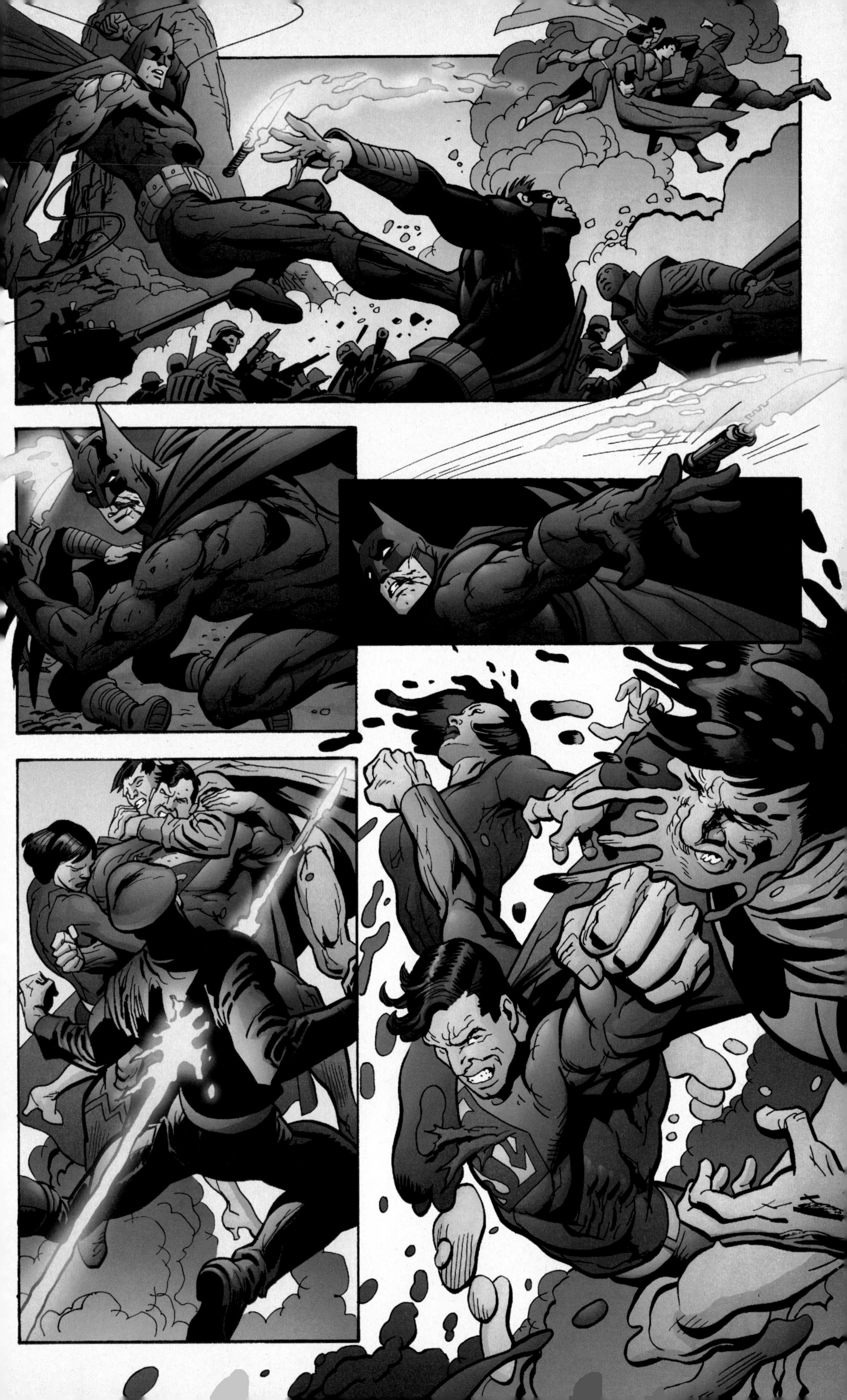

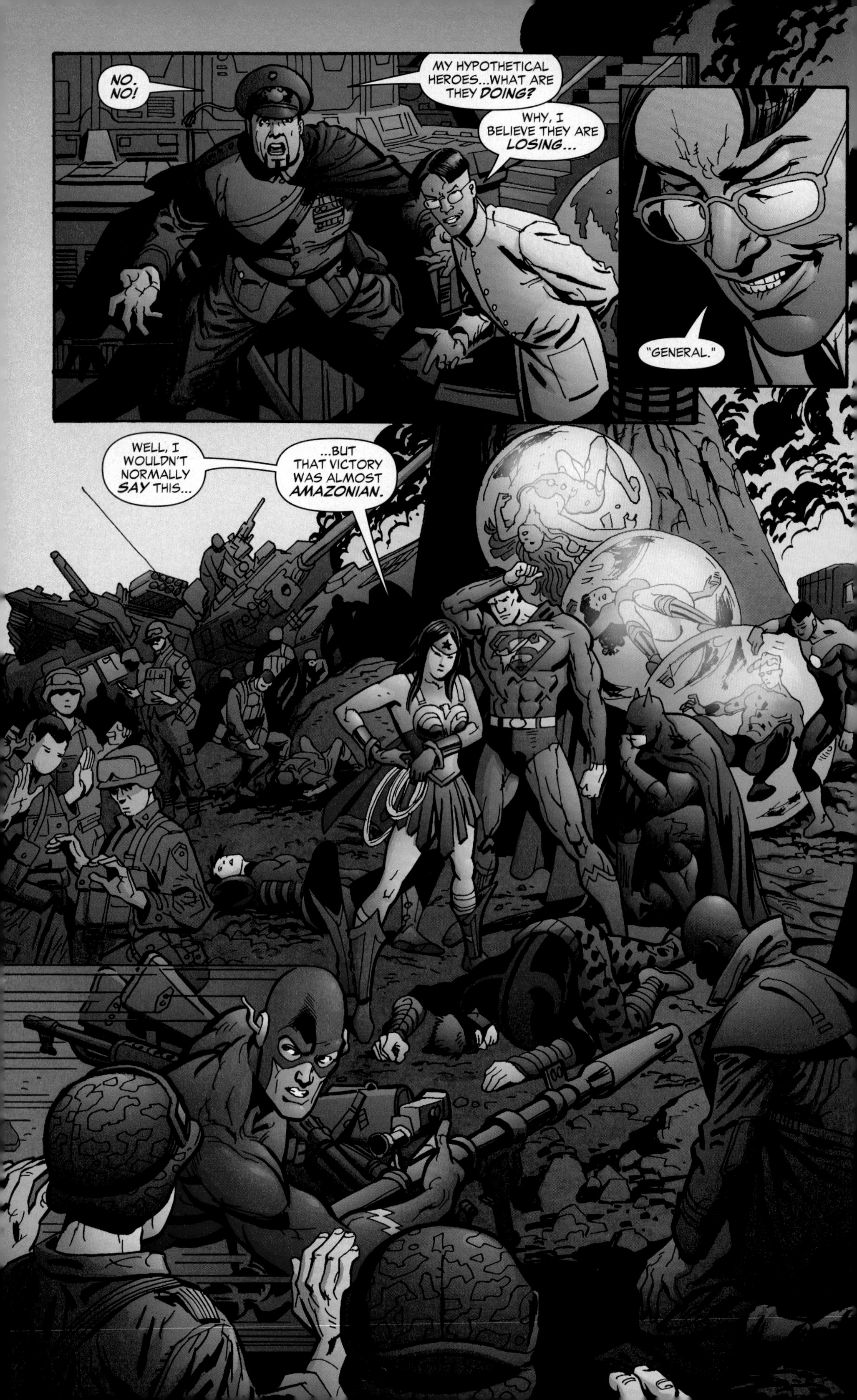
NO. NO!
MY HYPOTHETICAL HEROES...WHAT ARE THEY DOING?
WHY, I BELIEVE THEY ARE LOSING...
"GENERAL."
WELL, I WOULDN'T NORMALLY SAY THIS...
...BUT THAT VICTORY WAS ALMOST AMAZONIAN.

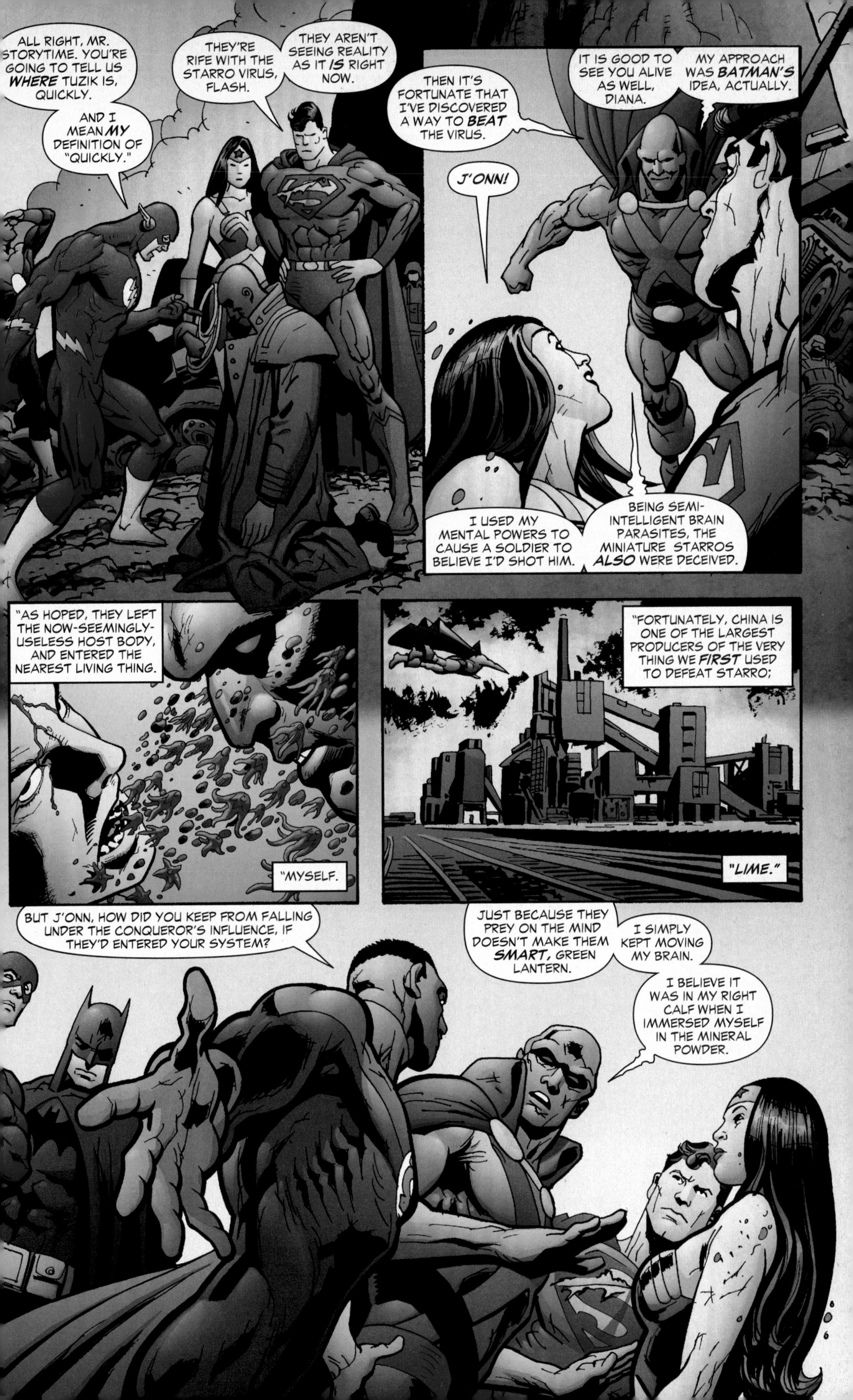
ALL RIGHT, MR. STORYTIME. YOU'RE GOING TO TELL US WHERE TUZIK IS, QUICKLY.
AND I MEAN MY DEFINITION OF "QUICKLY."
THEY'RE RIFE WITH THE STARRO VIRUS, FLASH.
THEY AREN'T SEEING REALITY AS IT IS RIGHT NOW.
THEN IT'S FORTUNATE THAT I'VE DISCOVERED A WAY TO BEAT THE VIRUS.
J'ONN!
IT IS GOOD TO SEE YOU ALIVE AS WELL, DIANA.
MY APPROACH WAS BATMAN'S IDEA, ACTUALLY.
I USED MY MENTAL POWERS TO CAUSE A SOLDIER TO BELIEVE I'D SHOT HIM.
BEING SEMI-INTELLIGENT BRAIN PARASITES, THE MINIATURE STARROS ALSO WERE DECEIVED.
"AS HOPED, THEY LEFT THE NOW-SEEMINGLY-USELESS HOST BODY, AND ENTERED THE NEAREST LIVING THING.
"MYSELF.
"FORTUNATELY, CHINA IS ONE OF THE LARGEST PRODUCERS OF THE VERY THING WE FIRST USED TO DEFEAT STARRO;
"LIME."
BUT J'ONN, HOW DID YOU KEEP FROM FALLING UNDER THE CONQUEROR'S INFLUENCE, IF THEY'D ENTERED YOUR SYSTEM?
JUST BECAUSE THEY PREY ON THE MIND DOESN'T MAKE THEM SMART, GREEN LANTERN.
I SIMPLY KEPT MOVING MY BRAIN.
I BELIEVE IT WAS IN MY RIGHT CALF WHEN I IMMERSED MYSELF IN THE MINERAL POWDER.
6

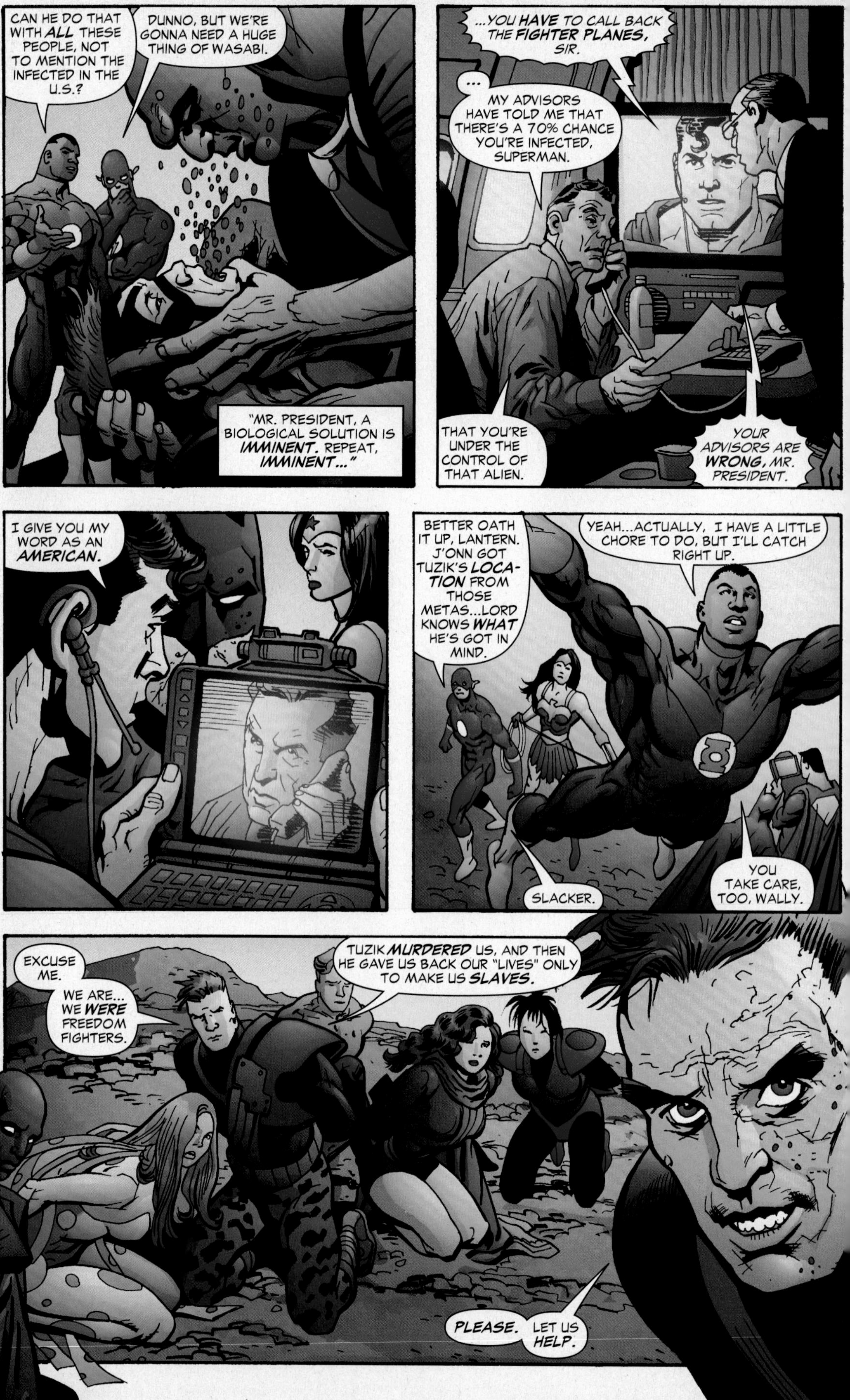
CAN HE DO THAT WITH ALL THESE PEOPLE, NOT TO MENTION THE INFECTED IN THE U.S.?
DUNNO, BUT WE'RE GONNA NEED A HUGE THING OF WASABI.
"MR. PRESIDENT, A BIOLOGICAL SOLUTION IS IMMINENT. REPEAT, IMMINENT..."
...YOU HAVE TO CALL BACK THE FIGHTER PLANES, SIR.
...
MY ADVISORS HAVE TOLD ME THAT THERE'S A 70% CHANCE YOU'RE INFECTED, SUPERMAN.
THAT YOU'RE UNDER THE CONTROL OF THAT ALIEN.
YOUR ADVISORS ARE WRONG, MR. PRESIDENT.
I GIVE YOU MY WORD AS AN AMERICAN.
BETTER OATH IT UP, LANTERN. J'ONN GOT TUZIK'S LOCATION FROM THOSE METAS...LORD KNOWS WHAT HE'S GOT IN MIND.
YEAH...ACTUALLY, I HAVE A LITTLE CHORE TO DO, BUT I'LL CATCH RIGHT UP.
SLACKER.
YOU TAKE CARE, TOO, WALLY.
EXCUSE ME.
WE ARE... WE WERE FREEDOM FIGHTERS.
TUZIK MURDERED US, AND THEN HE GAVE US BACK OUR "LIVES" ONLY TO MAKE US SLAVES.
PLEASE. LET US HELP.

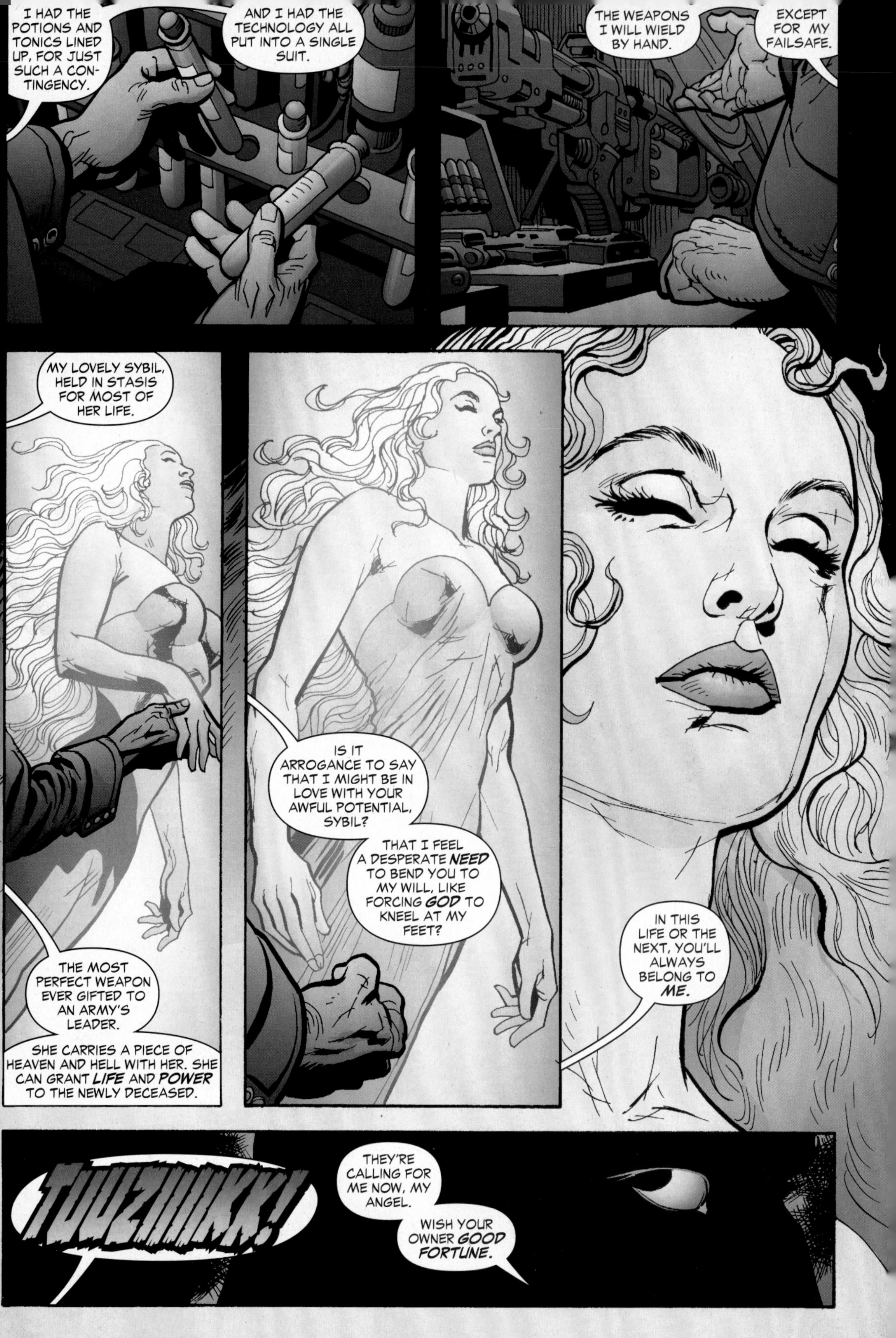
I HAD THE POTIONS AND TONICS LINED UP, FOR JUST SUCH A CON-TINGENCY.
AND I HAD THE TECHNOLOGY ALL PUT INTO A SINGLE SUIT.
THE WEAPONS I WILL WIELD BY HAND.
EXCEPT FOR MY FAILSAFE.
MY LOVELY SYBIL, HELD IN STASIS FOR MOST OF HER LIFE.
THE MOST PERFECT WEAPON EVER GIFTED TO AN ARMY'S LEADER.
SHE CARRIES A PIECE OF HEAVEN AND HELL WITH HER. SHE CAN GRANT LIFE AND POWER TO THE NEWLY DECEASED.
IS IT ARROGANCE TO SAY THAT I MIGHT BE IN LOVE WITH YOUR AWFUL POTENTIAL, SYBIL?
THAT I FEEL A DESPERATE NEED TO BEND YOU TO MY WILL, LIKE FORCING GOD TO KNEEL AT MY FEET?
IN THIS LIFE OR THE NEXT, YOU'LL ALWAYS BELONG TO ME.
TUUZHHKK!
THEY'RE CALLING FOR ME NOW, MY ANGEL.
WISH YOUR OWNER GOOD FORTUNE.

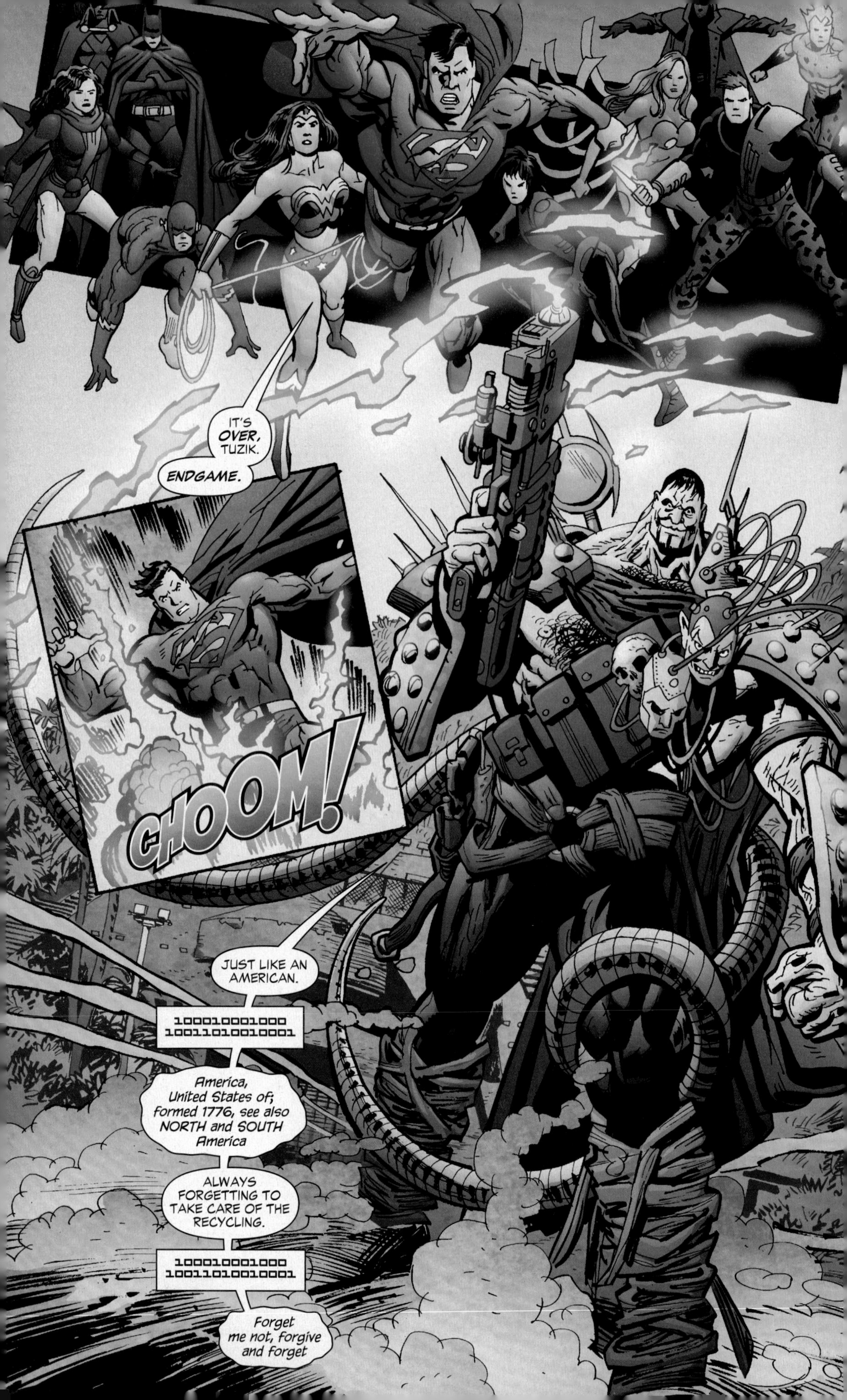
IT'S OVER, TUZIK.
ENDGAME.
CHOOM!
JUST LIKE AN AMERICAN.
100010001000
10011010010001
America, United States of; formed 1776, see also NORTH and SOUTH America
ALWAYS FORGETTING TO TAKE CARE OF THE RECYCLING.
100010001000
10011010010001
Forget me not, forgive and forget

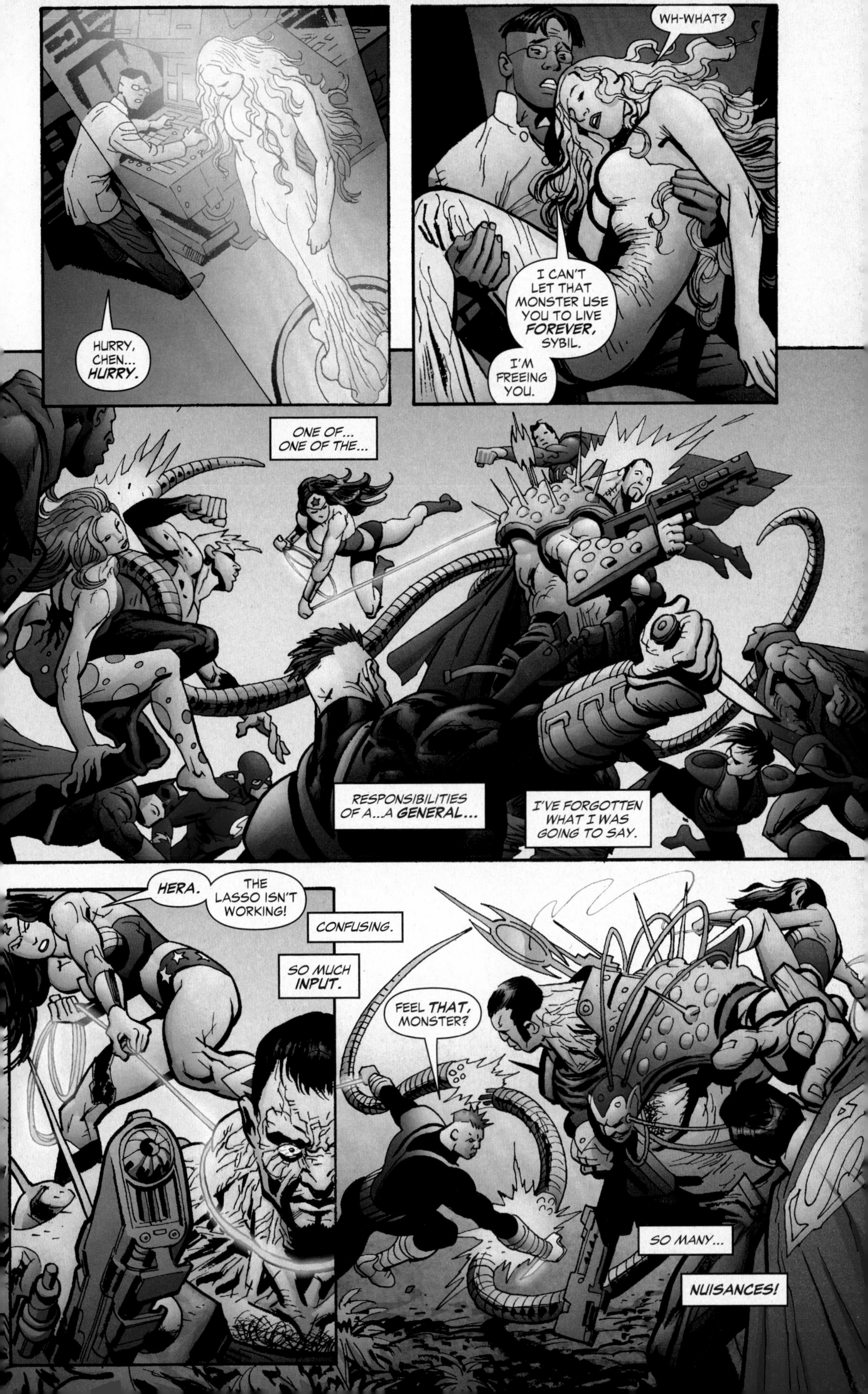

HURRY, CHEN... HURRY.
WH-WHAT?
I CAN'T LET THAT MONSTER USE YOU TO LIVE FOREVER, SYBIL.
I'M FREEING YOU.
ONE OF... ONE OF THE...
RESPONSIBILITIES OF A...A GENERAL...
I'VE FORGOTTEN WHAT I WAS GOING TO SAY.
HERA.
THE LASSO ISN'T WORKING!
CONFUSING.
SO MUCH INPUT.
FEEL THAT, MONSTER?
SO MANY...
NUISANCES!

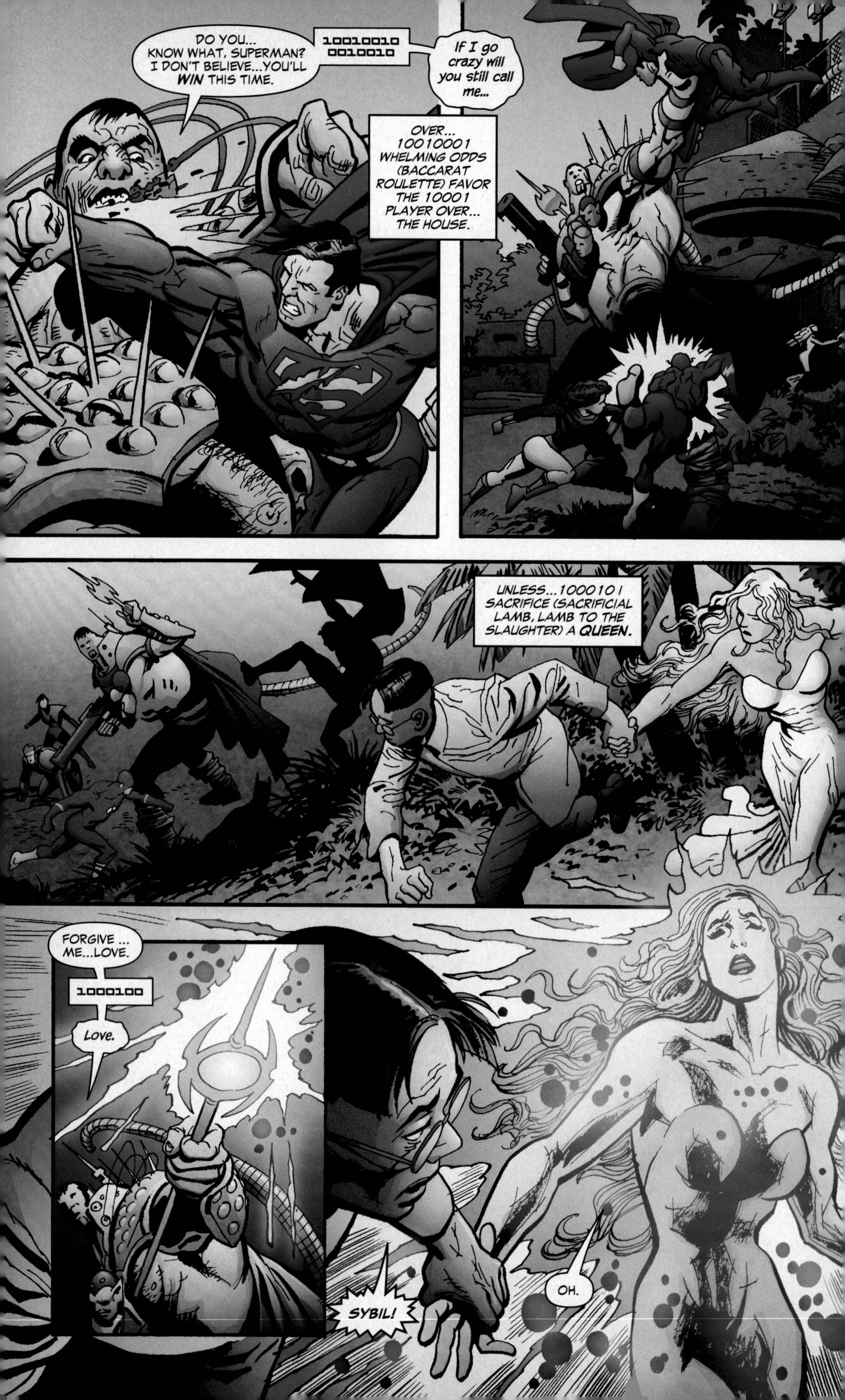
DO YOU... KNOW WHAT, SUPERMAN? I DON'T BELIEVE...YOU'LL WIN THIS TIME.
10010010 0010010
If I go crazy will you still call me...
OVER... 10010001 WHELMING ODDS (BACCARAT ROULETTE) FAVOR THE 10001 PLAYER OVER... THE HOUSE.
UNLESS...100010 I SACRIFICE (SACRIFICIAL LAMB, LAMB TO THE SLAUGHTER) A QUEEN.
FORGIVE ... ME...LOVE.
1000100
Love.
SYBIL!
OH.

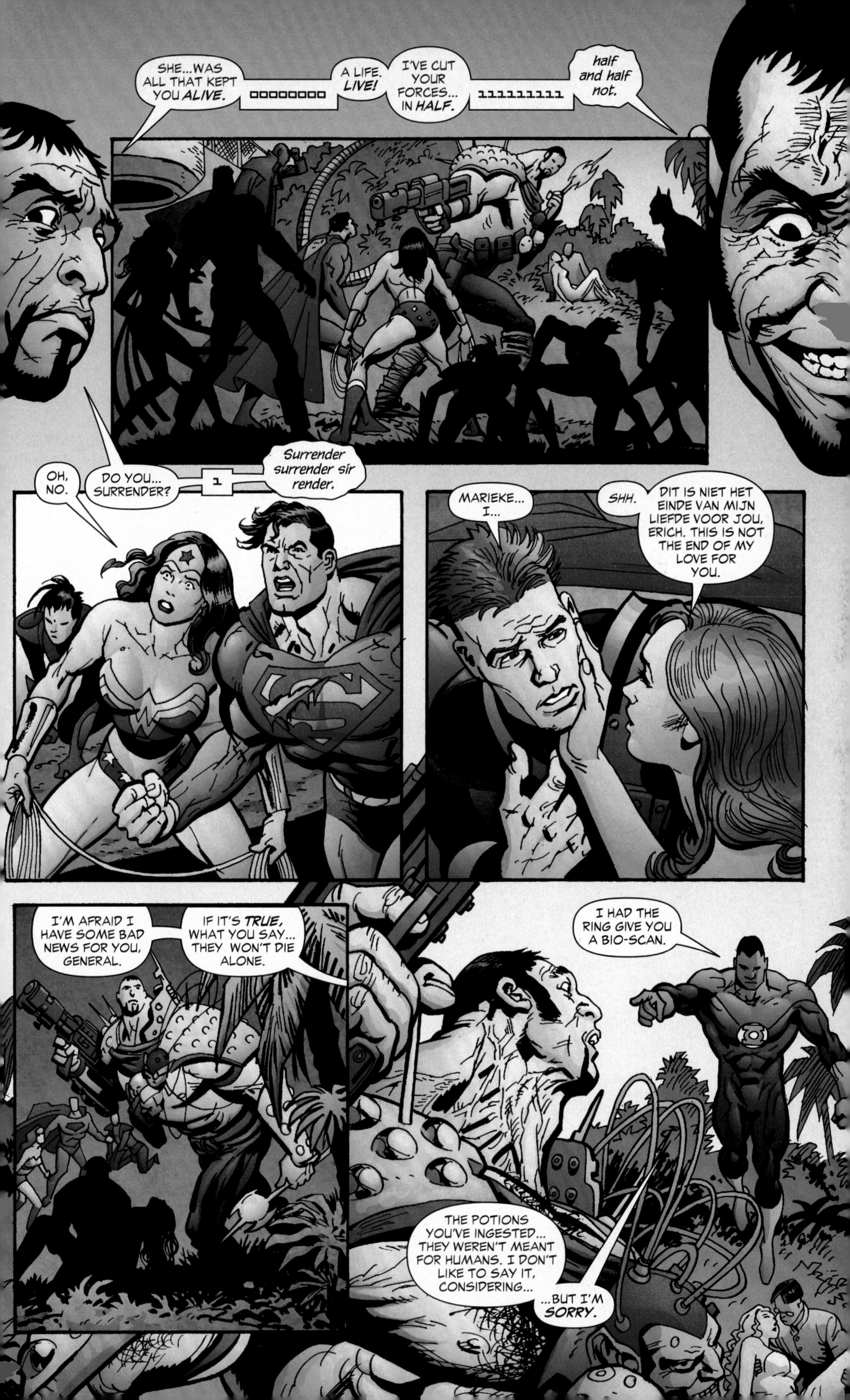
SHE...WAS ALL THAT KEPT YOU ALIVE.
oooooooo
A LIFE. LIVE!
I'VE CUT YOUR FORCES... IN HALF.
11111111
half and half not.
DO YOU... SURRENDER?
1
Surrender surrender sir render.
OH, NO.
MARIEKE... I...
SHH.
DIT IS NIET HET EINDE VAN MIJN LIEFDE VOOR JOU, ERICH. THIS IS NOT THE END OF MY LOVE FOR YOU.
I'M AFRAID I HAVE SOME BAD NEWS FOR YOU, GENERAL.
IF IT'S TRUE, WHAT YOU SAY... THEY WON'T DIE ALONE.
I HAD THE RING GIVE YOU A BIO-SCAN.
THE POTIONS YOU'VE INGESTED... THEY WEREN'T MEANT FOR HUMANS. I DON'T LIKE TO SAY IT, CONSIDERING...
...BUT I'M SORRY.

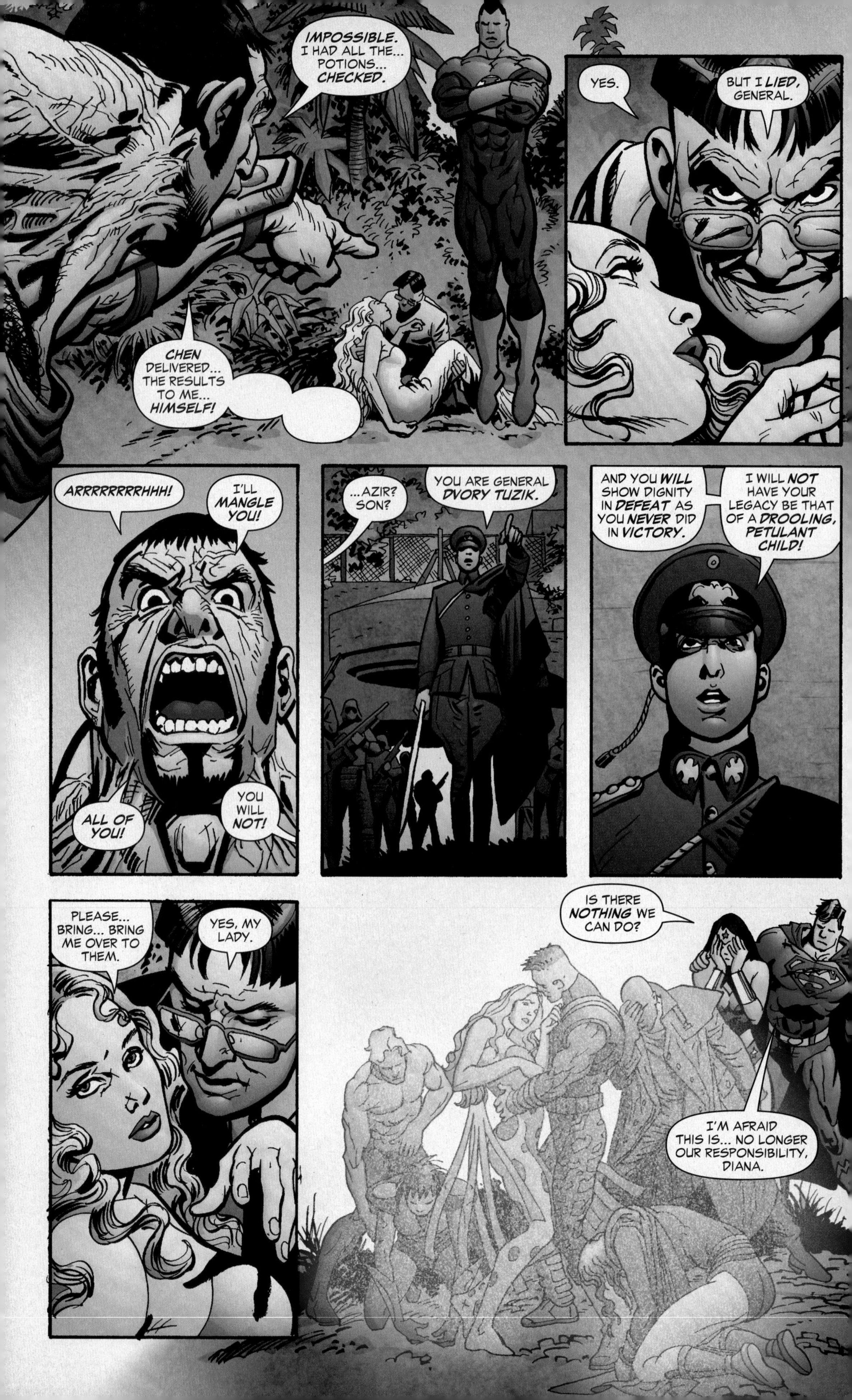
IMPOSSIBLE. I HAD ALL THE... POTIONS... CHECKED.
CHEN DELIVERED... THE RESULTS TO ME... HIMSELF!
YES.
BUT I LIED, GENERAL.
ARRRRRRRRHHH!
I'LL MANGLE YOU!
ALL OF YOU!
YOU WILL NOT!
...AZIR? SON?
YOU ARE GENERAL DVORY TUZIK.
AND YOU WILL SHOW DIGNITY IN DEFEAT AS YOU NEVER DID IN VICTORY.
I WILL NOT HAVE YOUR LEGACY BE THAT OF A DROOLING, PETULANT CHILD!
PLEASE... BRING... BRING ME OVER TO THEM.
YES, MY LADY.
IS THERE NOTHING WE CAN DO?
I'M AFRAID THIS IS... NO LONGER OUR RESPONSIBILITY, DIANA.

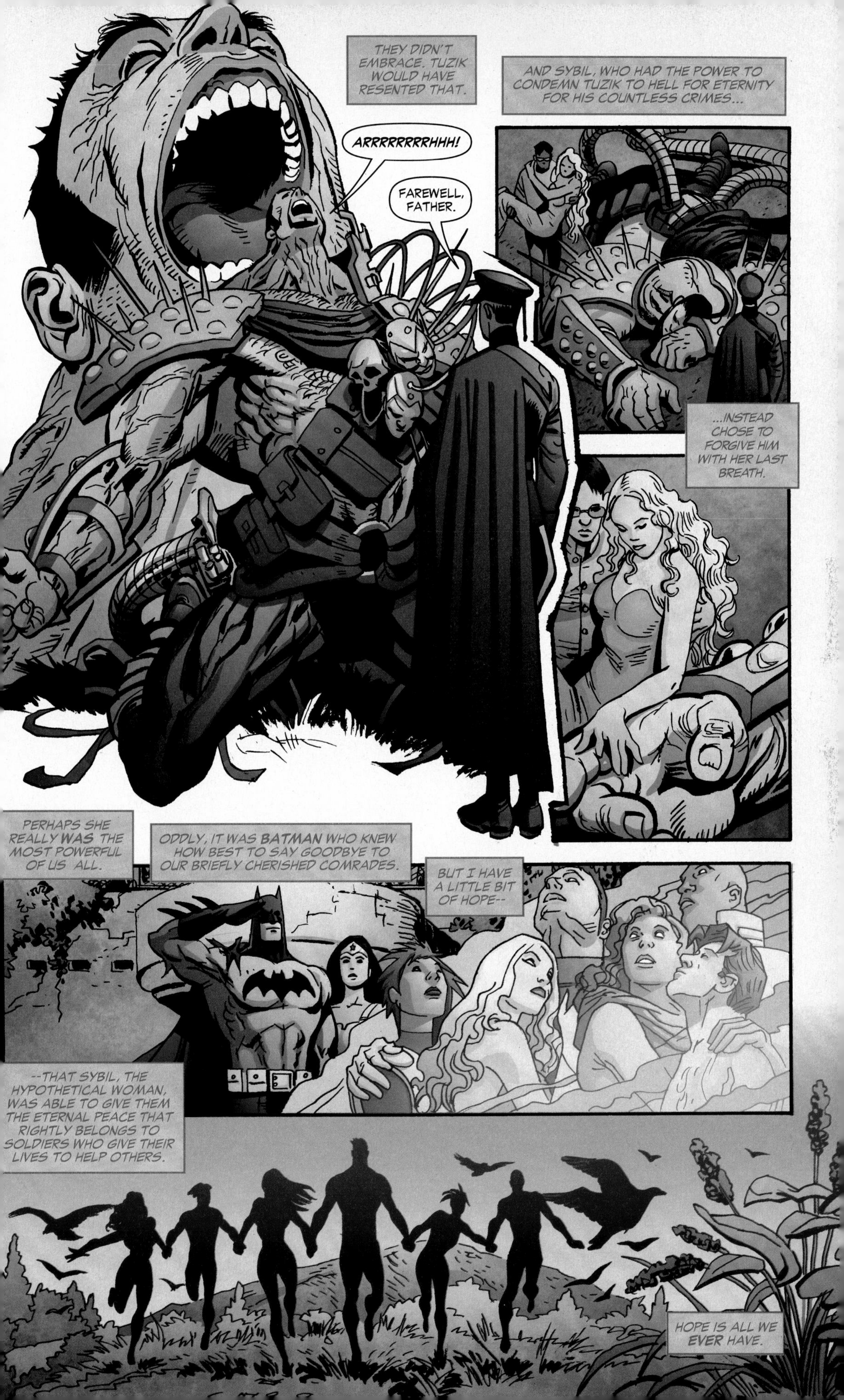
THEY DIDN'T EMBRACE. TUZIK WOULD HAVE RESENTED THAT.
ARRRRRRRRHHH!
FAREWELL, FATHER.
AND SYBIL, WHO HAD THE POWER TO CONDEMN TUZIK TO HELL FOR ETERNITY FOR HIS COUNTLESS CRIMES...
...INSTEAD CHOSE TO FORGIVE HIM WITH HER LAST BREATH.
PERHAPS SHE REALLY WAS THE MOST POWERFUL OF US ALL.
ODDLY, IT WAS BATMAN WHO KNEW HOW BEST TO SAY GOODBYE TO OUR BRIEFLY CHERISHED COMRADES.
BUT I HAVE A LITTLE BIT OF HOPE--
--THAT SYBIL, THE HYPOTHETICAL WOMAN, WAS ABLE TO GIVE THEM THE ETERNAL PEACE THAT RIGHTLY BELONGS TO SOLDIERS WHO GIVE THEIR LIVES TO HELP OTHERS.
HOPE IS ALL WE EVER HAVE.

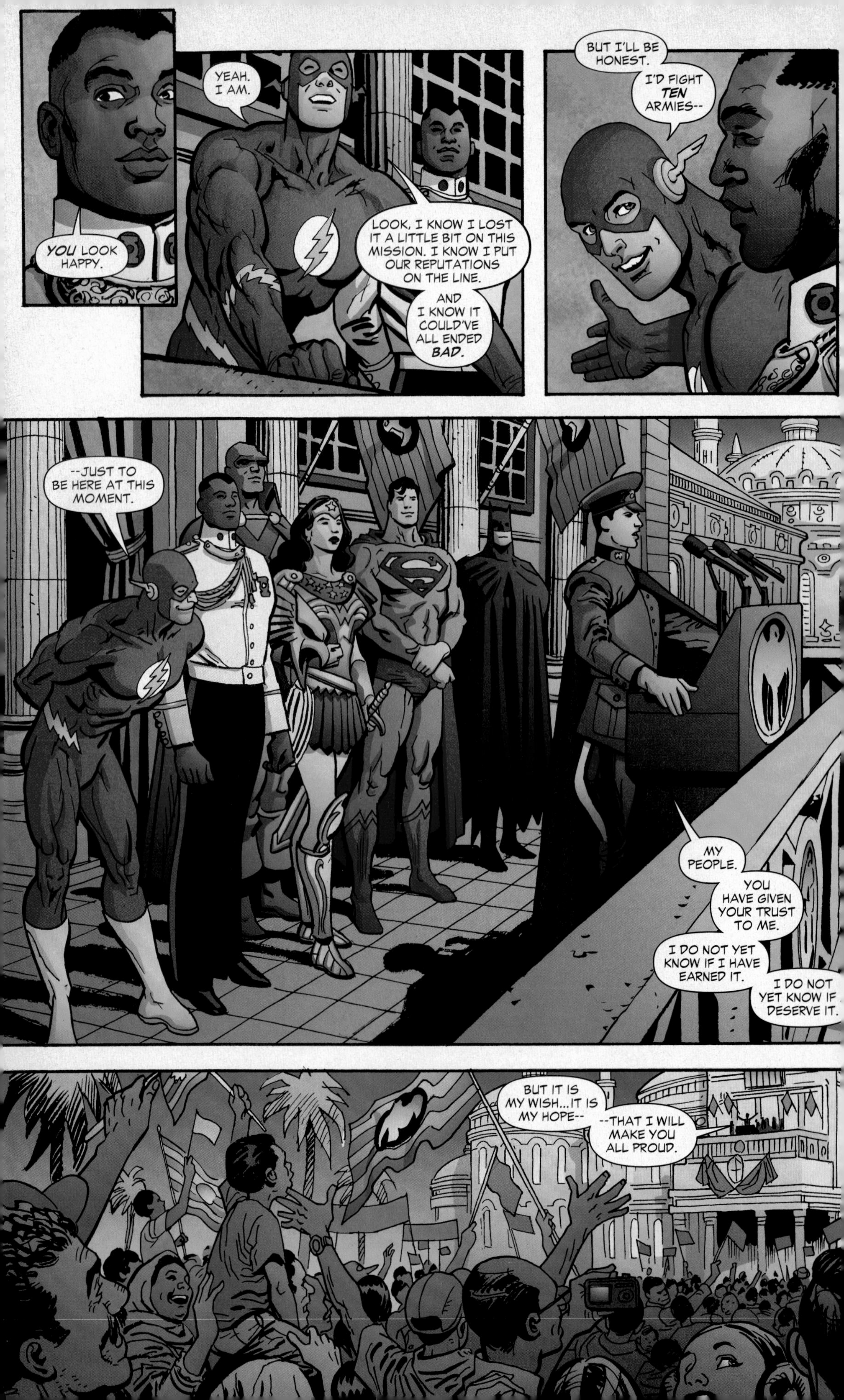
YOU LOOK HAPPY.
YEAH. I AM.
LOOK, I KNOW I LOST IT A LITTLE BIT ON THIS MISSION. I KNOW I PUT OUR REPUTATIONS ON THE LINE.
AND I KNOW IT COULD'VE ALL ENDED BAD.
BUT I'LL BE HONEST.
I'D FIGHT TEN ARMIES--
--JUST TO BE HERE AT THIS MOMENT.
MY PEOPLE.
YOU HAVE GIVEN YOUR TRUST TO ME.
I DO NOT YET KNOW IF I HAVE EARNED IT.
I DO NOT YET KNOW IF DESERVE IT.
BUT IT IS MY WISH...IT IS MY HOPE--
--THAT I WILL MAKE YOU ALL PROUD.

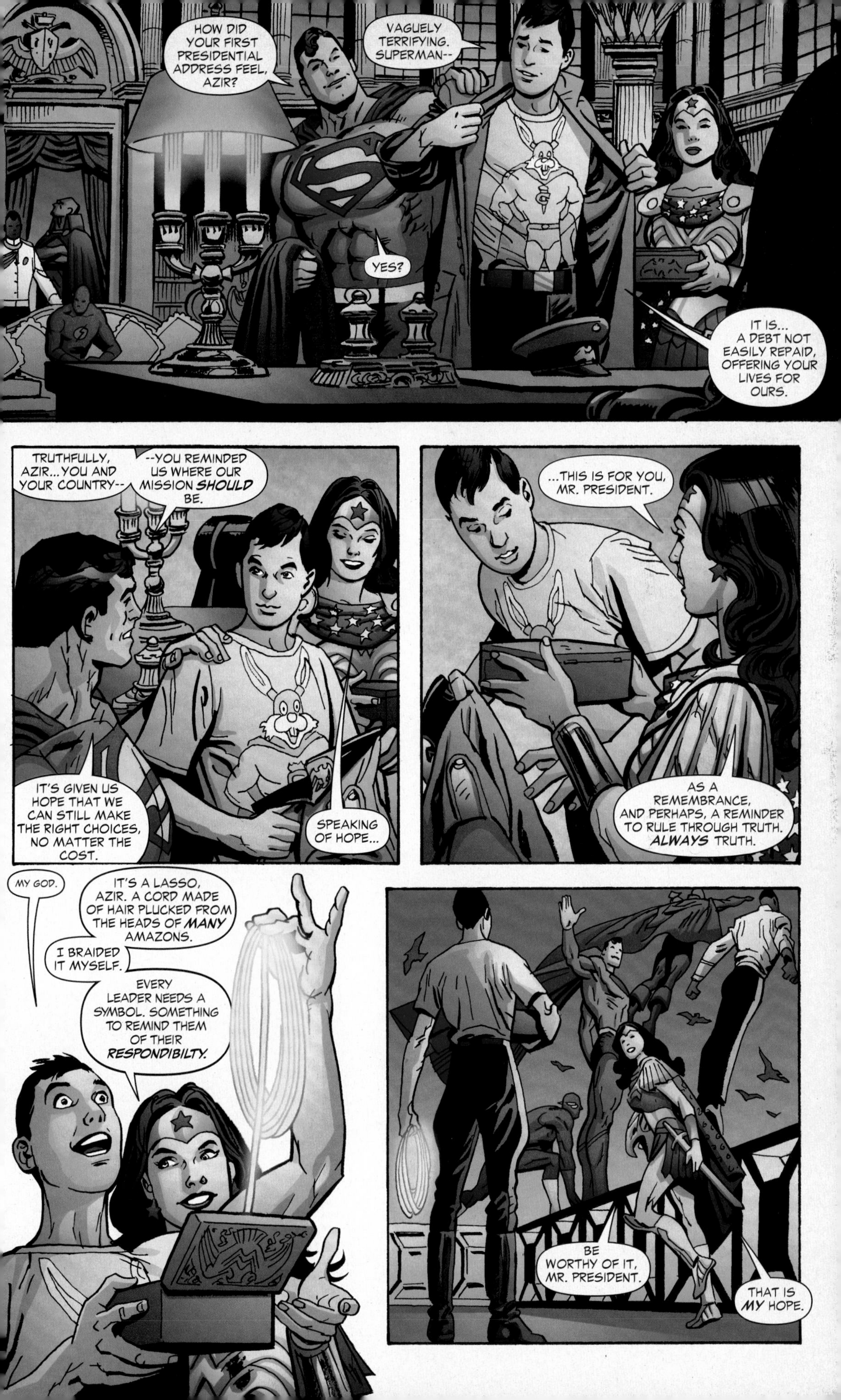

HOW DID YOUR FIRST PRESIDENTIAL ADDRESS FEEL, AZIR?
VAGUELY TERRIFYING. SUPERMAN--
YES?
IT IS... A DEBT NOT EASILY REPAID, OFFERING YOUR LIVES FOR OURS.
TRUTHFULLY, AZIR...YOU AND YOUR COUNTRY--
--YOU REMINDED US WHERE OUR MISSION SHOULD BE.
IT'S GIVEN US HOPE THAT WE CAN STILL MAKE THE RIGHT CHOICES, NO MATTER THE COST.
SPEAKING OF HOPE...
...THIS IS FOR YOU, MR. PRESIDENT.
AS A REMEMBRANCE, AND PERHAPS, A REMINDER TO RULE THROUGH TRUTH. ALWAYS TRUTH.
MY GOD.
IT'S A LASSO, AZIR. A CORD MADE OF HAIR PLUCKED FROM THE HEADS OF MANY AMAZONS.
I BRAIDED IT MYSELF.
EVERY LEADER NEEDS A SYMBOL. SOMETHING TO REMIND THEM OF THEIR RESPONDIBILTY.
BE WORTHY OF IT, MR. PRESIDENT.
THAT IS MY HOPE.

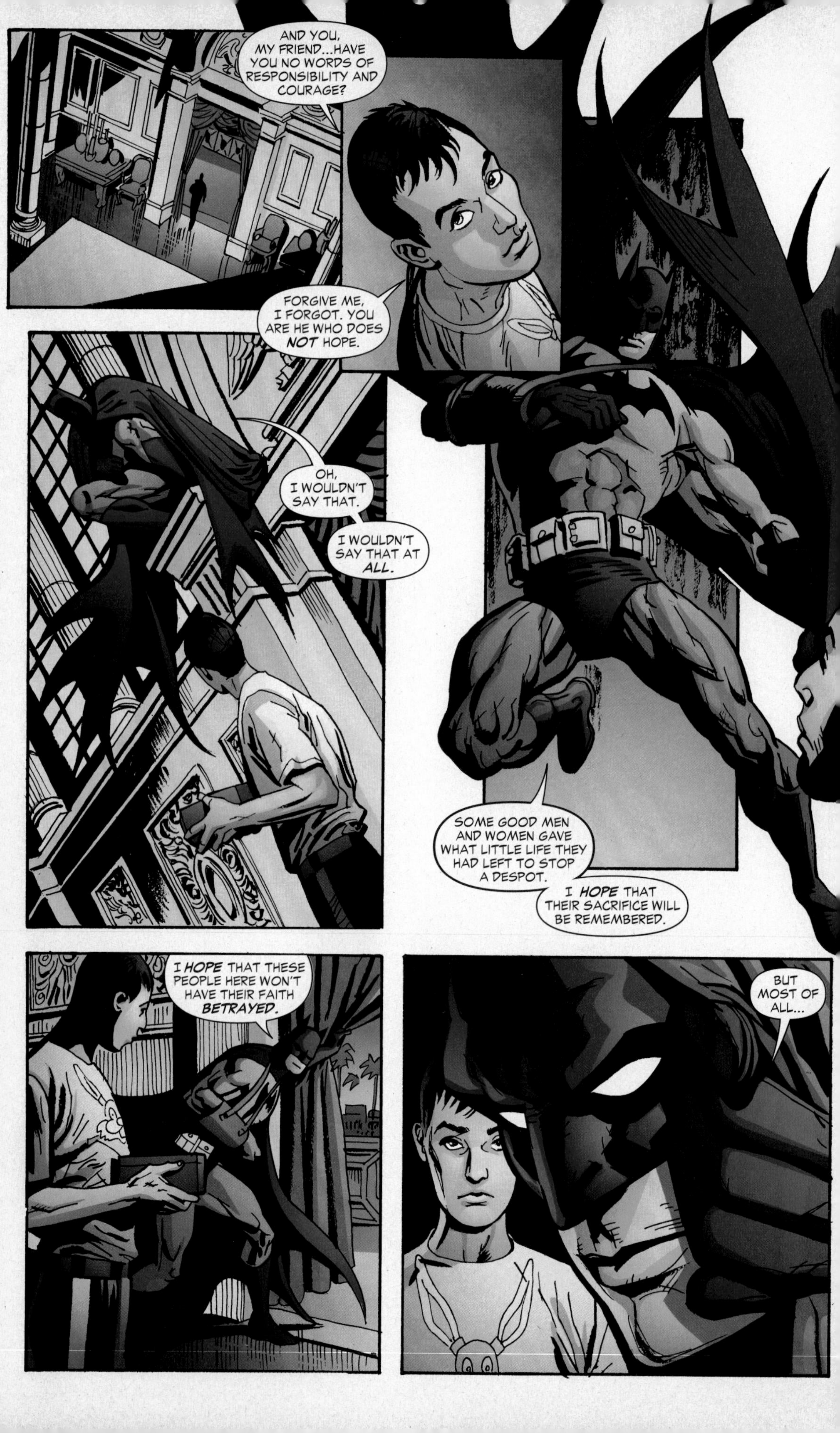

AND YOU, MY FRIEND...HAVE YOU NO WORDS OF RESPONSIBILITY AND COURAGE?
FORGIVE ME, I FORGOT. YOU ARE HE WHO DOES NOT HOPE.
OH, I WOULDN'T SAY THAT.
I WOULDN'T SAY THAT AT ALL.
SOME GOOD MEN AND WOMEN GAVE WHAT LITTLE LIFE THEY HAD LEFT TO STOP A DESPOT.
I HOPE THAT THEIR SACRIFICE WILL BE REMEMBERED.
I HOPE THAT THESE PEOPLE HERE WON'T HAVE THEIR FAITH BETRAYED.
BUT MOST OF ALL...

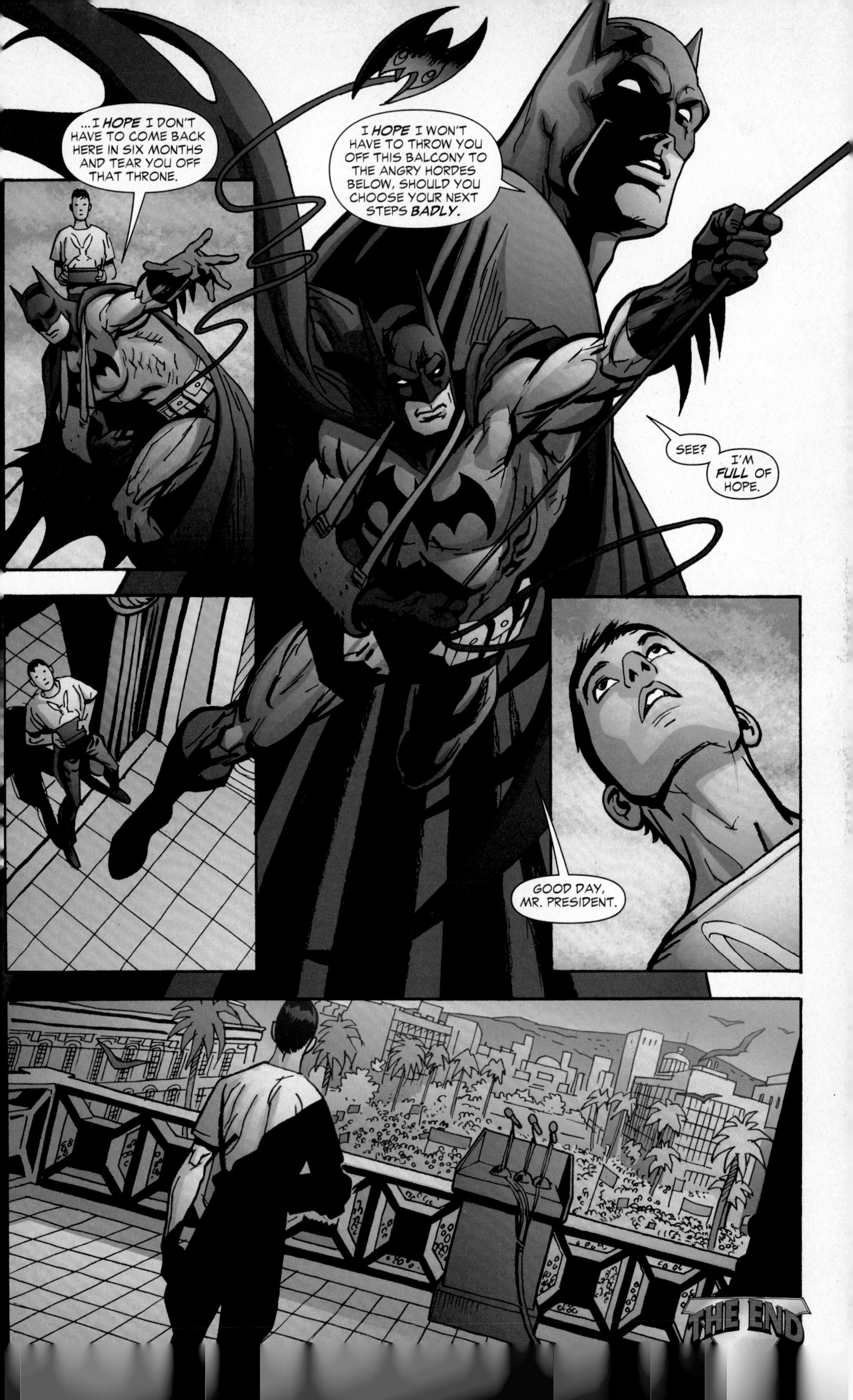
...I HOPE I DON'T HAVE TO COME BACK HERE IN SIX MONTHS AND TEAR YOU OFF THAT THRONE.
I HOPE I WON'T HAVE TO THROW YOU OFF THIS BALCONY TO THE ANGRY HORDES BELOW, SHOULD YOU CHOOSE YOUR NEXT STEPS BADLY.
SEE?
I'M FULL OF HOPE.
GOOD DAY, MR. PRESIDENT.
THE END

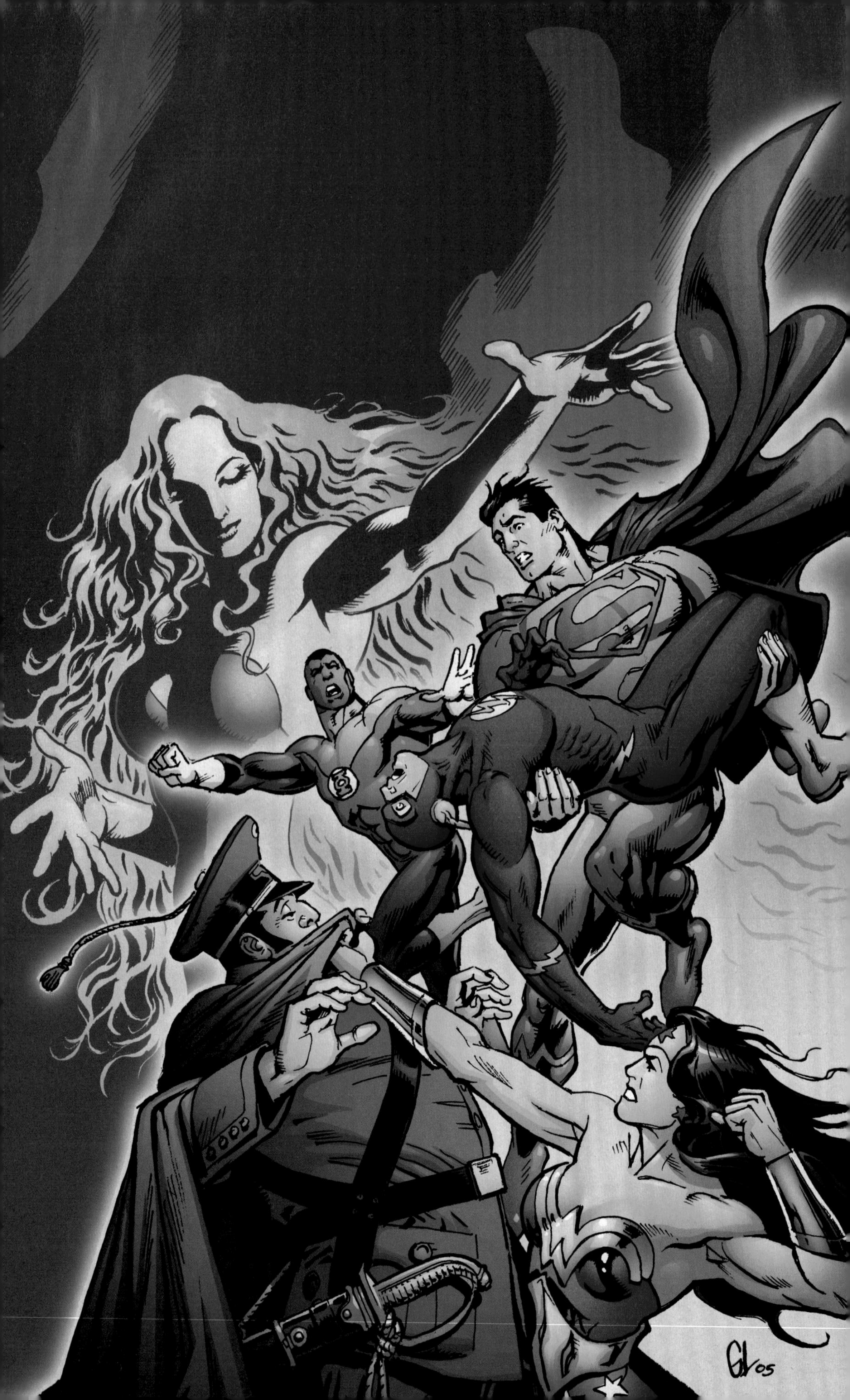

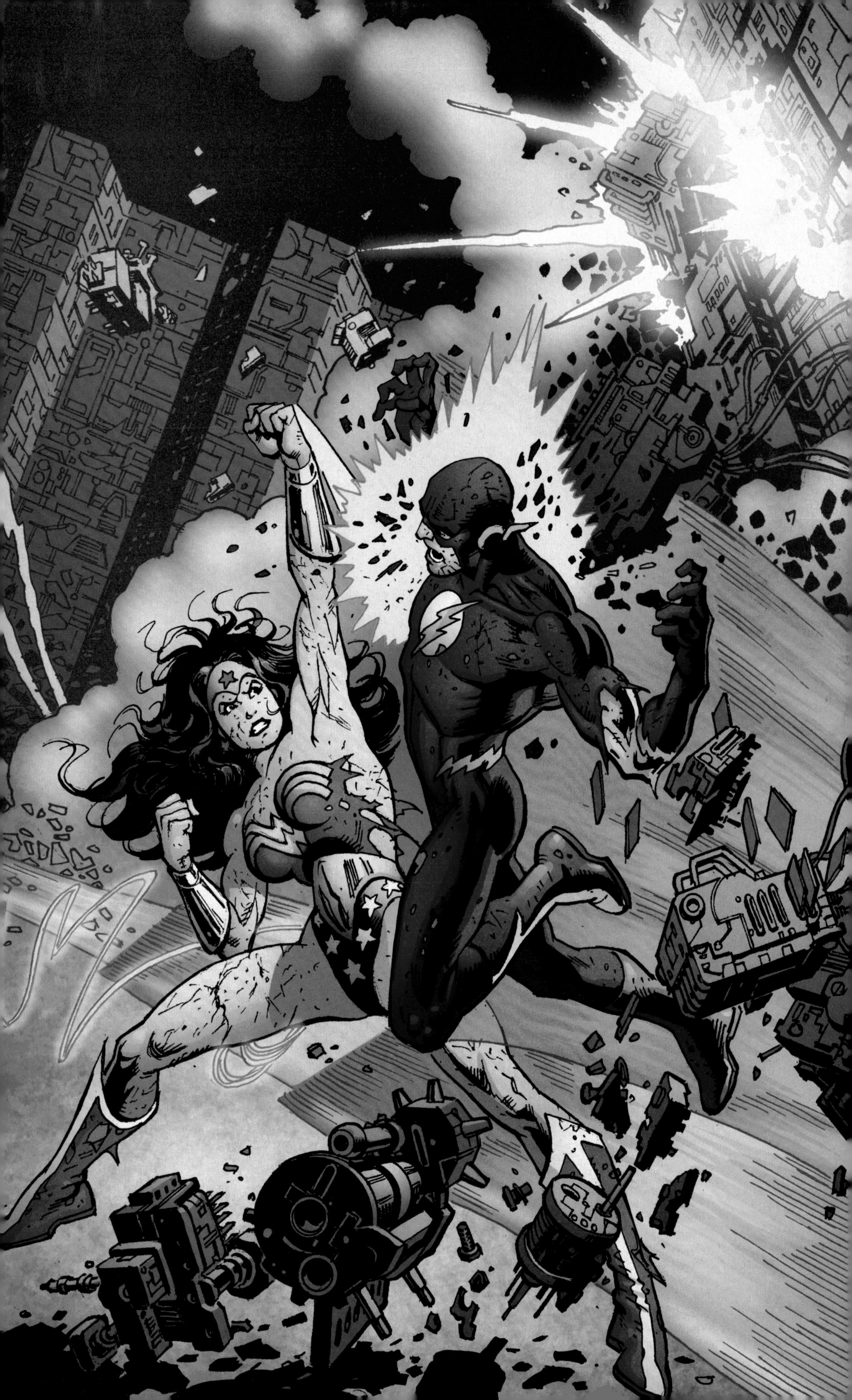

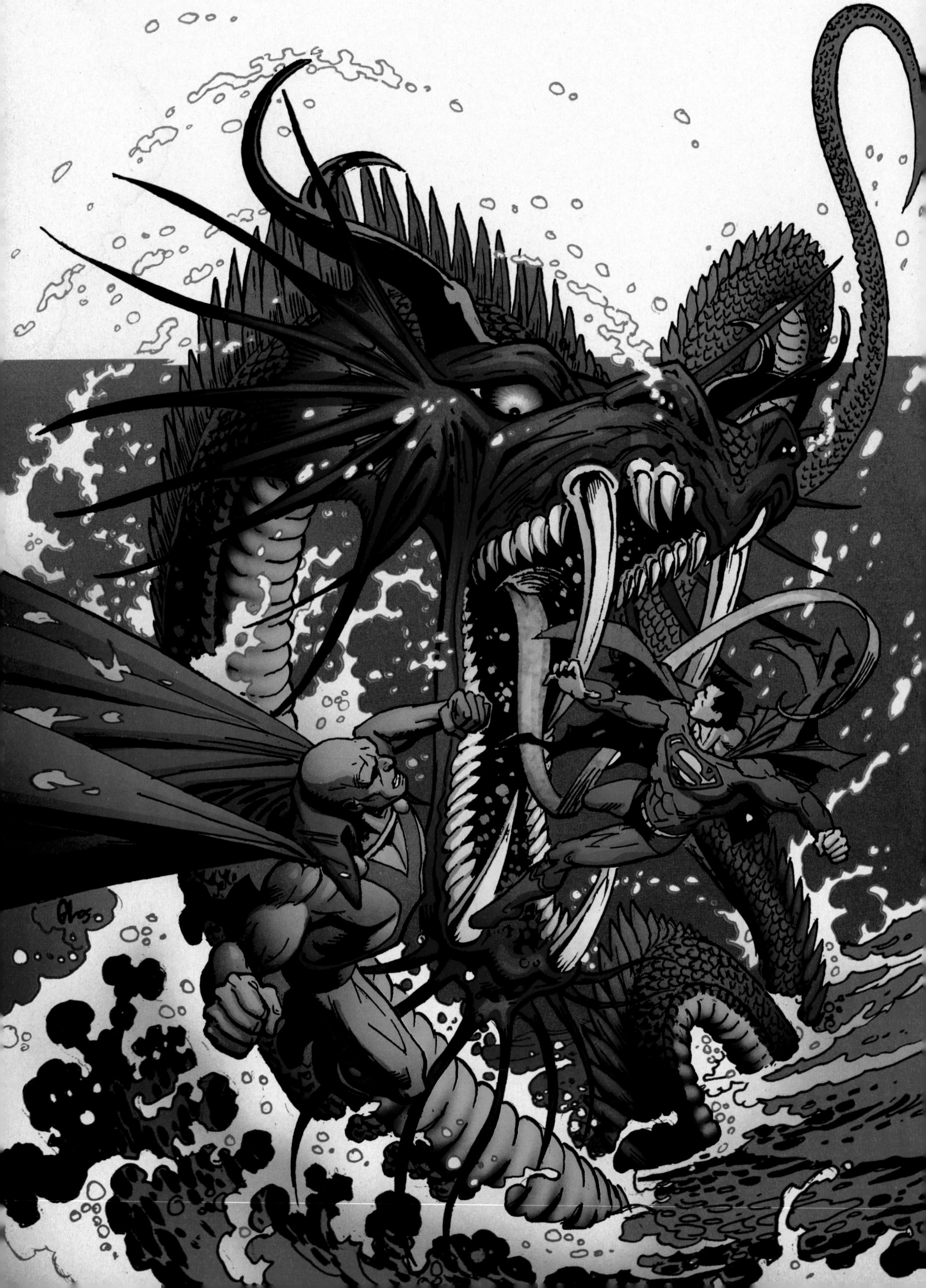

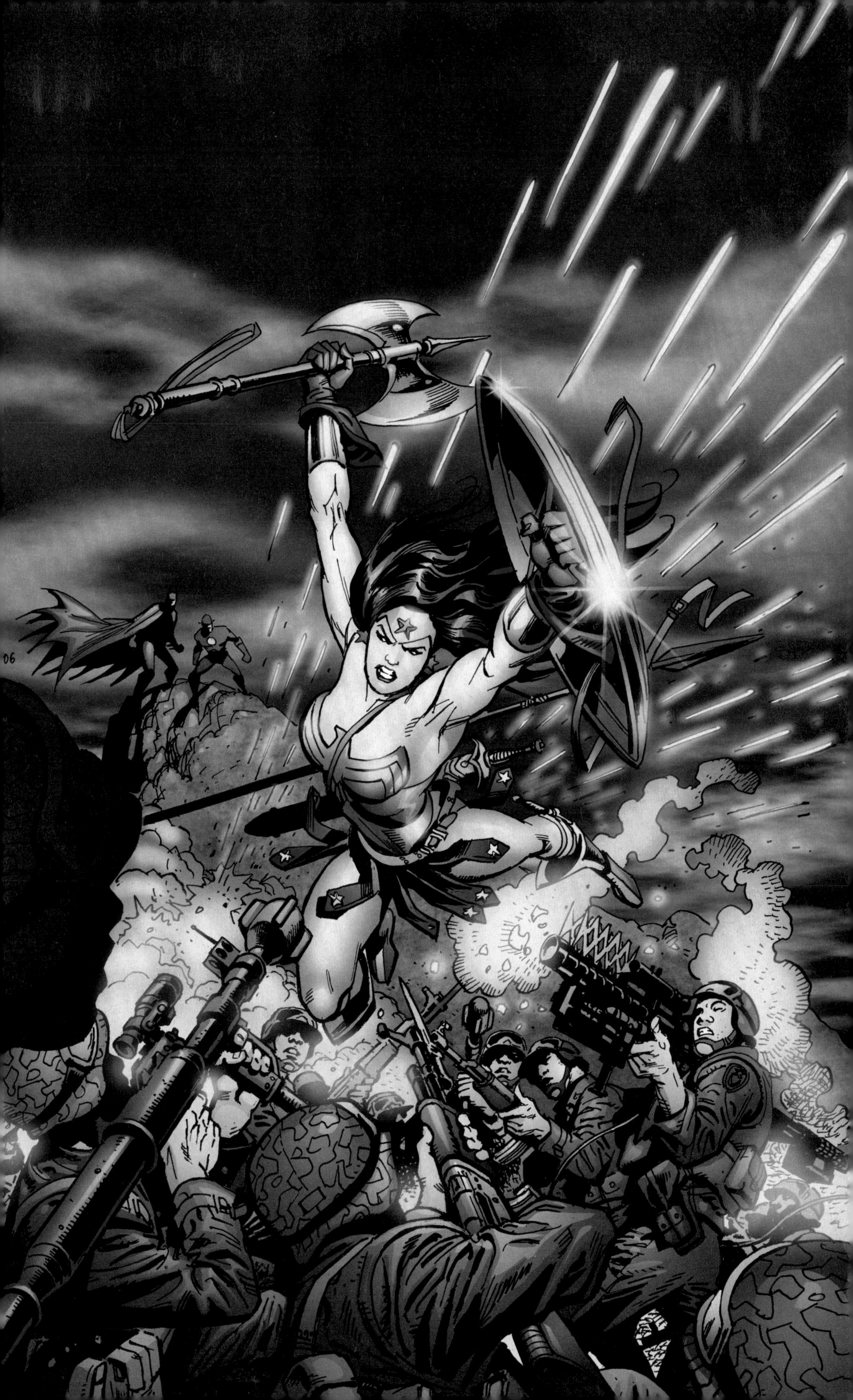

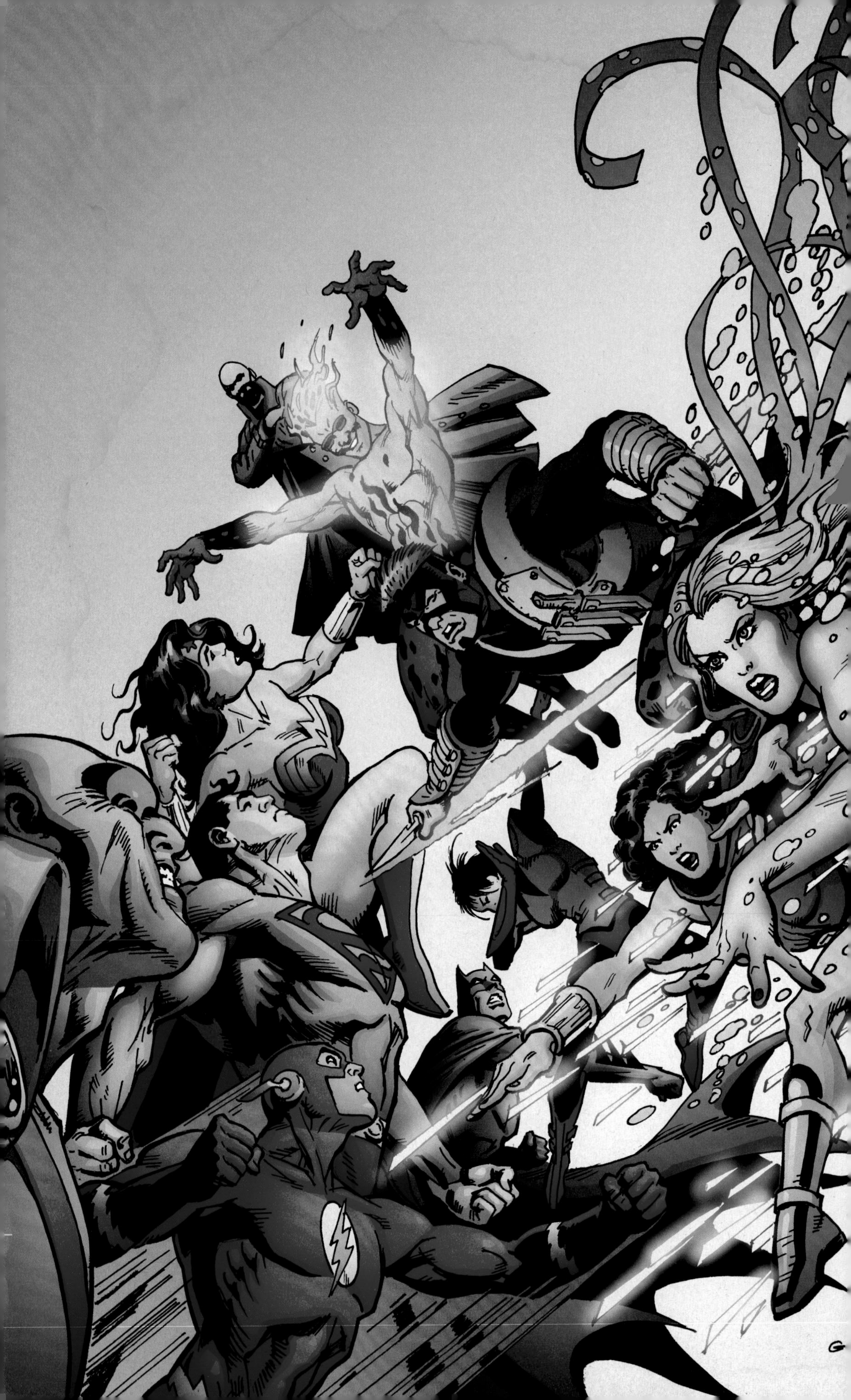

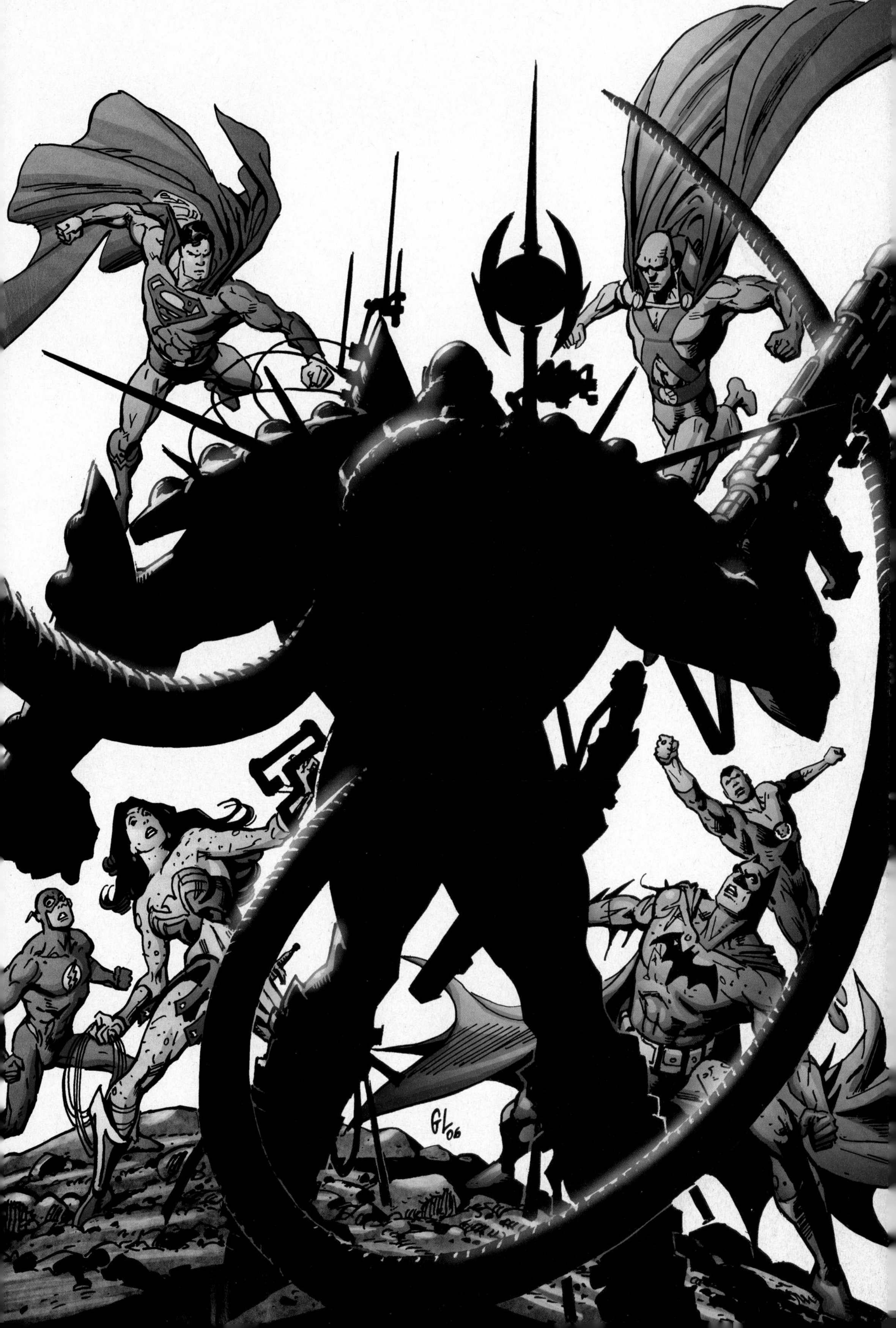

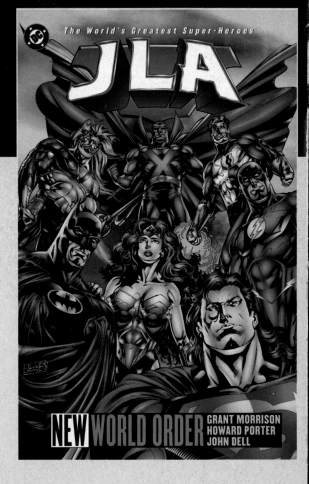